Adobe Digital Video How-Tos

100 Essential Techniques with Adobe Production Studio

Jan Ozer

Adobe Press

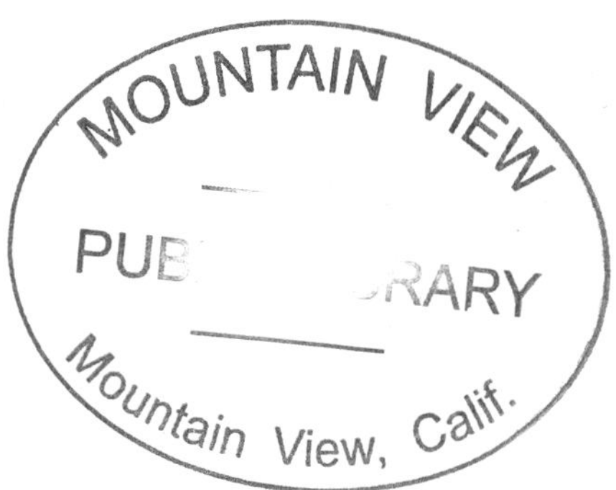

Adobe Digital Video How-Tos
100 Essential Techniques with Adobe Production Studio

This Adobe Press book is published by Peachpit

Peachpit
1249 Eighth Street
Berkeley, CA 94710
510/524-2178
800/283-9444
510/524-2221 (fax)

Peachpit is a division of Pearson Education

For the latest on Adobe Press books, go to www.adobe.com/adobepress

To report errors, please send a note to errata@peachpit.com

Project Editor: Karen Reichstein
Editor: Steve Nathans
Production Editor: Connie Jeung-Mills
Copyeditor: Joanne Gosnell
Compositor: ICC MacMillan
Indexer: Karin Arrigoni
Cover Design: Mimi Heft
Interior Design: Mimi Heft

ISBN 0-321-47381-7

9 8 7 6 5 4 3 2 1

Printed and bound in the United States of America

Dedication

To Marjorie Baer, my Peachpit fav, who got it all started and keeps it all going.

Acknowledgments

Wow, my first Adobe Press book—what an honor. Thanks to all the Adobe folks who helped form the vision of this book, and contributed some gems, including Giles Baker, Steve Kilisky, and Bob Donlon, and also Stephna May from A&R Edelman and her sidekick, Cara Porchia, both wonderful facilitators.

On the Peachpit side, my sincere thanks to world's best editor, Stephen Nathans (who I hope actually gets a copy of *this* book), Karen Reichstein, who kept us between the white lines, Karyn Johnson, who lured me into the book (in a Vegas sushi bar of all places), Connie Jeung-Mills, who figured out how to squeeze all the images in (as I knew she would). Additional thanks to ICC MacMillan for compositing and to Joanne Gosnell for copyediting.

Thanks to those whose videos contributed to the screens in this book, including Emma Ross, Congressman Rick Boucher, super models Rose and Whatley Ozer, Granddaddy Jack Ozer, David Kupsky, King Gary and Queen Heidi McLennan and the incomparable Rene Marie. All pictures used with permission.

As always, thanks to Pat Tracy for technical and other assistance.

Contents

Chapter One: Getting Started 1

#1: Choosing the Right Project Preset 2

#2: Changing Your General Settings 5

#3: Creating Custom Project Presets 7

#4: Customizing Your Workspace 9

#5: Working with Dual Monitors 12

#6: Introducing Adobe Bridge 14

Chapter Two: Editing Preliminaries 15

#7: Enabling Scene Detection During Capture 16

#8: Solving the Capture Device Offline Issue 17

#9: Creating Subclips 19

#10: Storyboarding in Premiere Pro 21

#11: Selecting Audio or Video in the Source Monitor 23

#12: Targeting Tracks for Input 25

#13: Overlay vs. Insert Edits 27

#14: Previewing with the Work Area Bar 29

#15: Working with Three-point Edits 31

#16: Working with Four-point Edits 34

Chapter Three: Using Premiere Pro and After Effects Together 37

#17: Getting Started with After Effects 38

#18: Copying and Pasting from Premiere Pro to After Effects 41

#19: Importing Premiere Pro Projects into After Effects 43

#20: Importing After Effects Projects into Premiere Pro with Dynamic Link 45

Chapter Four: Perfecting Video Quality 47

#21: Checking Brightness and Color with the YC Waveform Scope . . 48

#22: Setting Up for Color Correction 50

#23: Adjusting Brightness with Levels 51

#24: Fixing Backlight Issues with the Shadow/Highlight Filter. . .53

#25: Perfecting the Auto Color Effect. 55

#26: Adjusting White Balance with the Fast Color Corrector. 57

#27: Using the Three-Way Color Corrector 60

#28: Using the RGB Parade Scope 62

#29: Stabilizing Your Image in Premiere Pro 63

#30: Stabilizing Your Image in After Effects 64

#31: Pasting Effects 67

#32: Creating Effect Presets 68

Chapter Five: Multi-Camera Production in Premiere Pro 71

#33: Synching Clips with Markers 72

#34: Synching Clips on the Timeline 74

#35: Perfecting Source Clips 76

#36: Choosing Camera Angles with the Multi-Camera Monitor. . . .78

#37: The Tao of Multi-Camera Editing. 81

#38: Editing a Multi-Camera Sequence on the Timeline 82

#39: Setting Up Overlay Effects with the Multi-Camera Tool. 84

#40: HDV and Multi-Camera Editing, Part I 86

#41: HDV and Multi-Camera Editing, Part II 87

Chapter Six: Applying Cool Special Effects 91

#42: Producing Overlay Effects 92

#43: Customizing Effects with Keyframes 94

#44: Going Split Screen—Diagonal 96
#45: Producing a Picture-in-Picture Effect 98
#46: Converting Clips to Sepia in Premiere Pro 100
#47: Transitioning from Black and White to Full Color........102
#48: Perfecting Chroma Key in Premiere Pro 103
#49: Using After Effects' Keylight Plug-in................107
#50: Working with Mattes in Premiere Pro................109
#51: Creating Mattes in Premiere Pro 111
#52: Applying the Track Matte Key 113
#53: Animating Clips in Premiere Pro...................114
#54: Motion Tracking in After Effects 117
#55: Applying Motion-Tracking Data 120

Chapter Seven: Transitions and Titles 123

#56: Five Things You Don't Know About Premiere Pro Transitions . . 124
#57: Synch Your Titles and DVD Menus..................127
#58: Working with Premiere Pro Title Templates............129
#59: Designing with the Titler's Design Primitives 131
#60: Producing Rolling Credits 133
#61: Creating Titles in Photoshop 136
#62: Creating Titles in Illustrator 139
#63: Producing Title Backgrounds in After Effects 140
#64: Creating Simple Text Animations in After Effects 143
#65: Producing Matte Effects with Titles.................146

Chapter Eight: Creating Slide Shows in Premiere Pro 147

#66: Preprocessing Images for Premiere Pro in Photoshop.....148
#67: Understanding Square Pixels 150

#68: Managing Images in Premiere Pro 153
#69: Producing Pan-and-Zoom Effects in Premiere Pro 155
#70: Creating a Still Frame with Frame Hold Control 157
#71: Creating Slide Shows in Premiere Pro 159
Chapter Nine: Working with Audio 161
#72: Working with Audio in Premiere Pro 162
#73: Getting Started in Audition 164
#74: Normalizing Audio in Premiere Pro and Audition 166
#75: Reducing Noise in Audition 168
#76: Removing Irregular Pops and Clicks in Audition 171
#77: Creating Narrations in Audition 173
Chapter Ten: Sharing, Rendering, and Encoding Your Projects 177
#78: Sharing and Reviewing with Adobe Clip Notes 178
#79: Exporting Frames from Premiere Pro 182
#80: Exporting Audio from Premiere Pro 184
#81: Working with the Adobe Media Encoder 186
#82: Producing Flash Output 190
#83: Deinterlacing Video for Progressive Output 193
#84: Rendering in After Effects 195
#85: Creating Custom Output Presets in After Effects 198
Chapter Eleven: DVD Production in Premiere Pro 201
#86: Using Premiere Pro vs. Encore DVD 202
#87: Producing a Menu-less DVD in Premiere Pro 203
#88: Creating Scene Markers in Premiere Pro 205
#89: Choosing DVD Templates in Premiere Pro 207
#90: Customizing DVD Menus in Premiere Pro 209

#91: Creating Chapter Markers for Encore DVD in Premiere Pro . . 211

Chapter Twelve: Producing DVDs in Encore DVD 213

#92: Getting Started with Encore DVD 214

#93: Creating Text Buttons in Encore DVD. 217

#94: Editing Text Buttons in Photoshop 219

#95: Producing Motion Menus in After Effects 222

#96: Controlling Button Behavior in Motion Menus 225

#97: Controlling the DVD Viewing Experience 226

#98: Creating and Using Playlists 228

#99: Manually Arranging Button Routing 230

#100: Previewing Your DVD 232

Appendix 235

Index 239

Foreword

Adobe Production Studio, part of the Adobe Creative Suite family, brings extraordinary power and efficiency to anyone who wants to create films, videos, DVDs, and video for the Web.

At Adobe, we're proud of our digital video products. Adobe After Effects is the industry standard for creating motion graphics and visual effects. Adobe Premiere Pro continues to break new ground in digital video editing, and Adobe Encore DVD lets anyone produce professional-quality DVDs.

We understand, too, that video professionals need to be able to move easily and effortlessly between applications, and so individual components of Adobe Production Studio are designed to work as well together as they do apart.

Adobe Digital Video How-Tos is the ideal reference for videographers and filmmakers who want to learn to use Adobe Production Studio to streamline their digital video productions. In the 12 chapters of this book, you'll find helpful, standalone tips that show you the best of Production Studio and its integrated parts. Learn how to use Bridge to organize your assets and learn when to use Photoshop or Illustrator to create titles for your movie. Use After Effects to animate Illustrator graphics and to create motion menus for Encore DVD. Send audio from Premiere Pro and After Effects to Audition for detailed editing and cleanup, and learn how to copy effects and motion graphics from one clip to another.

Throughout this book, author Jan Ozer provides plenty of sidebars offering additional tips and hard-won advice to make your video productions efficient, rewarding, and fun.

Enjoy the book.

Giles Baker
Sr. Product Manager, Premiere Pro
Adobe Systems, Inc.

CHAPTER ONE

Getting Started

Adobe Creative Suite Production Studio Premium Edition includes a wealth of feature-rich programs—Premiere Pro, After Effects, Encore DVD, Audition, Illustrator, Photoshop—and two time-saving workflow technologies, Dynamic Link and Adobe Bridge. Most of these applications have several books from multiple publishers that explain how to use them. In this relatively short book, I won't try to describe how to use each program from scratch.

The purpose of this book is to help you save time and improve video quality by using the suite's integration-oriented features to reduce the number of times you render your video, and the number of editing generations. I'll also provide tips that simplify your workflow and help you use the video-related tools available in all the programs to maximum advantage.

I'll assume that you have a basic working knowledge of all programs in the suite, and that you'll spend most of your time in Adobe Premiere Pro, adding content funneled in from Adobe Photoshop, Adobe Illustrator, and Adobe After Effects.

I'll also assume that you'll want to edit your audio in Adobe Audition and output some of your projects to DVD in Adobe Encore DVD. As you can see from the Table of Contents, this book follows this workflow from start to finish. Overall, if you're looking for some ideas on how to boost creativity and productivity, especially via enhanced integration between the applications in the Production Studio, you'll find this book helpful. If you're looking for a soup-to nuts-guide from capture to output, you'll be better off with a Visual QuickStart Guide for the respective application.

The first chapter starts where most of your video projects will begin: choosing a preset in Premiere Pro. Then I'll discuss how to customize Premiere Pro's workspace, identifying principles that work similarly in all suite programs. I'll also talk a bit about Adobe Bridge, a great application for sifting through your content (and media provided by Adobe with Production Studio), and finish with an overview of the inter-program integration options available in Production Studio.

#1 Choosing the Right Project Preset

Download updates now

Adobe has issued updates for most Production Studio programs, so you could be running old code. Check www.adobe.com to see if you've got the latest version of the software.

The first step in starting a new Premiere project is choosing a project preset. Briefly, a project preset defines basic parameters that will govern any content you capture or import into your project. These include aspect ratio (e.g., 4:3 for standard TV); video resolution (e.g., 720x480 for standard-definition DV); video frame rate (e.g., 60i for 60 interlaced frames per second); and audio quality (e.g., 48kHz for DV-quality audio).

Most of the time, choosing a project preset is easy. If you shoot in standard (4:3) NTSC DV, you'll produce a standard NTSC DVD, so the correct preset is Standard DV-NTSC, which should also correspond to the audio setting used during your shoot. (I always shoot at 48kHz, which simplifies my preset selection).

Sometimes, however, the choice gets more complicated. For example, suppose you shoot in HDV format—say, 1080i, to be specific—and want to produce a Standard Definition (SD) 16:9 DVD. Which project preset should you choose?

Always choose the preset that corresponds with your ultimate output parameters. In other words, when producing an SD DVD from HDV video, you should use the Widescreen 48kHz DV-NTSC preset shown in **Figure 1a**. Here's why.

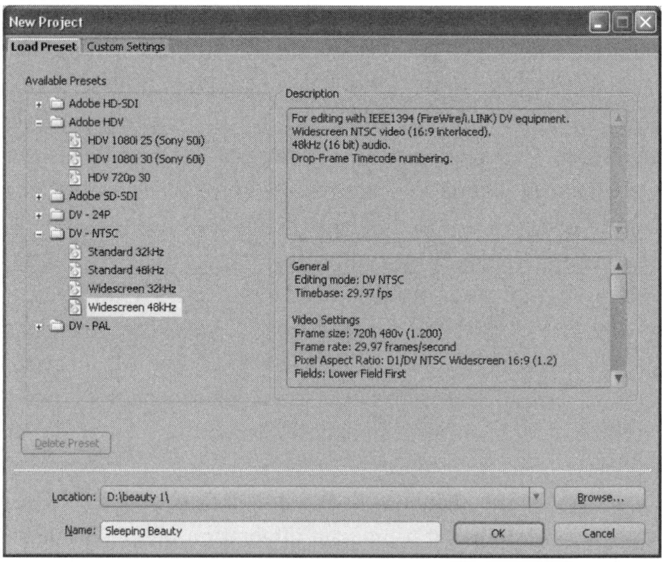

Figure 1a This is where you choose your project presets.

First, Premiere Pro produces higher-quality output when using this preset than when using the HDV 1080i 30 (Sony 60i) preset. Second, the Widescreen DV-NTSC preset provides a more accurate preview of the ultimate rendered video, which helps with details like title placement or with framing your shot when you're panning and zooming around an HDV image.

This principle is a bit easier to demonstrate when producing a 4:3 SD video from a 16:9 HDV stream, which I've done for several projects. If you use the HDV preset, Premiere Pro displays the complete HDV image in its native 16:9 resolution, which works well for full-resolution projects but provides little guidance regarding how the video will look at 4:3 (**Figure 1b**).

Figure 1b This is HDV video in an HDV project; it's kind of tough to figure out 4:3 positioning, isn't it?

However, if you use the DV-NTSC Standard preset, Premiere Pro provides a completely accurate preview, making it simple to zoom and pan to the appropriate framing (**Figure 1c**). For these reasons, you should always use the preset that corresponds with your target output parameters.

Choosing the Best Location for Your Project Files

Premiere Pro (like most Production Studio applications) stores most preview and other ancillary project files in the same folder as your project file. If you use a separate hard drive to store video, you should store your project file on that drive as well, rather than your system (usually your C drive), for better overall performance. Create a single folder for each project, and then store all project files associated with that project in that folder. When you're done with the project, simply delete one folder to reclaim all the hard drive space used by that project.

Working with HDV Video in SD Projects

Typically, when working with HDV video in SD projects, you'll have to scale the video down to about 46% of the original resolution. You'll do this in each clip's Motion controls in the Effect Controls panel.

Figure 1c The same video in an SD DV project, with a wonderfully accurate preview for framing. Now if I could just figure out how to apply the Rule of Thirds to that left arm...

The only potential wrinkle in this approach is that when it's time to capture, Premiere Pro will look for a DV device rather than an HDV device, and initially may not recognize your HDV camcorder. To fix this problem, do the following:

1. Go to File > Capture.
2. In the Capture window, choose the Settings tab.
3. Click Edit.
4. Change the preset to the appropriate capture device, as shown in **Figure 1d**.

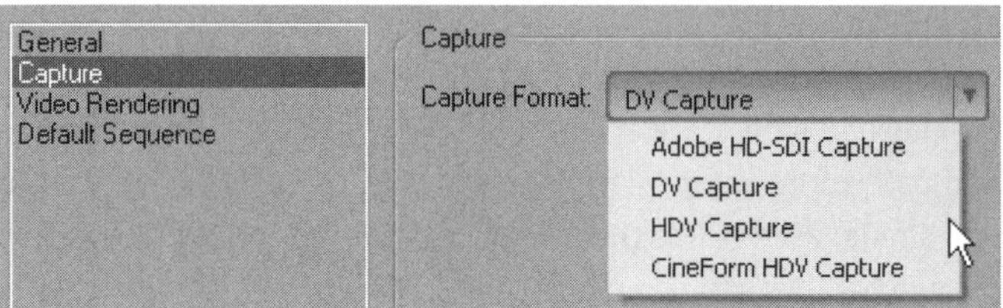

Figure 1d To ensure that Premiere recognizes your HDV camera, choose the correct capture format.

#2 Changing Your General Settings

Technically, you can't change your General settings; they're permanently grayed out as shown in **Figure 2a**. However, if you import a Premiere Pro project into another project, the imported project will assume the General settings of the project into which it's been imported.

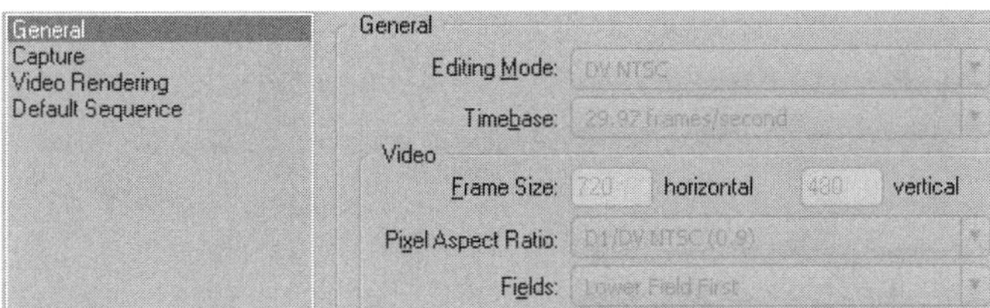

Figure 2a Yikes! How do you change the General presets? They're all grayed out!

Say, for example, you originally produced an HDV project using the HDV preset to render the result back to tape. Then your client asks for a 4:3 SD DVD. Rather than starting from scratch or blindly exporting a 4:3 file that could wreak havoc on titles and framing, you can remedy the situation by doing the following:

1. Create a new 4:3 project file.
2. Using the File > Import command (and *not* the File > Open Project command), *import* the HDV project into the new one (**Figure 2b**).

Changing the Default Number of Audio and Video Tracks

The fourth window in the Project Settings dialog box (Figure 2a) is the Default Sequence window. This is where you can control the default number of audio and video tracks that appear with each new project.

Figure 2b Fortunately, Premiere Pro allows you to import a project into another project, effectively changing the General presets to the new settings.

Premiere will import all files associated with the project and store them in a separate bin in your Project panel. It will then apply the new project settings to all sequences you've imported into the project. Presto, change-o, you've got new General settings, albeit in a different project.

#3 Creating Custom Project Presets

Sometimes, none of the presets supplied by Premiere Pro will work for you. For example, I frequently use Premiere Pro to compare videos for encoding or compression quality and will output in odd resolutions like 1280x480, which is two 640x480 videos side by side.

You may also want to use a nonstandard video resolution for a Flash video advertisement or other custom use. To guarantee an accurate preview of the video you're producing, you'll need to create a custom preset. Here's how to do it:

1. In the New Project window, select the Custom Settings tab (**Figure 3a**).

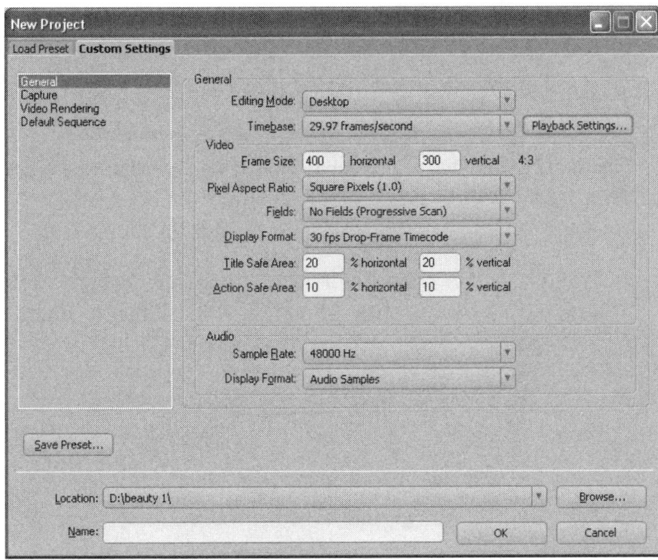

Figure 3a Here's how to create custom presets for nonstandard projects.

2. If you're producing a nonstandard resolution image, choose the Desktop option in the Editing Mode drop-down menu (**Figure 3b**).

3. Enter a Frame Size.

continued on next page

Producing Multiple Output Resolutions

What to do if you're outputting both MPEG-2 files for DVD and 320x240 Flash video for the Web? Two choices. Either produce at DVD resolutions and scale the video to the smaller resolution during rendering, or finish your project at the higher resolution, then import it into a 320x240 project (#2) and output from there. This gives you better visibility regarding the quality of the graphics and framing, but obviously requires more production time.

Never produce at the smaller resolution then scale to a larger resolution for rendering, which can noticeably degrade quality.

Working with Advanced Formats

The first time I shot in Sony Cineframe and Canon 24F modes and tried to capture the faux-progressive video in Premiere Pro, I was stumped by the lack of a capture preset. Sure, I could create my own, but I was concerned that one missed parameter would force a recompression during capture or a similar nightmare.

Fortunately, I found a third-party solution called Aspect HD from Cineform (www.cineform.com). Aspect HD provides capture presets for these modes and JVC's ("true" progressive) 24p and converts the incoming video into a high-quality wavelet-based AVI format. This format is less complex than native HDV and therefore easier for the system to decode, providing much more responsive editing. (Earlier versions of Premiere Pro used a Cineform intermediary codec for all HDV capture and editing.) The product costs $499, but you can download the complete program for a free 15-day trial before buying.

4. From the Pixel Aspect Ratio drop-down menu, choose a Pixel Aspect Ratio; this should be Square Pixels for most video produced for computer playback.

5. For streaming video, choose No Fields (Progressive Scan) in the Fields drop-down menu.

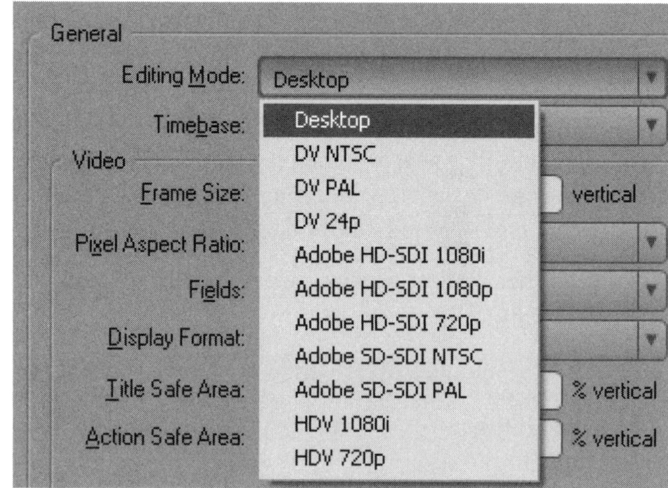

Figure 3b This Desktop editing mode is the only setting that expects you to set every parameter; others are pretty straightforward.

6. When finished, choose a name and storage location for your project file, then click OK in the New Project window to proceed to Premiere Pro and start your project.

#4 Customizing Your Workspace

Figure 4a shows the Premiere Pro interface in all its glory. You may already know what many of the windows are and what they do, but I want to make sure you know their official names (for example, it's the *Program Monitor*, not the *preview window*) before I started tossing them around.

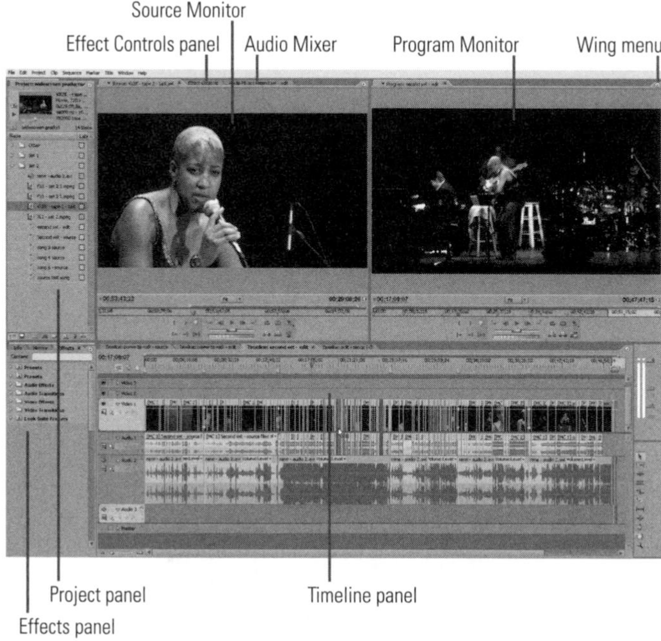

Figure 4a Here's Premiere Pro; please note the official names for all the windows (er... panels and monitors), since I'll be using these names throughout the book.

Adobe gives you lots of flexibility in using the various Production Studio applications by allowing you to drag and resize most panels in each program's workspace to your heart's desire. You can also choose between several "workspaces" designed to facilitate a particular editing or production activity.

The most obvious way to alter your workspace is by increasing the size of the preview window. It's easy enough to do, but in most cases you'll want to resize the window briefly then return it to its normal size. There are three more options that will save you time by eliminating workspace clutter and highlighting frequently used features.

Restoring Your Workspace

If your custom workspace gets too funky, you can always restore equilibrium by choosing Premiere Pro's Editing workspace (or pressing Shift+F9), which returns your workspace to its original positioning.

First is the ability to close panels that you don't typically use. For example, when editing, I want my Premiere Pro Timeline panel as wide as possible. In Premiere Pro's default workspace, however, a three-tabbed panel sits to the left of the Timeline, taking up space I'd rather allocate to the Timeline.

Two items you will rarely use in editing are the Info and History tabs. To close them permanently, do the following:

1. Select the appropriate tab.
2. Click the small x shown on the panel when selected. The tab will disappear.

You'll spend much more time in the third panel, "Effects." To make it more prominent, do the following:

1. Select the Effects tab.
2. Click the small "gripper" area on the left edge of the tab.
3. Drag it to the Project panel (**Figure 4b**).

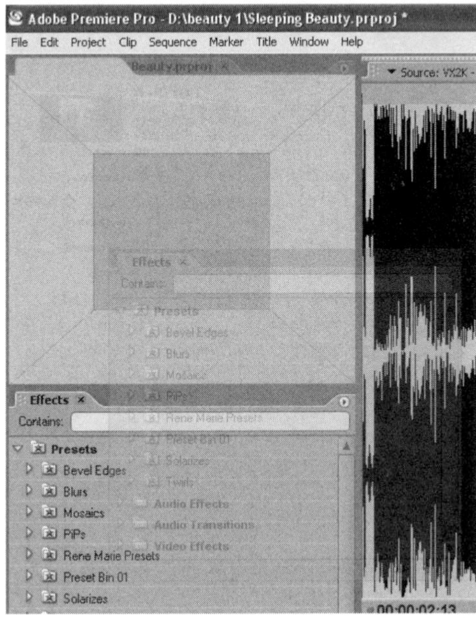

Figure 4b Drag the Effects panel alongside the Project panel by releasing the gripper area onto the middle (highlighted) panel.

When you do this, Premiere Pro divides the Project panel into five drop zones (see Figure 4b). To reposition the panel, do one of the following:

- Release the mouse when the middle drop zone is highlighted, and Premiere Pro will "group" the panel next to the Project tab, which is where you want it (**Figure 4c**).
- Choose any of the other drop zones, and Premiere will "dock" the Effects panel above, below, or alongside the Project panel, according to your preference.

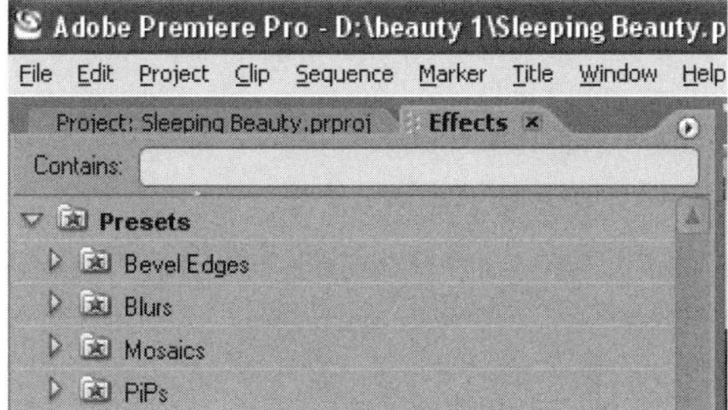

Figure 4c Now you've got the Effects Panel right where you want it.

Now you've got the Effects panel right where you want it. Once you've achieved your desired workspace, save it by choosing Window > Workspace > Save Workspace (**Figure 4d**).

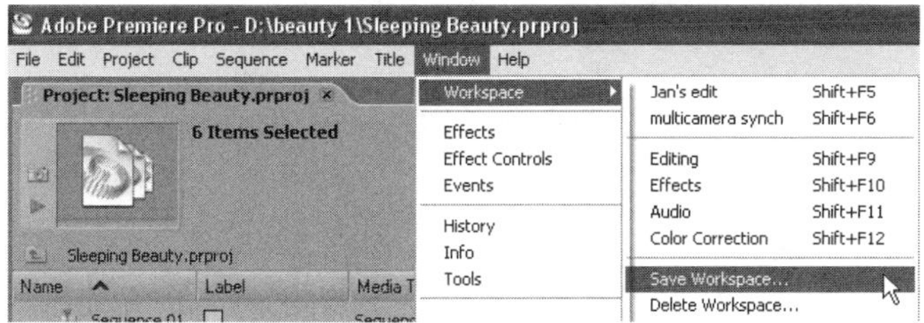

Figure 4d Now that I've got my workspace all prettied up, here's how I save it.

As you can see in Figure 4d, I've already saved two workspaces, "Jan's edit" and "multicamera synch."

Finding Lost Panels

Even with custom workspaces, you can lose a panel or two, or perhaps you may need to access a panel that's not available in that workspace. Note that you can open any panel by choosing Window > and then the target panel.

Restoring Your Workspace

If your custom workspace gets too funky you can always restore equilibrium by choosing Premiere Pro's Editing workspace (or pressing Shft+F9), which returns your workspace to its original positioning.

#5 Working with Dual Monitors

Editing on a single monitor can be a constant exercise in window shifting and resizing. Fortunately, it's fairly inexpensive to add a second monitor to your system, especially if you already have a dual-head graphics card. It's also quite easy to configure your dual-monitor system for effective editing in Premiere Pro and After Effects.

Essentially, there are three steps. The first step, as you might expect, is to connect the necessary cables and power on the second monitor. The next step is to extend your Windows desktop to support both monitors, and finally modify the Premiere Pro desktop to take advantage of the additional real estate. We'll pick up the story right after you get your monitor connected and powered on.

1. Right-click your desktop and choose Properties from the pop-up menu to bring up the Display Properties dialog box.
2. Click the Settings tab.
3. Choose the second monitor in the Display list box (**Figure 5a**).
4. Then select the Extend my Windows desktop checkbox, and Windows will do just that, blanking out your primary screen for a moment and then turning on both screens. Click OK to close the dialog and return to Premiere Pro.

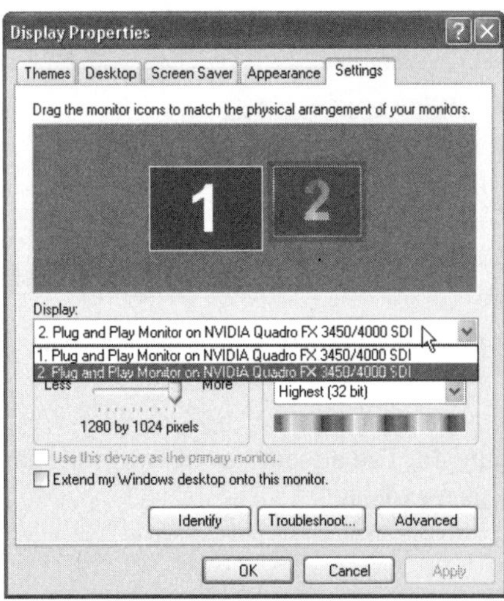

Figure 5a Set up your dual-monitor display by choosing the second monitor in the display list box.

VGA-to-DVI

If your current graphics card has two outputs, you should be able to configure your system for dual-monitor editing. If one or both of your connectors is an old-style blue VGA connector and you're installing a flat-panel monitor that connects via DVI, you should be able to buy a VGA-to-DVI adapter for under $10. Google "VGA to DVI adapter," and you should find lots of options. Less is more here. You don't need a $300 option; the sub-$10 unit will work just fine.

5. Now, working within the Premiere Pro interface, you can drag any Premiere Pro panel to the second monitor, perhaps pulling the Program Monitor over for a larger preview, or the Timeline for a larger editing surface. You can rearrange your configuration as you like and then save it as a workspace as discussed in step 4.

6. If you're editing DV video in 4:3 resolution, you can also display a full-screen preview on the second monitor. To accomplish this, click the small wing menu on the upper-right corner of the Program Monitor (see Figure 4a), and choose Playback settings to open the window shown in **Figure 5b**.

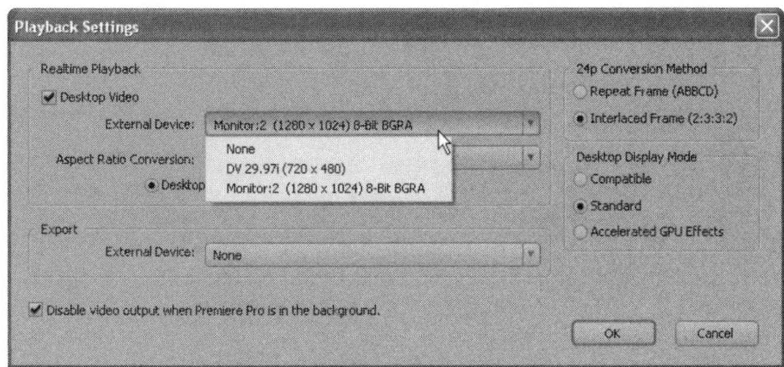

Figure 5b Using the Playback Settings control, you can preview your video in full screen on your second monitor.

7. Click the External Device list box, and choose Monitor:2 to display your full-screen preview on the second monitor.

If you have a DV camcorder connected, you can also choose that option and display the full-screen preview on an NTSC monitor or television attached to your camcorder.

Buying a Dual-Head Graphics Card

If your current graphics card doesn't have two outputs, you'll need to install one that does to take advantage of dual-monitor display in Premiere Pro. You should be able to find a suitable card for under $200. Remember that there are multiple video bus architectures out there, from PCI to AGP to PCI Express. Check your system documentation to determine which architecture your computer uses, and/or bring your current graphics card to the computer store when you make your purchase.

#6 Introducing Adobe Bridge

By the time you've finished with some complicated projects, you'll have literally dozens of audio, video, and still image files floating around, and finding the right content can consume valuable production time. Fortunately, Adobe Bridge, which is included in all versions of Production Studio, can help you to quickly zero in on almost any file you need.

Bridge can display still image files and play audio and video files. I find it particularly useful for browsing through the many templates, behaviors, and presets offered with Adobe After Effects (**Figure 6**).

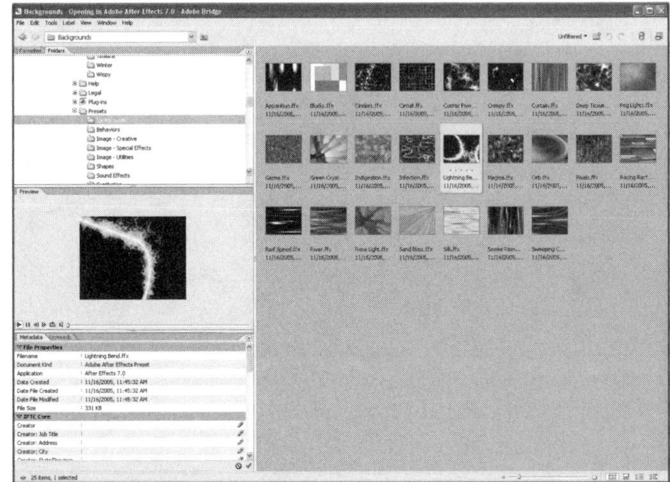

Figure 6 Adobe Bridge provides a great environment for finding and organizing your project assets and for previewing templates and other design elements from After Effects.

In addition, it offers advanced search capabilities and the ability to insert metadata into a file. To access Bridge, do one of the following:

- Select it from your Windows Start menu to open it as a separate application.
- Choose File > Browse in any Production Studio application, and it will open automatically.

Adobe Stock Photos

With over 750,000 royalty-free images to select from, Adobe Stock Photos is a great source of images for menus and other design elements. Bridge gives you direct access to the Adobe Stock Photos Web site, with the ability to search, sample, download, and manage your purchased images.

Simplified File Selection

If you access Bridge via the File > Browse command, double-click any file to load it into that host application. Or, as with Windows Explorer, you can insert a file into any Production Studio application by dragging it into the Project panel or equivalent.

CHAPTER TWO

Editing Preliminaries

Every project has a bunch of lowest common denominator activities—the unglamorous work of capturing or importing your videos, trimming and sequencing them, and getting them to the timeline. Fortunately, Premiere Pro has a number of tools and techniques that streamline these steps to make them faster and more efficient.

This chapter includes essential techniques on expediting these editing preliminaries, starting with capture, working through sequencing in the Project panel, and concluding with a look at three- and four-point editing.

#7 Enabling Scene Detection During Capture

As you may know, DV camcorders and some other devices store time codes on the tape that record the starting and stopping point of each shot taken while shooting. During capture, Premiere Pro can scan the tape and identify "scenes" using these time codes. If you enable scene detection, Premiere Pro will produce a separate captured file for each scene.

If you're shooting a concert, ballet, or other linear real-time event, where you shoot continuously from start to finish, this feature has little value. For most other productions, where you start and stop the camera frequently, scene detection can save a lot of time during editing.

Note that Premiere Pro can't detect scenes *after* capture, or from footage that you've imported from other sources. So you get one shot, during capture, and that's it.

To enable scene detection during capture, do one of the following:

- Select the Scene Detect checkbox in the Capture panel (**Figure 7**).
- Click the Scene Detect button in the Device controls beneath the capture preview window.

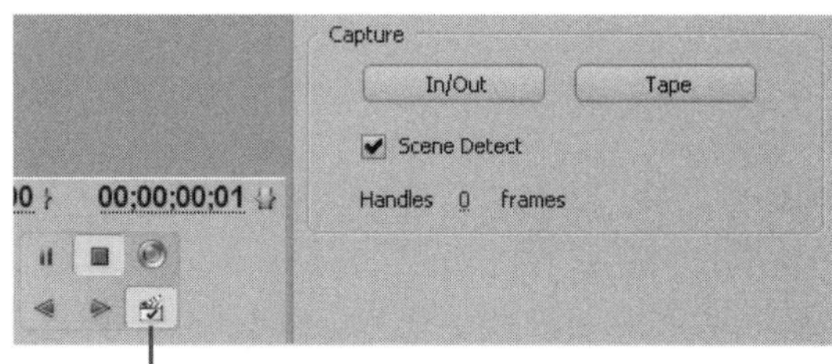

Figure 7 Enable scene detection by selecting the Scene Detect checkbox or clicking the Scene Detect button.

Remember to Name Your File Before Capture

I'm not trying to be a nag, but if you don't name your file and capture with scene detection enabled, you could end up with dozens of clips named "untitled clip 1 0avi" that you might have to rename to make useful. If you name your captured clips, Premiere Pro will increment the selected file name, providing some clue as to what's in the file. You can name your file in the Capture panel in the Clip Data section of the Logging tab.

Set the Time and Date in Your Camcorder

You've probably already set the time and date in your camcorder, but if not, note that you may not be able to detect scenes unless you set it.

#8 Solving the Capture Device Offline Issue

One issue I've noticed with the latest crop of HDV camcorders is that sometimes Premiere Pro has trouble finding the camcorder when first connected, leading to the error message "Capture Device Offline"(**Figure 8a**). Sometimes Premiere Pro will instruct you to turn the camcorder on and off, which is certainly the first step to try.

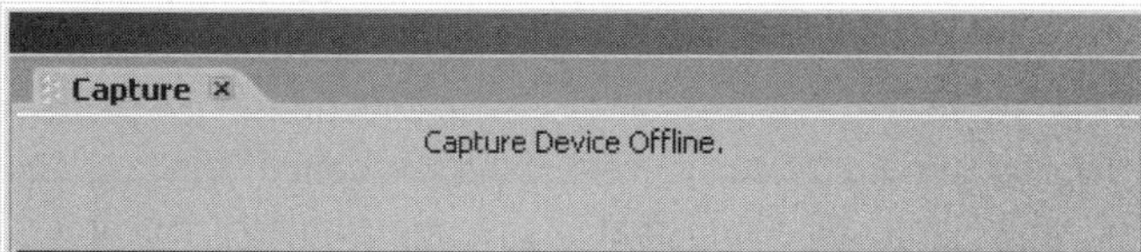

Figure 8a This error message can lead to hours of frustration. Try these steps.

If that doesn't help, consider the following steps to resolve the problem.

1. Make sure all cables in your camcorder are properly seated in the connectors.
2. Close and reopen the Capture panel.
3. Make sure you've selected the correct capture format. I often forget to do this when capturing HDV video into an SD project.
4. Manually play a short section of the tape in the camcorder. Sometimes dual HDV/DV camcorders stay in HDV mode even after you insert a DV tape (or vice versa) and send the incorrect signal to Premiere Pro, preventing capture. This is particularly true with the Canon XL H1. Often, playing a short section of the tape will reset the camcorder into the proper format and allow it to synch with Premiere Pro.
5. Close and reopen Premiere Pro.
6. Reboot your computer, and check Windows Explorer to make sure that Windows recognizes the camcorder (**Figure 8b**).

continued on next page

Other Digital Formats

In some instances, you may need to capture video from consumer camcorders that store video in MPEG-2 or other formats on Flash or DVD media. Though Premiere Pro can't interface directly with these devices, if you can get the video to your hard drive, there's a good chance Premiere can import it. Also, be aware that consumer sibling Adobe Premiere Elements offers excellent support for most consumer camcorders and can retrieve video from unprotected DVDs. If you're looking for a tool to interface with these devices, consider downloading a trial version of Premiere Elements.

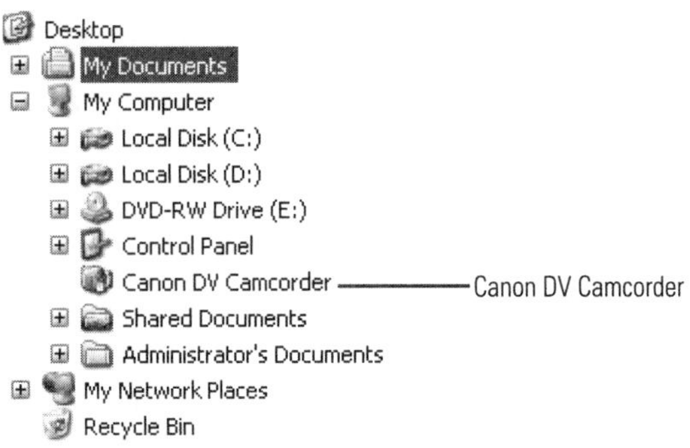

Figure 8b If Windows doesn't recognize your camcorder, Premiere Pro can't recognize it either. We're in good shape here.

7. Try turning the camcorder on and off again; if Windows doesn't give you some sign that it's recognizing the camcorder, like the Digital Video Device dialog box shown in **Figure 8c**, you either have a faulty cable or faulty (usually burned out) FireWire connectors on either the camcorder or computer. In ten years of working with digital camcorders, I've unfortunately experienced all three problems.

Figure 8c Each time you turn your camcorder on, Windows should display a dialog like this, letting you know that it recognizes the camcorder. If you don't see this dialog or one like it, it's likely that there's some type of hardware failure.

#9 Creating Subclips

Subclips are sections of a longer video that you can edit separately from the original source. Here's a scenario where I'll use them.

My wife's ballet company recently performed *Sleeping Beauty*, and to produce the credits, I'll display a short video of each performer or group, just long enough to display their name and a twirl or two. Subclips are perfect for this task. Whenever I see short clip that's suitable for the credits, I identify it as a Subclip. Here's how it's done:

1. Set the In and Out points in the Source Monitor as normal.
2. Still in the Source Montor, right-click and choose Make Subclip (**Figure 9a**).
3. In the dialog that opens, enter a name for your clip and click OK.

Figure 9a Here are Heidi and Gary, the perfect queen and king. Making this snippet a Subclip will simplify producing the credits.

Be a Neat Freak

When it comes to Premiere Pro projects, storing relevant sets of content in separate bins will save you loads of time down the road. In Figure 9b, you can see that I've got separate bins for the three major sets in the production: the Fairy Tale for the creative movement girls (two- to four-year-olds), and two sets of the ballet. Once I start collecting still-frame grabs for the DVD menu, I'll store these in a separate, appropriately named folder.

Premiere Pro inserts the Subclip in the Project panel, where it looks and functions just like any other clip (**Figure 9b**). You can trim it in the Source Monitor, drag it to the timeline, and add effects and transitions just like any other clip.

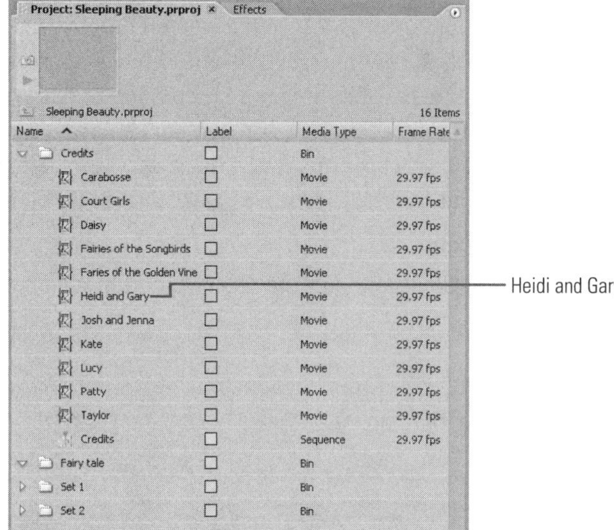

Figure 9b Here's the Subclip in the Project panel; though the icon is different from regular video clips, Subclips act just like regular clips during editing.

#10 Storyboarding in Premiere Pro

Unlike many editing tools, Premiere Pro doesn't have a formal storyboard feature. But you can still gain the benefits of storyboard editing for getting an overview of your project by using the Project panel as a storyboard and then automatically inserting your clips into the timeline. It's perfect for producing the credits video I started in the last technique (#9) and still-image slide shows, which we'll talk about later in the book. Here's how it works:

1. Start by dragging the bottom-right corner of the Project panel to the right to create more working room.
2. Click the Icon view icon in the lower-left corner of the Project panel, which displays the first frame of your Subclips in individual frames in the Project panel (**Figure 10a**).

   In this view, you can click and drag your clips to place them in any desired order. Note that you can also set In and Out points in the Source Monitor for these clips or Subclips in the Project panel to create a "rough cut" of the sequence.

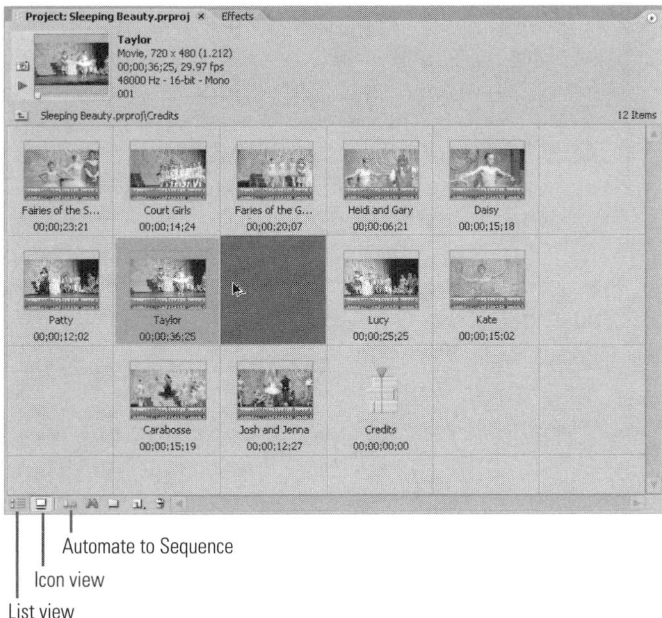

Figure 10a In Icon view, you see the first frame of each clip or Subclip and can move them around like pieces on a chessboard.

continued on next page

Cleaning Up the Project Panel

Icon view and the ability to drag the Project panel out to see more of your images and videos are great features. However, when you resize the Project panel back to its original viewing area, the images don't automatically snap back so you can see them. Some stay hidden behind the Source Monitor, which can be a pain if you're trying to hunt one down.

A quick solution is in the fly-out menu that you access by clicking the small triangle in the top-right corner of the Project panel (see Figure 10a). Choose Clean Up in the fly-out menu, and Premiere Pro will snap all content back to where you can see it and eliminate any space-consuming blank boxes.

Another useful option in the fly-out menu is the ability to set thumbnail sizes (small, medium, and large), which can be very helpful if you're working at 1600x1200 resolution or so, even on a large monitor.

3. Select the clips you wish to add to the sequence.
4. Click the Automate to Sequence button in the lower-left corner of the Project panel (see Figure 10a). Premiere Pro opens the Automate to Sequence dialog enabling several options, including Clip Overlap (which determines the length of transitions in frames or seconds) and insertion of the default audio and video transitions (**Figure 10b**).
5. Make your choices, click OK, and the sequence will appear in the timeline, ready for fine-tuning.

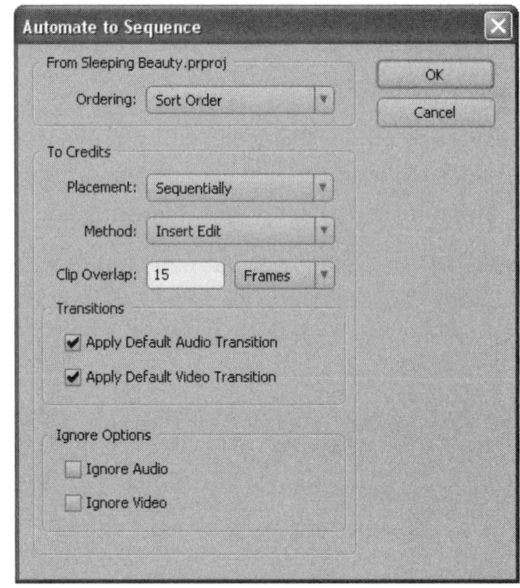

Figure 10b Now you can send the clips to the timeline in the desired sequence, even adding transitions as you go.

Note that I describe how to set the default audio and video transitions in #56.

#11 Selecting Audio or Video in the Source Monitor

Sometimes you want to include just the audio from a video clip in a project.

Other times, particularly when you're attempting to set up multiple-camera streams for synchronization, you'll prefer to view only the audio waveform in the Source Monitor because it offers more precision than video frames for making your edit decision. Interestingly, you can accomplish both goals with the same button in the Source Monitor (**Figure 11**).

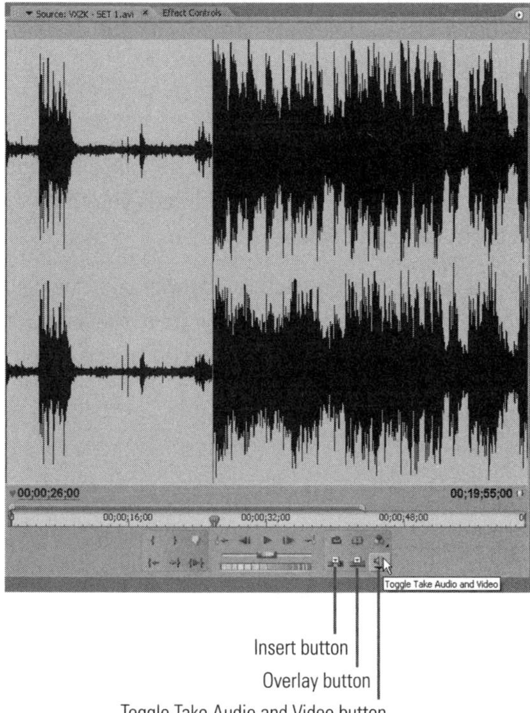

Figure 11 The audio-only view can be a great way to find a precise point in the video file.

To show only audio in the Source Monitor, do the following:

1. Drag your clip to the Source Monitor.

continued on next page

When Would You Import a Clip for Audio Purposes Only?

There are many scenarios in which importing only the audio component of a video clip might be helpful. The possibilities extend and vary widely, but two common examples come from stage event and wedding videography.

For instance, you may have one camera patched into the soundboard when shooting a concert or other performance and be using that camera for no other purpose. Or let's say you're shooting a wedding reception and synching live audio from one song to the best clips of fast dancing throughout the evening. You may not use any video from that one song, or you may not use any video from the camera you used to capture the audio from the song, but you'll still need to get the complete song into your audio track so you can cut your music video to it.

In both cases, the only reason you are importing a video clip from a particular camera source is to use the audio track, and that's all you'll place in the timeline.

So What Is Added?

Even if I've set In and Out points in the file in the audio-only view, as long as I click back to the audio and video view before adding the content to the project, Premiere Pro will add both audio and video to the project. Basically, Premiere Pro adds the content selected when you add the file to the project, not when you set In or Out points.

2. In the bottom panel of the Source Monitor, you'll find the Toggle Take Audio and Video button at the far right, as shown in Figure 11. The button has three states: audio, video, or both. Click the button until you see only the waveform. The selected state dictates what's added to your project when you add the content to the timeline.

Obviously, Figure 11 shows only the audio waveform from the selected clip. If you click the Insert or Overlay buttons to add the content to the project (or use any other technique), only the audio from the file will be inserted, not the video.

In this example, I'm using the audio file to find similar locations in the three video files from the ballet shoot, and I ultimately want to include *both* the audio and video files portions of the file in the project. To include both components after using the audio-only view for editing, do the following:

1. Set the In and Out points.
2. Click the Toggle Take Audio and Video button until both a tiny filmstrip and speaker appear, which tells you that you've selected both audio and video.
3. Drag the file down, or right-click anywhere in the Source Monitor and select Insert or Overlay from the menu that appears, and Premiere Pro will add the clip to the timeline.

#12 Targeting Tracks for Input

Premiere Pro is very flexible regarding ways to add content from the Source Monitor to the timeline: you can drag the file down, click the Insert or Overlay buttons that we saw in Figure 11, or use the keyboard shortcuts (,) and (.), respectively. (The only limitation is if you have toggled to audio only and try to drag the clip into a video track, or vice versa.) But if you use the button or keystroke commands, how do you control to which tracks the content is sent?

Figure 12a shows an example from a recent piano concert that I produced. On the timeline at the bottom of the frame, you can see that a new pianist, Kimberly Wells, is about to start playing. At the beginning of her mini-concert, I wanted to insert a title with her name and the name of the songs she was about to play. The title is currently in the Source Monitor and the current-time indicator at the start of her performance.

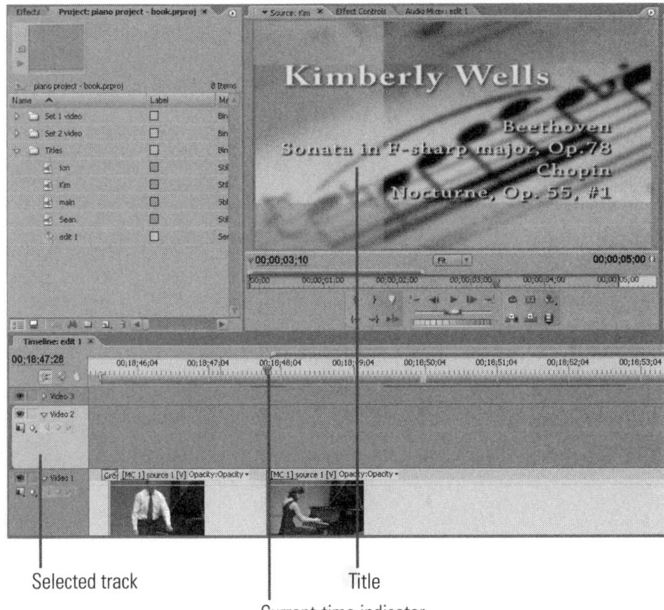

Figure 12a Let's insert this great title (from a Premiere Pro preset, by the way) at the start of Kimberly's performance (where the current-time indicator is now positioned).

Working with Audio

This technique works with audio and video. In fact, you can specify different tracks for the audio and video content coming from the same file—say Video 2 for the video frames and Audio 3 for the audio. This mixed target feature can be particularly useful when you're trying to shoehorn in some content during late-stage edits when the timeline is already crowded with audio and video.

If you look to the extreme left of the timeline, you'll note that Video 2 is highlighted and is a lighter color gray than Video 1. This is because I clicked the Video 2 track within the area that is now highlighted to select it. If you click the Overlay button (see Figure 11), Premiere Pro will insert your title at the current-time indicator on track Video 2 as shown in **Figure 12b**.

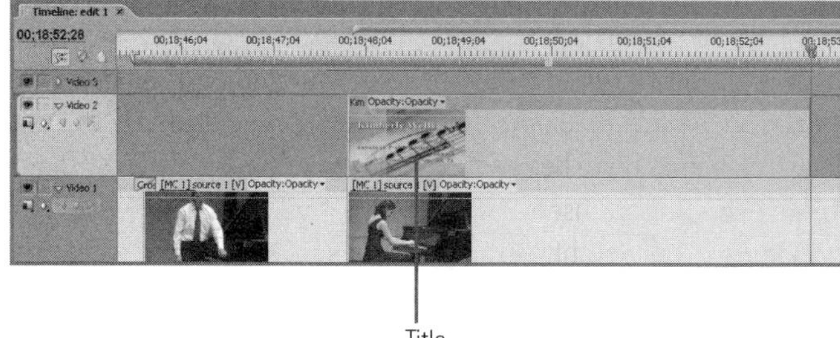

Figure 12b Here's the title inserted in the targeted track.

#13 Overlay vs. Insert Edits

When you add content to existing footage on the timeline, you have two choices. You can push the content back the duration of the new content, which is called an *insert edit*, or you can replace the content with the new content, which is called *overlay*.

In #12, I used an overlay edit, which inserted the title directly above the start of Kimberly's performance. This means that the viewer will see the title while hearing Kimberly play, then see her play. Another option is to use an insert edit to insert the title and move the rest of the concert to the right. I could just use the Insert button at the bottom of the Source Monitor, but I'll drag the track down, this time to Video 1, to illustrate another Premiere Pro feature (**Figure 13a**).

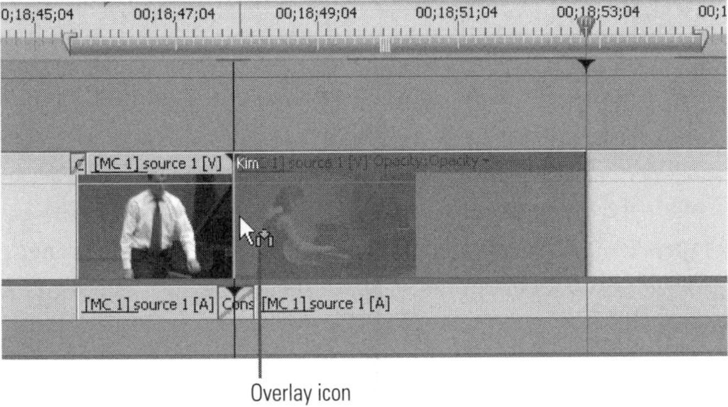

Figure 13a The Overlay icon means that the title will overwrite the selected video track.

When you drag the image to the timeline, Premiere Pro defaults to an overlay edit, where the clip will overwrite any content on the selected track. You can see the tiny Overlay icon attached to the pointer in Figure 13a. If you release the clip at this point, you'll get the result shown in **Figure 13b**.

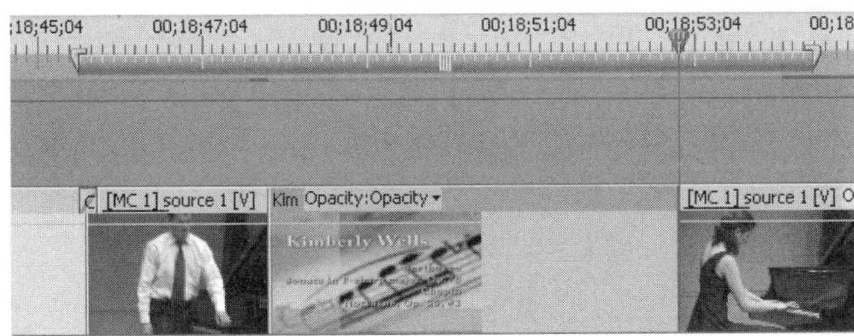

Figure 13b See? The title overwrote the video of Kimberly playing.

Which Tracks Shift During an Insert Edit?

Good question! An insert edit shifts all "unlocked" tracks. If there are tracks that you don't want to shift during the insert edit, lock those tracks by clicking the empty box immediately to the left of the track name on the left of the timeline. Premiere Pro will display a diagonal pattern on the locked tracks and prevent you from editing them in any way.

Overlay Edits and Overwrite Edits

Premiere Pro's usage of the term *overlay edit* is industry-standard language. However, overlay edits often refer to edits involving multiple tracks and blending effects like transparency, chromakey, and picture-in-picture. We deal with all three types of overlay edits throughout Chapter 6.

However, if you press and hold the Ctrl key while dragging the clip to the timeline, Premiere Pro changes into Insert mode, shown by the tiny Insert icon attached to the pointer in **Figure 13c**. Premiere Pro also displays white triangles on the current-time indicator on all video and audio tracks. This indicates that *all of these tracks* will be pushed back as part of the insert edit.

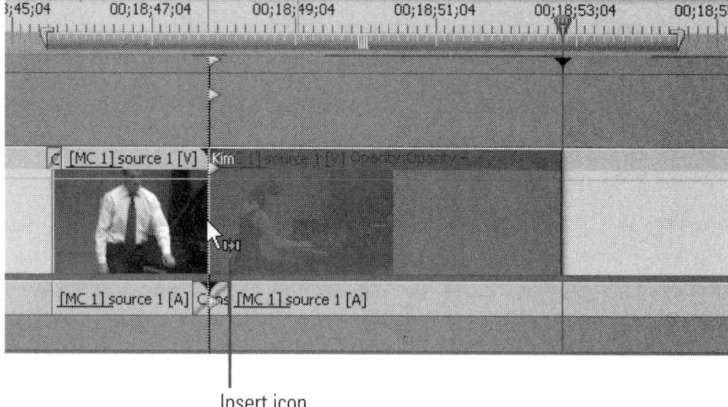

Figure 13c The Insert icon tells you that the dropped clip will push all unlocked tracks back, which is indicated by the white triangles.

Release the mouse, and you'll get the results shown in **Figure 13d**. Kimberly is shown from the very first note of her performance, and all audio tracks are pushed back, just as the triangles promised.

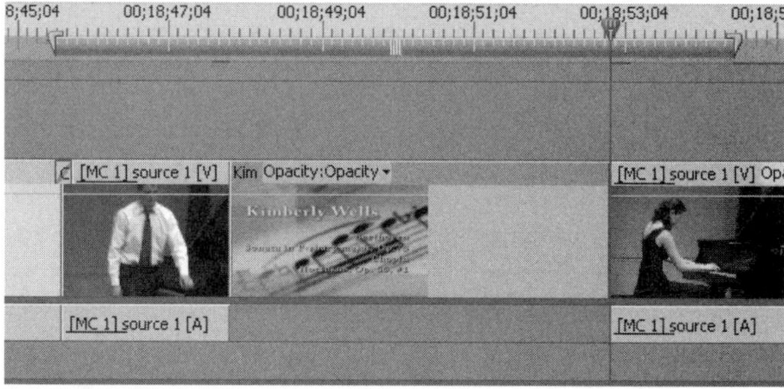

Figure 13d Here's what we want: the title inserted and Kimberly's performance shown from the first note.

#14 Previewing with the Work Area Bar

Though Premiere Pro's unrendered real-time transitions are usually accurate enough, you should always check these scene transition points with rendered audio and video, just to be sure. You do so by rendering a specific area of your project known as the *work area*. The work area is designated by the gray bar found immediately beneath the time ruler above the timeline (**Figure 14a**).

As a default, the work area stretches over the entire project, which means that the markers used to adjust the beginning and end of the bar are generally not visible when you're zoomed in as we are in Figure 14a.

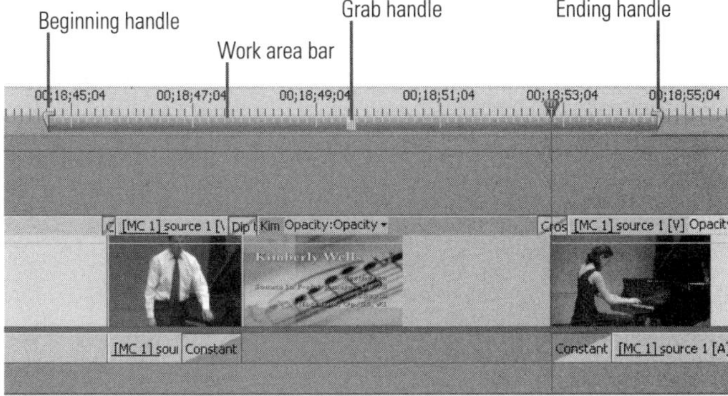

Figure 14a Let's render the transitions. Click and drag the handles of the work area bar so it's just outside all the edits you want to preview.

To render a specific area, do the following:

1. Double-click the work area bar to make the handles appear within the current viewable timeline area; Premiere Pro will insert handles at the edges of the timeline.
2. Drag the handles over the target preview area.
3. Click and drag the grab handle in the middle of the bar to move the work area bar itself. (If you click anywhere else, you'll just move the current-time indicator to that location.)

continued on next page

The Work Area Bar During Rendering

The work area bar can also limit the footage produced by Premiere Pro during actual rendering, and thus reduce the time required to render. For example, if you just want to render a short chunk of video to burn to DVD for a quick test, or get a representative sample of how your video will look at a given bit rate for streaming, you can set the work area as described here, and then choose to render only the work area. (See #71 for more details.)

4. Once you've set the work area bar in the desired area, press the Enter key to start the preview. If the area is as tiny as in our example, it should only take a few minutes to render before playing (**Figure 14b**).

Figure 14b Preview should be only a minute or two away because you're rendering so few frames.

#15 Working with Three-point Edits

The most fundamental action in editing is adding a section from a source clip to a sequence on the timeline. There are four relevant points to this activity: the In and Out points of the source clip and the In and Out points of the sequence.

In a three-point edit, you select any three points and the fourth takes care of itself. For example, in **Figure 15a**, I set the In and Out points in some crowd shots to insert as B-roll on Video 2 and set the current-time indicator exactly 20 minutes into the concert. These are three of the four points.

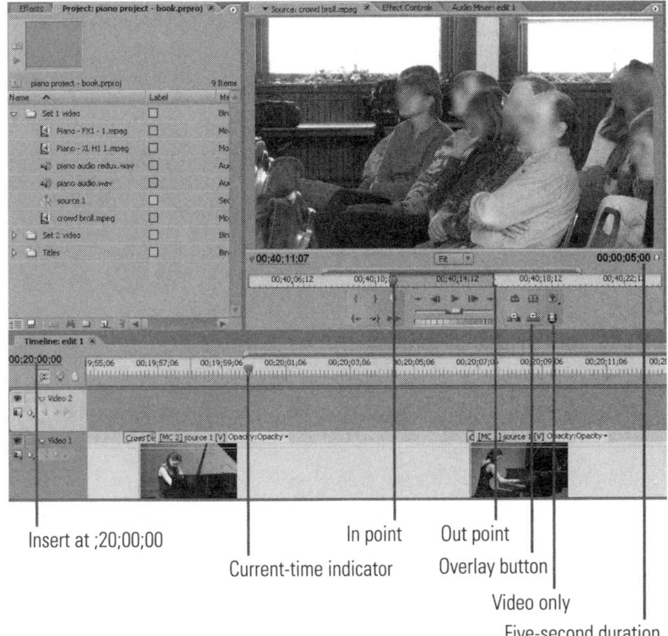

Figure 15a These are the three points in the three-point edit: the In and Out points in the Source Monitor, and the current-time indicator in the sequence.

When I click the Overwrite icon, Premiere inserts the 5 seconds of B-roll into Video 2 at the 20-minute mark, where the B-roll ends at precisely 20:04.29, the fourth point of the edit.

Now let's address a different problem. Say while you were shooting, the person sitting in front of you abruptly stood up and stretched, blocking your view. Now you've got 4 seconds of video to hide with B-roll.

Rather than setting the In and Out points in the Source Monitor, you set them in the sequence using controls in the Program Monitor. Here's how:

1. Set the In point on the last good frame before your shot was obscured.

2. Set the Out point on the first frame after your field of view was restored. This creates the selection shown in both the timeline and Program Monitor in **Figure 15b**—essentially, the bad video you need to hide with B-roll.

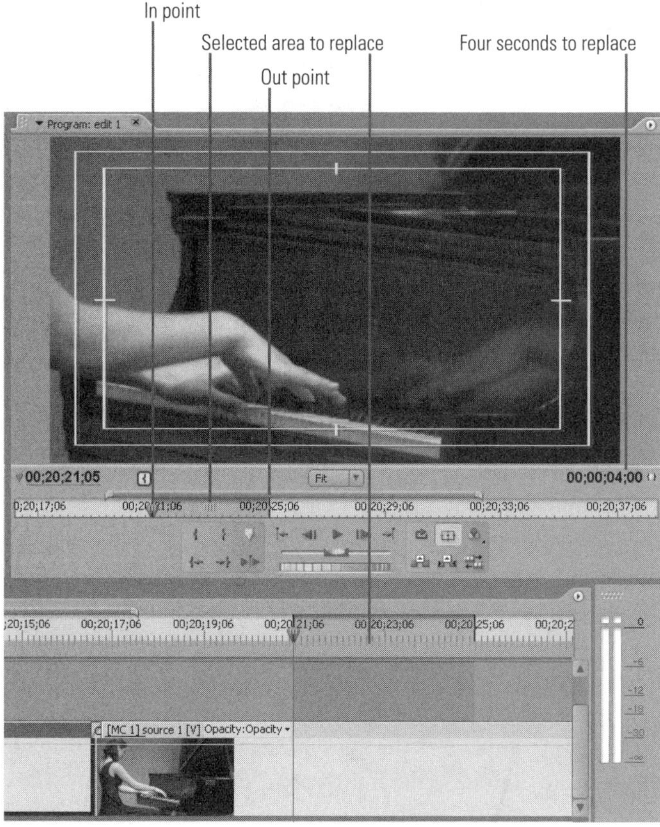

Figure 15b Now let's mark two points in the timeline and one in the Source Monitor.

3. Next, load your crowd scene into the Source Monitor, and set the In point.

4. Click the Overlay icon in the Source Monitor, and Premiere Pro will automatically fill the selected area in the sequence with B-roll from the Source Monitor (**Figure 15c**). In this example, we set two points in the sequence and one in the Source Monitor, and Premiere Pro set the fourth.

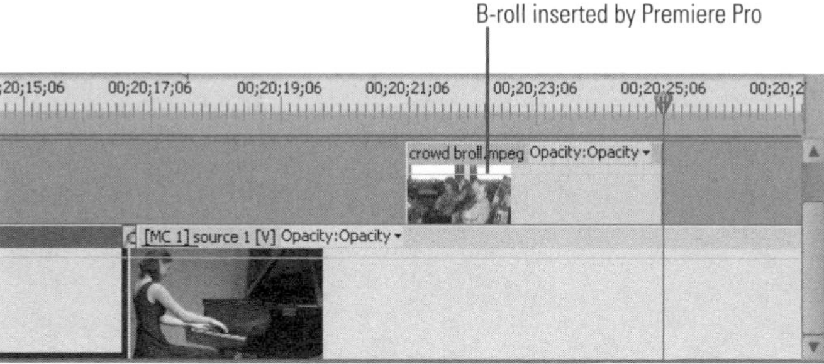

Figure 15c Here's the B-roll inserted by Premiere Pro. Note that Premiere Pro clears the In point and Out point in the sequence so you can go on to the next edit.

Insert? Overlay? Both?

You can perform three-point editing using both insert and overlay editing, but for adding B-roll as I was doing, overlay is definitely the way to go.

The sharp-eyed reader will also note that I've got the Toggle Take Audio and Video buttons in Figure 15a set to video only, since I don't want to overwrite the carefully captured audio, just the video. This is a perfect example of when you'd want to use this feature to isolate only the video portion of the clip in the Source Monitor.

B-Roll

Just to make sure we're on the same page, *B-roll* refers to footage that's ancillary to but not the main event. In this project, the main event is the concert, while B-roll is the video of folks watching and hopefully applauding. B-roll serves a lot of purposes, including hiding poor quality A-Roll (when you accidentally kicked the tripod) and helping to retain the viewer's interest.

#16 Working with Four-point Edits

Suppose you have only three good seconds of B-roll, but a four-second gap to fill? This is the classic four-point edit.

Start by setting the In and Out points in the Source Monitor for the good B-roll that you have and your In and Out points in the sequence representing the video you have to hide (**Figure 16a**). Next, do the following:

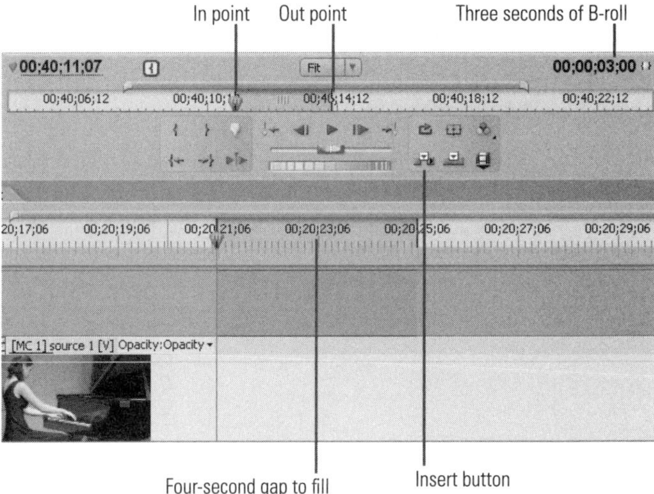

Figure 16a Now we're selecting all four points–In and Out points in both the Source Monitor and Program Monitor/timeline.

1. Click the Overlay button, and Premiere Pro displays the dialog box shown in **Figure 16b**.

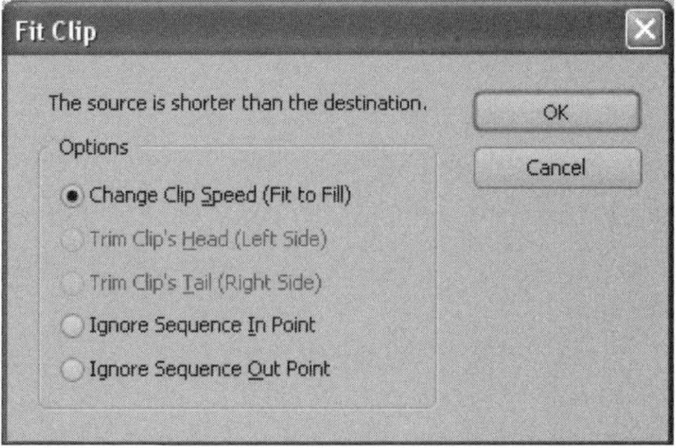

Figure 16b The four-point edit only makes sense when you choose the first option; all others essentially perform a three-point edit.

2. Choose Change Clip Speed (Fit to Fill), and Premiere Pro will slow down the B-roll to make it fill the space. Since there's not a lot of bouncing, cheering, or waving arms in the B-roll (it's a piano recital, after all, not a Springsteen concert), most viewers probably won't even notice that we slowed it down.

Neither of the final two alternatives makes sense, since this would leave one second of blocked video in the front or back of the inserted B-roll. Note that if the selected area of the B-roll exceeded the selected area in the sequence, the second and third choices (grayed out in Figure 16b) would become active.

Again, however, neither of these choices would make sense; if you wanted to trim the Clip's Head (left side), you would have performed a three-point edit and just set the Out point. The only time it makes sense to use a four-point edit is when the duration of your source video and the duration of the sequence you need to fill don't match, and Premiere Pro either needs to slow the video down to fit, or speed it up.

CHAPTER THREE

Using Premiere Pro and After Effects Together

If you're unfamiliar with After Effects, you should know that the program is a gold mine of content, particularly motion backgrounds and text effects. In addition, for many key functions, including chroma key, variable slow motion, color correction, and scaling, After Effects has more features than Premiere Pro and produces much higher output quality.

Most importantly, you should know that you don't really need to master After Effects to retrieve these gold nuggets. Understand a few simple concepts about how the program works, and you can use it to quickly and easily improve the quality and variety of your videos and DVDs. This chapter starts with these concepts.

Then you'll learn the integration option available between After Effects and Premiere Pro to help you work more efficiently. First you'll learn alternatives for getting Premiere Pro content into After Effects, then how to get the results back into Premiere Pro.

#17 Getting Started with After Effects

Working in After Effects

Working in After Effects is a lot like Premiere; generally, you apply effects or presets by dragging them from the Effects and Presets panel onto clips on the timeline and customizing the controls. The procedure for rendering is definitely different, as described in #84.

You can start After Effects projects many ways, and you'll learn many of them in this book. The most straightforward way is to insert a file into After Effects, and create a new composition manually (what Premiere calls a *sequence* and After Effects calls a *composition*). Here's how.

1. In After Effects, choose File > Import.
2. Select the file(s). After Effects loads them into a Project panel that looks comfortingly like Premiere Pro's (**Figure 17a**). In the figure, I'm loading a song called "Power to Rock."

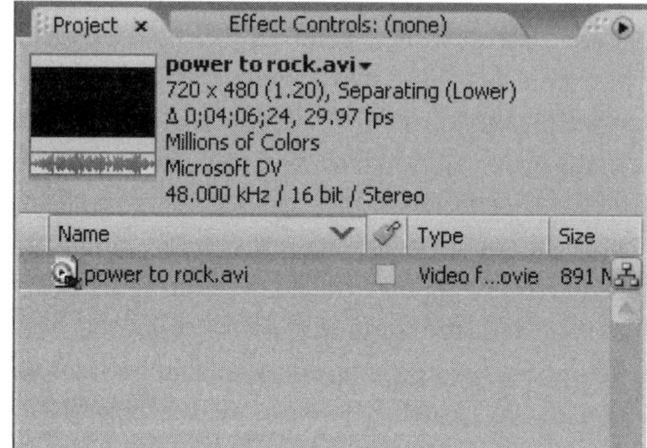

Figure 17a After Effects' Project panel looks just like Premiere Pro's. Here's the imported file.

3. Drag the video file into the timeline. This creates a composition that's the same duration as the video file. You should see the file on the timeline (**Figure 17b**) and a new composition in the Project panel.

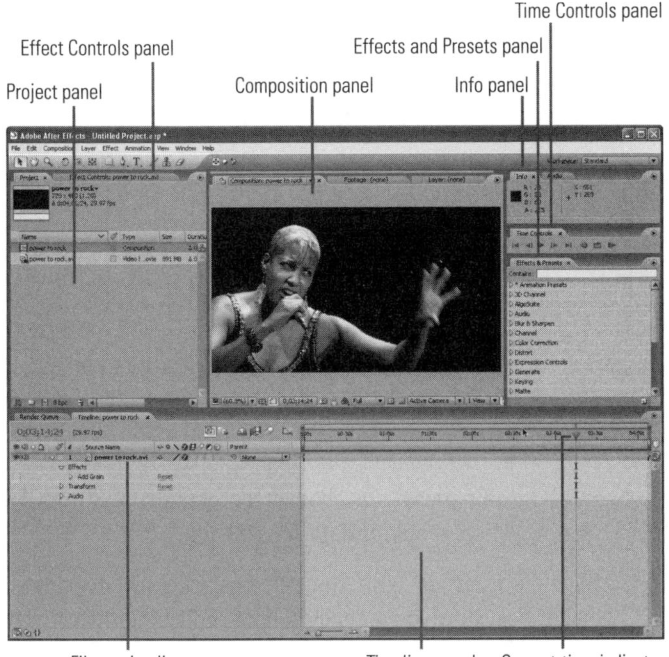

Figure 17b Drag the video file into the timeline to create a composition of equal length. Here's After Effects in all its glory.

4. Next, choose Composition > Composition Settings to open the Composition Settings window (**Figure 17c**). The Duration is 4:06:24, matching the inserted song perfectly.

continued on next page

Creating an After Effects Project from Within Premiere Pro

If you create your After Effects project from Premiere Pro, After Effects will automatically use the correct composition settings, a nice error-prevention feature. See #20 to learn how.

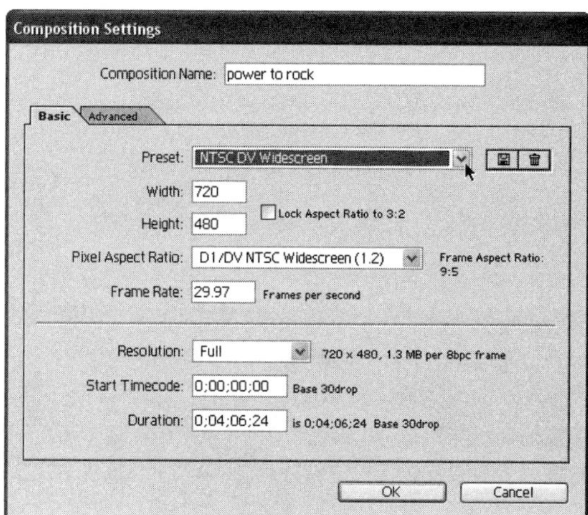

Figure 17c After Effects' Composition Settings window.

5. Click the Preset drop-down menu, and you'll see a number of presets.
6. Select a new preset, or choose the default, NTSC DV Widescreen, which is appropriate for this file.
7. If you're satisfied with the settings, click OK to close the dialog box. Now you're ready to start editing in After Effects.

#18 Copying and Pasting from Premiere Pro to After Effects

Adobe offers a number of ways to pass content back and forth between Premiere Pro and After Effects. First is copying and pasting content from Premiere Pro to After Effects. This works well for getting content into After Effects, but you may have some issues returning them to Premiere Pro if that's your goal.

For example, suppose you're editing in Premiere Pro and decide to apply a chroma key effect in After Effects. Here's how it works:

1. In Premiere Pro, select the clips, right-click, and choose Copy from the pop-up menu (**Figure 18a**).

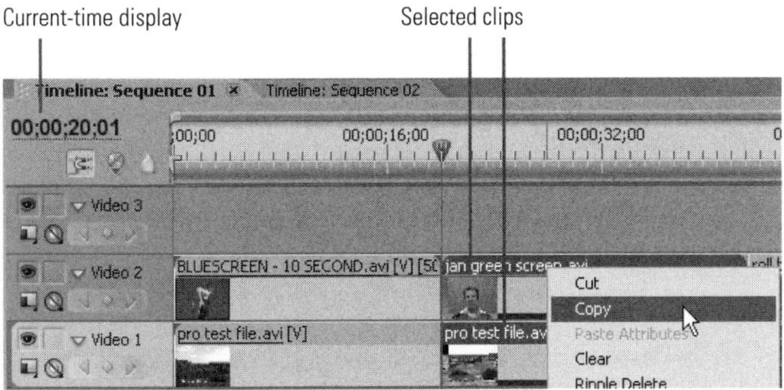

Figure 18a To copy from Premiere Pro to After Effects, select the clips, right-click, and choose Copy.

2. Open After Effects, and select Composition > New Composition to open a new composition.

3. In After Effects, click the timeline panel and choose Edit > Paste. After Effects inserts the clips into the composition at the same location as the clip in Premiere Pro (**Figure 18b**).

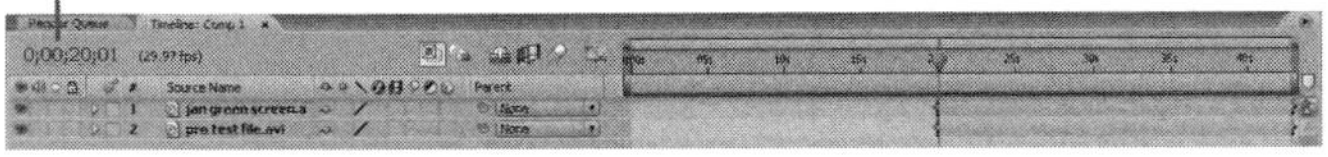

Current-time display

Figure 18b Here are the pasted clips in an After Effects composition. Note that After Effects pasted them at the exact same timeline position as Premiere Pro.

continued on next page

Filter unavailable?

What should you do? Save your work as an After Effects project and import it into Premiere Pro via Dynamic Link, which is technique #20. Or render the file to DV format and import the resulting file back into Premiere Pro.

Visit www.adobe.com/support/techdocs/330388.html for a complete list of items that won't copy and paste from Premiere Pro to After Effects.

Ways to Create a New Composition

The most obvious way to create a new composition to contain pasted content is by choosing Composition > New Composition as mentioned above. Another way is to create it from within Premiere Pro as described in #20. Either way, you should choose duration carefully; life is simpler when duration matches that of your content.

Saving a Premiere Pro Project from After Effects

After Effects can save compositions as Premiere Pro projects (choose File > Export > Adobe Premiere Pro Project), but if you apply effects in After Effects that aren't available in Premiere Pro, Premiere Pro can't load them. Overall, the easiest and most powerful way to share your work from After Effects into Premiere Pro is to use Dynamic Link, as described in #20.

Note

According to the current time display in both figures, the clips start at 20:01 on both timelines. This means that once you paste it back into Premiere Pro, the starting point of the chroma key clip will be exactly where you want it, at 20:01.

4. With your clip now placed in an After Effects composition, apply the After Effects effect of your choice. For example, I use the fabulous Keylight chroma key plug-in on the green-screen clip.
5. Once you've applied the effect to your satisfaction, copy and paste the clip back into Premiere Pro, making sure that the current-time indicator is set at the desired insertion point.

Note

There are limitations as to the types of effects and other project elements that you can copy from Premiere Pro into After Effects. Premiere Pro won't recognize any After Effects filters that it doesn't share. There are also a number of other After Effects content types that don't paste into Premiere Pro, like text layers.

*In the example described in this how-to, you'll notice that the green-screen clip reappeared in Premiere Pro totally un-chroma keyed! Click the Effect Controls tab, and you'll see the message "Offline (filter unavailable)" (**Figure 18c**).*

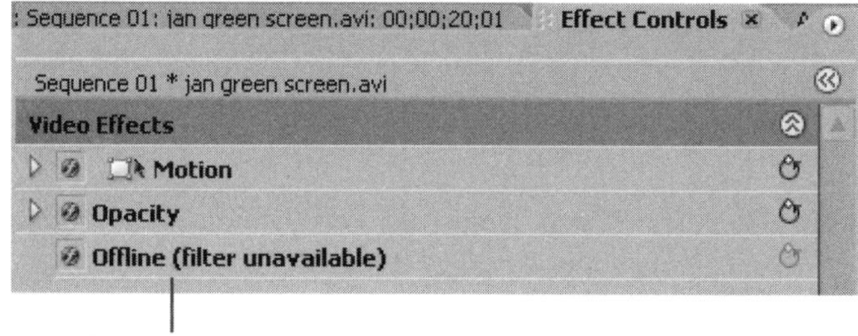

Figure 18c Yikes! Premiere Pro can't import any After Effects filters it doesn't share.

#19 Importing Premiere Pro Projects into After Effects

Sometimes you want to import a Premiere Pro project or sequence into After Effects for final tweaking and output. Here's how to do it.

1. To start, choose File > Import > Project then navigate to and select the Premiere Pro project file. After Effects will open the dialog box shown in **Figure 19a**; choose the desired option and click OK.

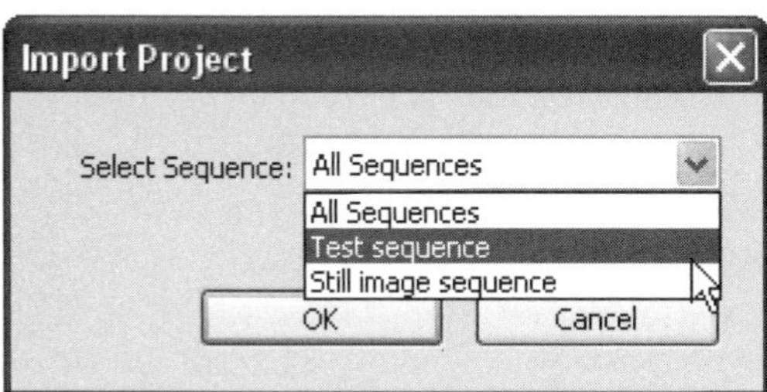

Figure 19a When you import a Premiere Pro project into After Effects, you can choose all or any sequence.

2. Once imported into After Effects, you can open any Premiere Pro sequence as a composition by double-clicking the sequence in the Project panel (**Figure 19b**). As you can see, the After Effects timeline presents an individual layer for all project content, very much like Photoshop.

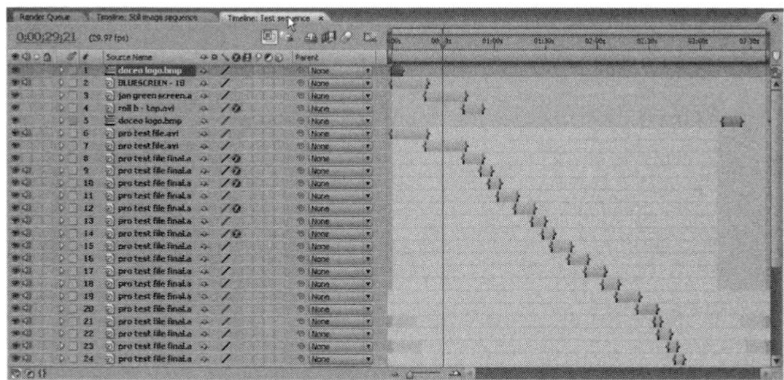

Figure 19b This timeline will be quite a shock if you're used to Premiere Pro, but will make tons of sense if you're a heavy Photoshop user.

continued on next page

Overcoming Interapplication Incompatibilities

Only the effects shared by After Effects and Premiere Pro will import with the project. If such critical incompatibilities affect your project, the most straightforward option is render a DV-AVI file, import that into After Effects, and re-render to your final target output. Alternatively, you could start by applying the After Effects filter to your target clip, saving it as an After Effects project, and importing and editing it via Dynamic Link. This would make the project slightly more complex, but would likely save at least one rendering generation.

Applying an Effect to Multiple Layers

You can apply an effect to multiple layers in After Effects by clicking Ctrl+A to select all layers, then dragging the target effect onto any layer. Changes made to the Effects panel flow through to all layers until you deselect them by clicking Ctrl+Shift+A.

3. To ensure that changes made to the Premiere Pro project in After Effects flow back to the original project, save the After Effects project and import it back into Premiere Pro via Dynamic Link (see #20). (You might consider doing the same for rendering, since the rendering options in Premiere Pro are much easier to use than the options in After Effects.)

#20 Importing After Effects Projects into Premiere Pro with Dynamic Link

Adobe Dynamic Link allows you to create an After Effects composition in Premiere Pro (and Encore) or import one directly. This potentially saves a rendering generation and delays what can be a lengthy After Effects rendering cycle until you render the final project. The After Effects project can contain *any* After Effects filter or other content, even those not directly supported in Premiere Pro. So even if you can't paste the content and related effects from After Effects into Premiere Pro, you can bring them in via Dynamic Link.

Moreover, any changes made to the original project in After Effects automatically flow through to the imported project in Premiere Pro, saving another time-consuming rendering cycle. For serious integration between Premiere Pro and After Effects, Dynamic Link is your best option.

To open an After Effects composition in Premiere Pro, start by doing one of the following:

- If you've already started your After Effects composition, import it by choosing File > Adobe Dynamic Link > Import After Effects Composition. Premiere Pro opens the dialog box shown in **Figure 20a**, where you can navigate to the folder with the After Effects projects and choose the target composition.

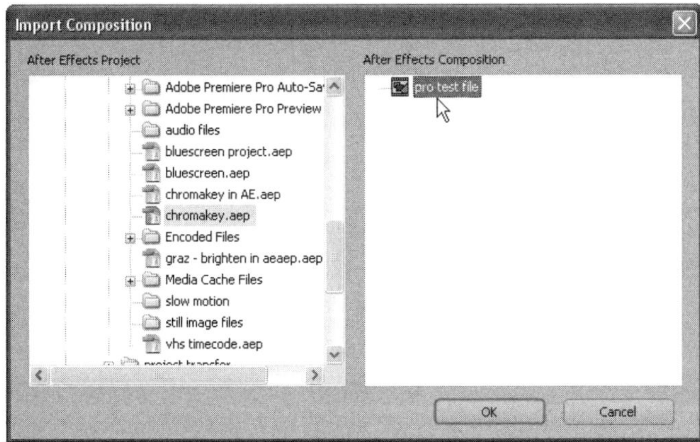

Figure 20a Here's how you import an After Effects composition into Premiere Pro.

Making Changes in After Effects

To re-edit the composition in After Effects, select the composition, right-click, and choose Edit Original. Note that all edits made in After Effects instantly appear in Premiere Pro; you don't have to wait to save the After Effects project to preview them.

- Or create a new After Effects Composition by choosing File > Adobe Dynamic Link > New After Effects Composition. I like this approach because After Effects automatically chooses composition settings that match your current Premiere Pro project, minimizing error, and imports the composition into your project, saving a step.

Note

*Once in the Project panel, the composition looks and acts just like any other video file. You can drag it to the Source Monitor, trim it, drag it to the timeline, and add audio and video effects (**Figure 20b**).*

Figure 20b And here's said composition, looking and—more importantly—acting just like any other video clip in the Project panel and timeline.

CHAPTER FOUR

Perfecting Video Quality

If you shoot live events outside of a studio, you're very good, very lucky, or you spend lots of time fixing the color and exposure of your videos. Fortunately, Adobe Production Studio has a wealth of tools to identify and correct these issues.

In this chapter, we'll start with brightness and contrast adjustments, and then move to color correction and image stabilization, and conclude by explaining how you can apply these effects efficiently to multiple clips. After Effects has great tools for color and brightness adjustments, but in this chapter we'll work mostly in Premiere Pro, where it's easier and faster to correct most videos.

While various Production Studio scopes offer some objectivity for adjusting brightness and color, many adjustments are just plain subjective. If the color or brightness of your computer monitor or NTSC display isn't accurate, your adjustments will be off. At the very least, you should run Adobe Gamma to calibrate your monitor (for a helpful knowledgebase article on the subject, visit www.adobe.com/support/techdocs/321608.html). You should also consider a third-party calibration tool for both your computer monitor and NTSC monitor or television (check www.colorvision.com for several options).

When producing for DVD, burn some corrected footage to DVD early in the process and view it on several television sets to gauge your adjustments. Otherwise, when you jump from the computer to DVD, you may be unpleasantly surprised by the inaccuracy of your adjustments.

Much of the footage shown in the examples discussed in this chapter comes from a test project I use to evaluate video editors. Essentially, it's a series of mistakes like underexposed video, white-balance issues, handheld shots, and other detritus. If you see text and/or time code on a screen, that's because it's part of my test project.

#21 Checking Brightness and Color with the YC Waveform Scope

100% Intensity

When you open your YC Waveform, the intensity level should be set at 50%. In Figure 21b, I boosted the level to 100% to produce a more visible screenshot. Note that varying the intensity level doesn't change the pixel values for the videos on the timeline, just the pixels in the YC Waveform, shown in Figure 21a.

Premiere Pro's YC Waveform scope (**Figure 21a**) displays the intensities of the luminance signal, essentially brightness (called *luma*, or Y) and color signal (called *chroma*, or C). In the onscreen chart, luma is presented as green and chroma blue, and both are measured as IRE values, which stands for Institute of Radio Engineers (go figure). The brighter the pixel value, the higher the IRE rating, which is shown on the vertical axis.

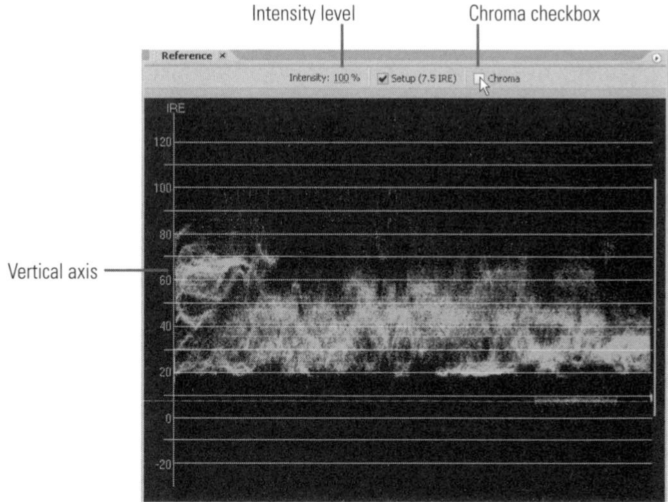

Figure 21a Here's Premiere Pro's YC Waveform scope. Note how all the pixels are grouped in the middle, indicating poor contrast.

You can display the scope by clicking the Output button in the Program Monitor or Source Monitor, just above the timeline, as shown in **Figure 21b**.

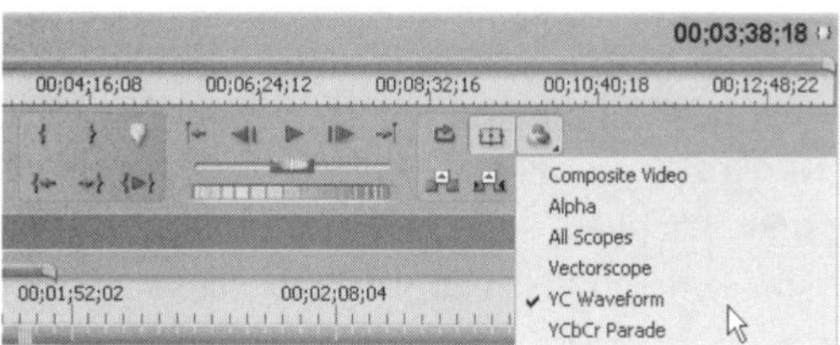

Figure 21b Here's how you choose scopes in both the Program Monitor and Source Monitor.

For broadcast television, producers keep their signals between 100 IRE (pure white) and 7.5 IRE (pure black), a range referred to as *broadcast legal*. Computer monitors and television sets can display pixels that exceed these limits, but you shouldn't necessarily consider the full spectrum available on your computer as appropriate to your project, for several reasons.

First, if too much of the signal exceeds the broadcast-legal limits, the image will be over- or underexposed and lose detail at either end. Conversely, if the signal is bunched in the middle, the image will lack contrast and appear faded. This is the problem with Figure 21a, where most pixels are clustered between 20 and 90. You'll learn how to deal with insufficient contrast in #23.

Finally, when correcting the brightness and contrast of your videos, you should check the YC Waveform to assess the levels and spread of both your starting point and subsequent adjustments.

Viewing Chroma Only

Note that you can display only the luminance signal by clicking the Chroma checkbox above the scope. This approach is helpful when adjusting video brightness and contrast. When it comes time to make color adjustments, turn Chroma back on.

#22 Setting Up for Color Correction

Reference Monitor During Color Correction

Using a separate Reference Monitor, usually set to RGB Parade (#28), can prove absolutely essential when performing manual color correction, especially in Multi-Camera projects.

Color correction works best when you can see all relevant information. Adobe has created a Color Correction workspace in Premiere Pro that does just that. You can access it by choosing Window > Workspace > Color Correction.

Or you can create your own workspace with reference monitors added by clicking the Program Monitor fly-out menu and choosing New Reference Monitor (**Figure 22**). This opens a second monitor you can configure with the Output button found in the six-icon panel in the lower-right corner of the Program Monitor.

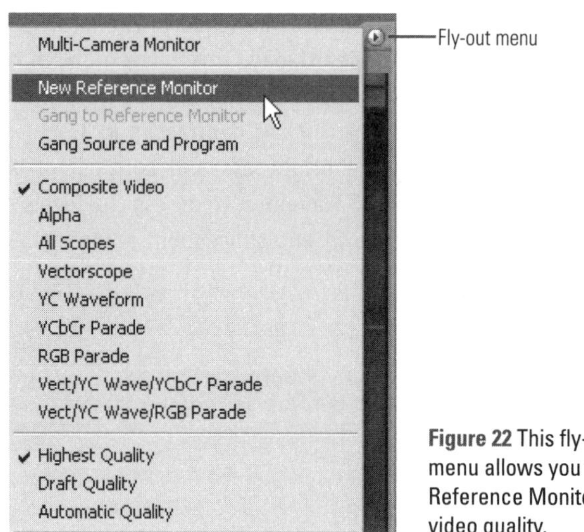

Figure 22 This fly-out menu allows you to open a Reference Monitor and set video quality.

To set video quality, do one of the following:

- Click the Output button and select Highest Quality Output (selected in Figure 22) to display video at full resolution during preview, which is most accurate but can produce dropped frames, especially when editing HDV video.
- Select Draft Quality to display video at one-half resolution during preview, which improves frame rate but can make your video look grainy.

Note that whenever you stop the preview, Premiere Pro always displays a full-resolution still frame.

#23 Adjusting Brightness with Levels

I find the Levels effect the most intuitive and visual brightness adjustment tool in Premiere Pro's repertoire (After Effects too). Here's how it works.

1. Select Premiere Pro's Video Effects folder in the lower-right panel and open the Adjust subfolder.
2. Select the Levels effect and drag it onto your clip.
3. Click the Effect Controls tab in the Source Monitor to open the Effect Controls panel.

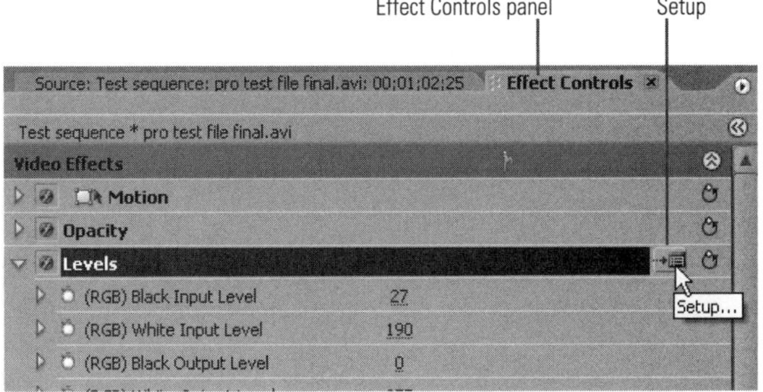

Figure 23a Working in the Effect Controls panel, click Setup to view the histogram shown in Figure 23b. This clip has insufficient contrast.

4. Click Setup to open the Levels Settings dialog (**Figure 23b**).

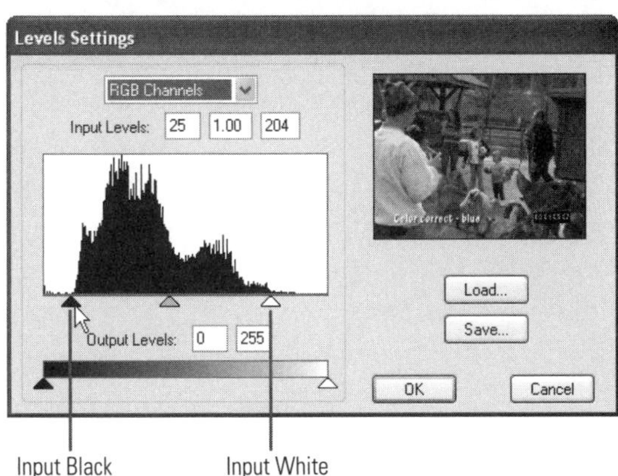

Figure 23b Now "bracket" the histogram, dragging Input Black to the first significant group of pixels on the left, and the Input White to the first significant group of pixels on the right.

continued on next page

Auto Levels

Premiere Pro's Auto Levels effect performs a similar operation, but is more conservative, often producing less contrast. For example, in Figure 23b the pixels to the right of the Input White triangle will likely be overexposed and obscured (often called "crushed"), but there are so few that the result is insignificant (though obviously you should preview to be sure). Though similar controls aren't available in the Auto Levels effect, it appears that Adobe (wisely) prefers to err on the safe side, preventing any under- or overexposure, but limiting the improvement in brightness or contrast.

What About Gamma?

While "bracketing" (what you did in Step 5) is very objective, adjusting gamma—the middle triangle in Figure 23b—is largely subjective. Technically, gamma adjustments change brightness in the midtones of the frame, leaving the darkest and lightest areas unaffected. If your clip still doesn't look right after bracketing, go ahead and wiggle the gamma triangle around and see if it helps.

What if My Levels Show a Flat Line?

This can happen when shooting stage productions with a black backdrop, and potentially other shots with lots of black. As a result, you won't have sufficient information on the line to make a decision. In these instances, switch to the Brightness & Contrast effect, and keep the YC Waveform scope open while making your adjustments.

That Sneaky Brightness & Contrast Effect

When you apply this effect, Premiere Pro automatically adjusts both brightness and contrast to keep them broadcast legal—even when the values are set to zero! Watch the YC Waveform and toggle the effect on and off, and you'll see. In this manner, it works more like an auto-correcting brightness and contrast tool than a manual one.

Note:

The Levels Settings histogram displays the brightness values of all pixels in the current frame on a scale from 0 to 255, shown on the bottom X-axis from darkest to brightest. The Y-axis represents the total number of pixels at the particular brightness value. Figure 23b confirms that most pixels are bunched in the middle, with few approaching the extremes.

5. Move the black triangle (Input Black) inward to the first value with significant numbers of pixels. Then do the same with the white triangle (Input White).

Note:

*This tells Premiere Pro to ignore the pixel values outside the triangles, and to convert the Input Black value to 7.5 IRE and the Input White value to 100 IRE. As shown in **Figure 23c,** the luma pixels are spread over a much larger range, indicating increased contrast.*

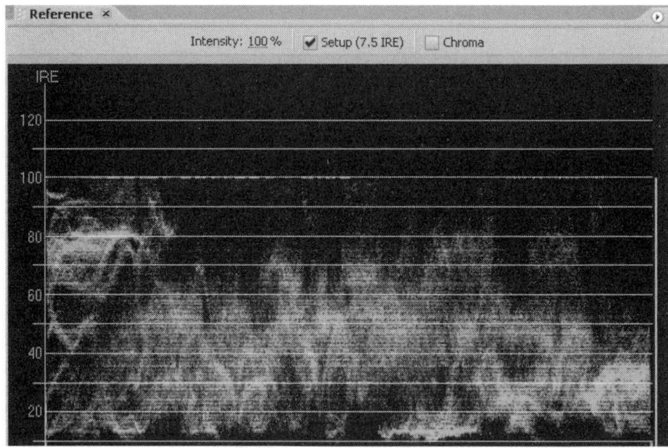

Figure 23c Now the pixels are much more broadly spread vertically, indicating better contrast.

#24 Fixing Backlight Issues with the Shadow/Highlight Filter

Backlighted videos are shot with a bright light behind the subject with automatic exposure enabled. To avoid overexposure, the camera darkens the entire image, often obscuring the subject as shown on the left in **Figure 24a.**

Figure 24a The Shadow/Highlight effect boosts the foreground lighting without touching the back. This figure shows a clip before (left) and after (right) the effect is applied.

If you checked this image in the YC Waveform (see #21), you'll be surprised to see that the overall contrast and brightness is great; the lighting is just in the wrong places. You need a tool to brighten the foreground image without boosting the background light. Fortunately, Premiere Pro has such a tool. It's called the Shadow/Highlight filter, and it works like absolute magic on backlighted images. To apply this filter, do the following:

1. Select Premiere Pro's Video Effects folder in the lower-right panel and open the Adjust subfolder.
2. Select Shadow/Highlight and drag it onto your clip.
3. Open the Video Effects panel and you'll see the controls located in **Figure 24b.**

continued on next page

Caveats

When you apply the Shadow/Highlight effect, watch for a slight strobe effect in Auto mode, which you can minimize by applying Temporal Smoothing. This averages the effect over adjacent frames. Unfortunately, this option is unavailable in manual mode, which is why it's grayed out in Figure 24b.

Also watch for "banding" where adjacent pixels coagulate into bands that dance around lights in the video frame. If this occurs, adjust the Highlight Amount downward.

How to Toggle the Shadow/Highlight Effect on and off

See the little *f* in a circle to the left of the Shadow/Highlight effect in Figure 24b? Click it to toggle the effect on and off in the Program Monitor to assess how well it's working.

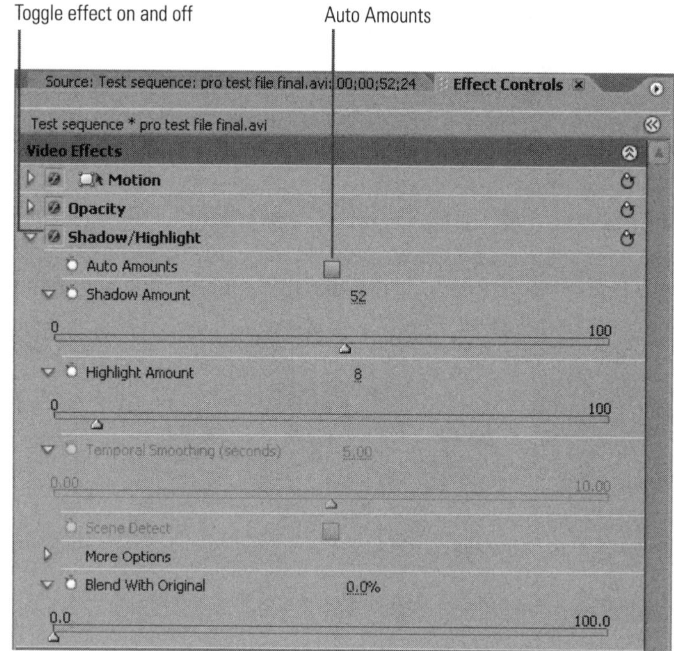

Figure 24b I usually end up going manually with this tool by deselecting the Auto Amounts box.

4. To make manual adjustments (the effect defaults to Auto Amounts; I've deselected the box in the figure), use the slider bars below the Shadow Amount and Highlight Amount headings. In the example shown in Figure 24b, I had to boost the Shadow Amount (the lighting applied to the shadows in the image) and reduce the Highlight Amount (the lighting applied to the highlighted areas). The result is shown on the right in Figure 24a.

#25 Perfecting the Auto Color Effect

I have a four-level hierarchy for color correction in Production Studio. First, in Premiere Pro, I try the Auto Color effect. If that doesn't get the job done, I move on to the Fast Color Corrector, and then the Three-Way Color Corrector. If my results are inadequate, I try Color Finesse in After Effects, but I won't demonstrate that here.

Basically, my goal is to make color correction as automatic as possible, and each tool requires more manual input than the last. Before starting, check the YC Waveform monitor (#21) and apply the Levels or Brightness & Contrast effect (#23), if necessary. To apply the Auto Color effect, do the following:

1. In Premiere Pro, double-click the target clip on the timeline to bring it up in the Source Monitor.
2. Click the Effect Controls tab to open that panel.
3. Click and drag the Auto Color effect from the Effects panel's Adjust subfolder to the space above the Levels or Brightness & Contrast effect in the Effect Controls panel, if you've already applied those effects to your clip. Otherwise drag the effect to the slot just below the Opacity effect (**Figure 25a**).

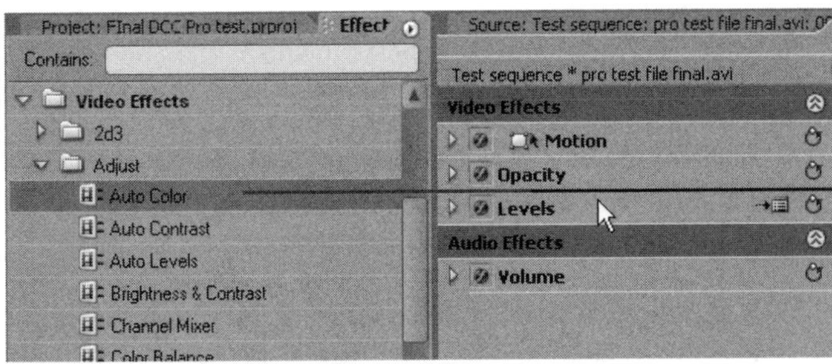

Figure 25a Drag the effect directly to the Effect Controls panel, so you can control its placement order.

Note:

I typically get better results when the Auto Color effect is above the Levels effect. Order does matter, and you can experiment by dragging the effects up and down in the Effect Controls panel to change the sequence in which they're applied, and previewing the impact in the Program Monitor. You can always restore the original order if you don't like the results.

continued on next page

When to Use Auto Color

Not to beat a dead horse, but I get much better results with the Auto Color effect if brightness and contrast are properly adjusted, and I get poor results when they're not. So check and adjust Levels if necessary before applying this effect.

4. Preview the image in the Program Monitor. If acceptable, skip to step 7. If not, continue to step 5.

5. Click the triangle to the left of the Auto Color effect to reveal its configurable properties (**Figure 25b**).

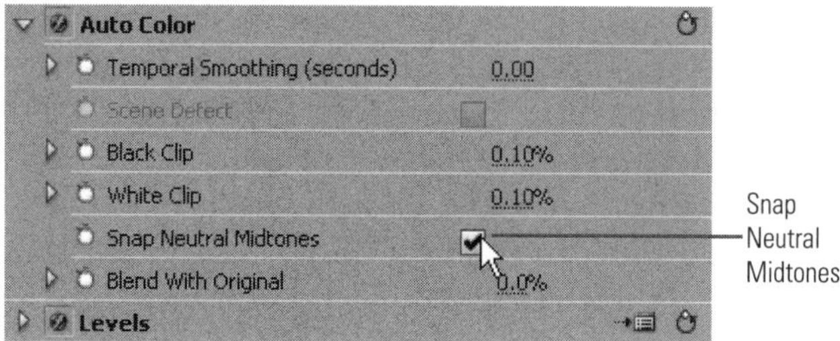

Figure 25b Select the Snap Neutral Midtones checkbox to adjust the Auto Color effect.

6. Select the Snap Neutral Midtones checkbox. If this doesn't produce the desired quality, delete the effect by right-clicking the effect and choosing Clear. Then move to #26. If the results are acceptable, continue to step 7.

   Note:
   Technically, when you "snap" the neutral midtones, you're adjusting the gamma values in the clip, which often adds significant contrast and vividness to the Auto Color effect.

7. Render at least a 30-second segment of the clip (#14), and then preview, watching for flicker.

8. If there's flicker in your rendered clip, set Temporal Smoothing (found in the Auto Color configurable controls) to 5 seconds, re-render, and preview.

9. If the flicker persists, adjust duration of smoothing and toggle the Scene Detect button (also in the Auto Color controls) on and off to see if this resolves the problem. If not, delete the effect and refer to #26.

#26 Adjusting White Balance with the Fast Color Corrector

If the Auto Color effect doesn't resolve color problems in your video, try white balancing your clip using the Fast Color Corrector effect. Here's how:

1. Double-click the target clip on the timeline.
2. Click the Effect Controls tab to open that panel.
3. In the Effects panel, click and drag the Fast Color Corrector effect from the Color Correction subfolder to the Effect Controls panel, to the space below the Levels or Brightness & Contrast effect, if applied. Otherwise drag it to the slot just below the Opacity effect.

   Note:
   The Fast Color Corrector seems to work best when inserted below the Levels effect. You can easily shift the order by dragging the effects up and down in the Effect Controls panel.

4. Click the triangle to the left of the Fast Color Corrector to reveal its configurable properties (**Figure 26a**).
5. If desired, select the Show Split View checkbox and adjust options to your liking (Horizontal or Vertical view in the Layout drop-down list and percentage in the Split View Percent).
6. Click the eyedropper next to the White Balance chip, press the Ctrl key, and click a spot in the video frame that should be pure white. I'm using the white shirt of the girl in the coat. Sample a few white areas to see which provides the best result. If this resolves your problem, skip to step 8. If not, move to step 7.

   Note:
   If there are no white patches in a particular frame, move to a frame from the same scene that contains some white. If there are no frames that contain white, see #28 on using the RGB Parade scope.

continued on next page

What the Fast Color Corrector Tools Do

There are several tools within the Fast Color Corrector to help you fine-tune your video. Top to bottom, here's what they do:

Hue Angle controls the outer ring of the color wheel; rotating left shifts the colors toward green; rotating right shifts them toward red.

Balance Magnitude controls correction intensity. This corresponds to the ball on the end of the Color Correction widget, with more intense adjustments produced further from the center.

According to the user manual, **Balance Gain** controls the "coarseness or fineness of the Balance Magnitude and Balance Angle Adjustments," and corresponds to the crossbar in the middle of the Color Correction widget. I use it to fine-tune these adjustments, and find it easier to adjust by dragging over the numerical values than dragging the crossbar directly.

Balance Angle controls which colors are adjusted. Generally, when fixing a colorcast, you're moving *away* from a color, as shown in Figure 26b, which is pointed away from blue to cure a bluish colorcast.

Saturation controls color saturation, or the intensity of the color. When adjusting Balance Magnitude or Balance Angle, you're changing the actual colors in the frame, while saturation makes these colors more or less vivid.

Don't Sample Pure White Pixels

Even if your video has a colorcast, pixels that are overexposed (e.g., over 100 IRE) are "pure white." If you choose one of these pixels, the Fast Color Corrector will assume that your whites are white, and won't correct the cast. Keep your eye on the color chip next to the eyedropper as you choose your pixels in the frame, and if it's pure white, don't click that pixel.

By the way, pressing the Ctrl key while making your selection forces Premiere Pro to sample a group of pixels, rather than a single pixel, which reduces the risk of aberrant results.

What About the Other Controls?

Immediately under the Saturation controls are Auto Black Level, Auto Contrast, and Auto White Level controls and individual eyedroppers for Black Level, Gray Level, and White Level. These largely duplicate the controls used in the Levels tool (#22) Levels Settings histogram (Figure 23c). For this reason, I typically don't use these adjustments.

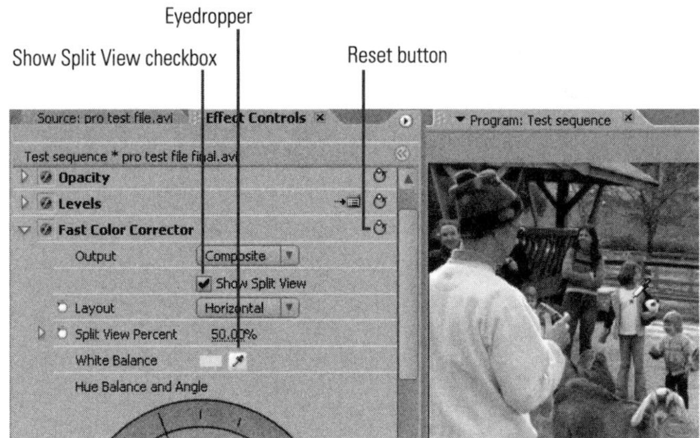

Figure 26a Click this eyedropper to make it active, and then click a region that's supposed to be pure white in the frame.

7. Drag the outside color wheel and/or the Color Correction widget to get close, then fine-tune it with the numerical controls (**Figure 26b**).

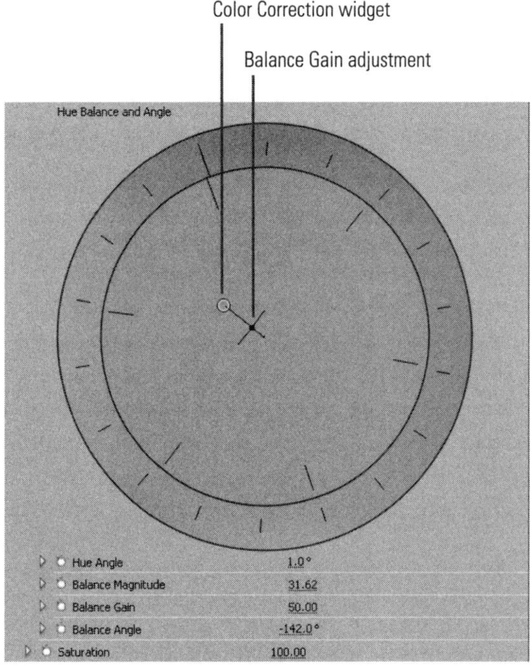

Figure 26b You're now in the "wiggle the controls until it looks right" phase of the adjustment; here's your toolset.

8. When you've completed your adjustment, remember to deselect the Show Split View checkbox you selected in Step 5; otherwise Premiere Pro will render your video with the split view intact.

What About Scene Changes?

If there's a scene change in your project, you may have to reapply the Fast Color Corrector, as you will if you white balance your camera. However, if multiple shots from the same basic setup are on your timeline, there are strategies for quickly applying effects to multiple clips on the timeline (refer to #31 and #32).

#27 Using the Three-Way Color Corrector

When correcting a general colorcast issue, the Auto Color and the Fast Color Corrector effects should get the job done. On the other hand, if you need to adjust the shadows, highlights, and midtones individually in an image, the Three-Way Color Corrector is your best option. **Figure 27** shows what I mean.

Less Is More

Don't use the Three-Way Color Corrector to correct white balance and color casts because uneven adjustments between the three tonal ranges can produce bizarre results. For simple problems like these, try the Auto Color Corrector and Fast Color Corrector effects (in that order).

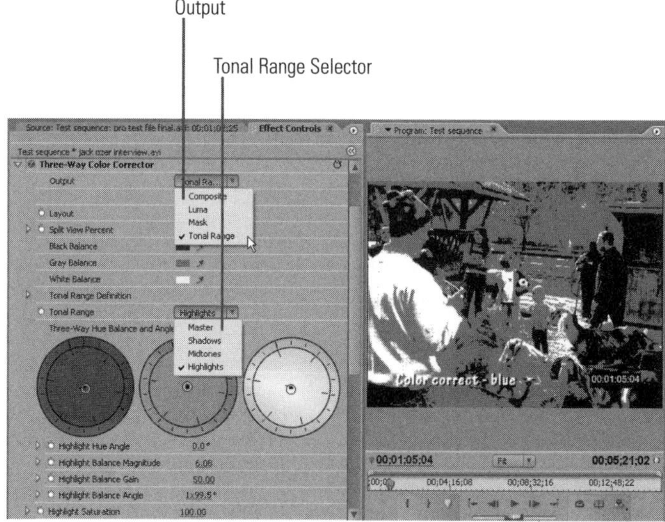

Figure 27 This tonal view shows the three ranges adjusted by the Three-Way Color Corrector effect: shadows, midtones, and highlights.

In Figure 27, the Program Monitor shows the image with Tonal Range Output, which splits the image into shadows (blacks), midtones (gray), and highlights (white). The three color wheels apply separately to each tonal range, so you can adjust them separately.

To operate the effect, do the following:

1. In Premiere Pro, select Effects > Color Correction > Three-Way Color Corrector, and drag the effect onto your clip.
2. Click the Effect Controls tab and when the panel opens, click the triangle to the left of Three-Way Color Corrector. The controls shown in Figure 27 will appear.

3. Choose the eyedropper that corresponds to the tone you need to correct and click it on the whitest white, grayest gray, and blackest black in the frame, then adjust further in the color wheel.

4. Fine-tune these adjustments as needed with the numerical controls found at the bottom of the window, accessed for each tonal range via the Tonal Range drop-down menu (set to Highlights in Figure 27).

How to Reset and Start Over

The Yiddish term *farblunget* (flah–bun'jet) refers to a state of being all messed up, kind of like SNAFU. Growing up in a Jewish household, I heard this term quite often (homework, room, priorities, hair, clothing, and so on).

Oftentimes, when you're working with color correction, things get so farblunget that it's best to just start over rather than trying to fix what you've got. In these instances, click the Reset button to the far right of the Effect name in the Effect Controls panel (see Figure 25a), and you'll be presented with a tabula rasa.

#28 Using the RGB Parade Scope

Multi-Camera Color Correction

The RGB Parade is especially helpful with Multi-Camera color correction. Generally, I pick the camera with the most accurate color and compare its RGB Parade to those of the other cameras. This provides the clues necessary to get the colors close enough so that most viewers won't notice the difference.

You can access the RGB Parade scope (**Figure 28**) by clicking the Output button in the Program Monitor. This scope displays the levels of Red, Green, and Blue in the video signal on a scale from 0 to 100 IRE. In my view, unlike the YC Waveform (#21), which shows nearly absolute information (the frame doesn't reach 100 IRE, therefore it's too dark), you can only draw inferences from the RGB Parade.

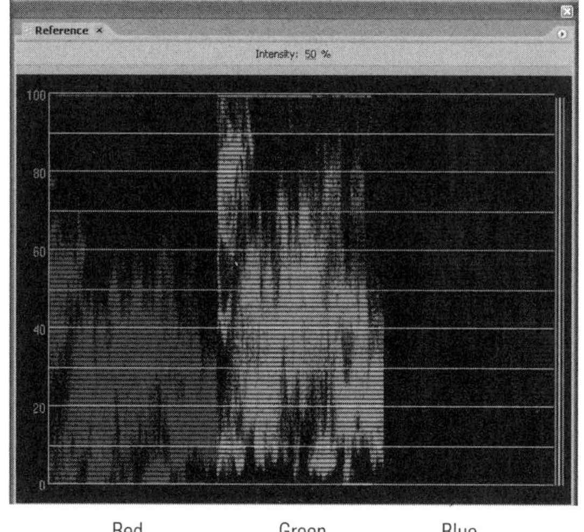

Figure 28 The RGB Parade scope helps diagnose color problems, especially with Multi-Camera projects.

For example, in Figure 28, the blue and green signals tower above the red signal. This tells me that the video probably has a bluish green. If I was using the Fast Color Corrector and there were no white pixels to sample, I would drag the Balance Angle of the Color Correction widget *toward* the red and *away from* the blue and green sections, and then fine-tune as described in #26.

#29 Stabilizing Your Image in Premiere Pro

While you should always shoot with a tripod, sometimes you can't. Fortunately, Premiere Pro provides an effective, extraordinary image stabilization effect called SteadyMove from 2d3 Ltd (www.2d3.com).

It's a third-party plug-in, which means that (even though it comes free with Production Studio) you have to install it manually from the suite's main installation menu. Once installed, it lives in its own 2d3 folder in the main Video Effects folder. To apply it in your project, drag it to your handheld clip and open the Effect Controls window to see the controls in **Figure 29**.

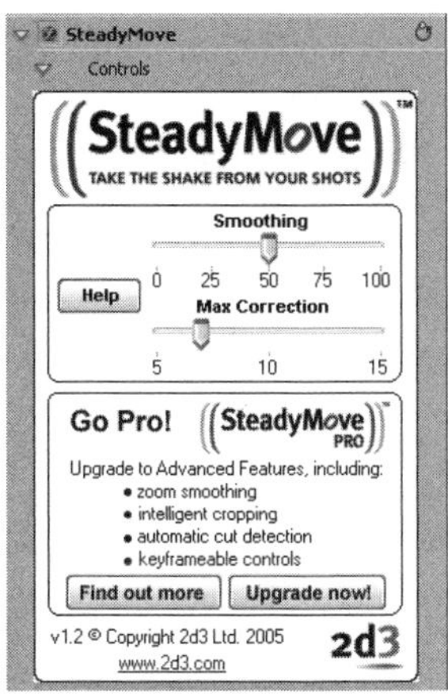

Figure 29 SteadyMove is as close to a "get out of jail card" for shaky video as I've ever seen.

In my experience, this effect is binary. Sometimes, it works with the default settings enabled, both stabilizing the image and zooming in to hide the adjustments, with no additional configuration from the user. The rest of the time, it doesn't work at all, and it's off to After Effects' image stabilization tool, which is discussed in #30.

Don't Count on Image Stabilization

Image stabilization should be considered a last resort, not a leg to stand on. Sometimes, it works well, and other times it doesn't. It's impossible to tell when and why. So keep using that tripod or steadycam when you can, and don't count on fixing shaky video "in post."

Why Is My Video Larger?

All digital image stabilization techniques work by shifting the frame around to stabilize the video. Shifting a frame, say, to the right, leaves a black stripe on the left where the frame used to be. To cover these stripes, most stabilization techniques zoom into the video sufficiently to eliminate the stripes. As we'll see in #30, however, After Effects lets you zoom manually, providing a bit more control.

#30 Stabilizing Your Image in After Effects

Preview Carefully

All digital image stabilization techniques make minor adjustments to the entire frame, which can create visual distortion. Render and preview your adjustments at full quality, and make sure the cure isn't worse than the disease.

After Effects' Image Stabilizer is a component of the Tracker feature that allows you to track motion in a video, and, for example, attach an arrow to a moving car or apply a blur filter to a running suspect. We'll learn how to do that in #39.

Here, After Effects tracks what's *not* moving in a video, which allows the program to adjust for random up-and-down and side-to-side motion. In the example, I'm shooting a concert with a handheld camera. In essence, I tell After Effects that the microphone isn't moving (Step 3) and After Effects analyzes the video, shifting each frame to keep the microphone in the same place.

After Effects performs this automatically, but if you see it go off course, you can stop the analysis, nudge the tracker control back to the desired object, and restart the tracking.

There are three controls in After Effects' Image Stabilizer, as follows:

- + sign—This marks the exact spot of the key frame stored during the motion tracking. Drag this to the middle of the object you're attempting to track, which is also called the "Feature region."
- Feature region—This is the inner box; drag this to and around the object that you're tracking.
- Search region—This outer box defines the area that After Effects will track. It needs to be large enough to contain the frame-to-frame motion of the object, but if it's too large, it will slow the search process.

Here's a simple step-by-step example to get you started with image stabilization in After Effects.

1. Import the video file into After Effects and create a new Composition (#18)
2. Choose Animation > Stabilize Motion to apply the effect.
3. Click the Stabilize Motion button (**Figure 30a**).

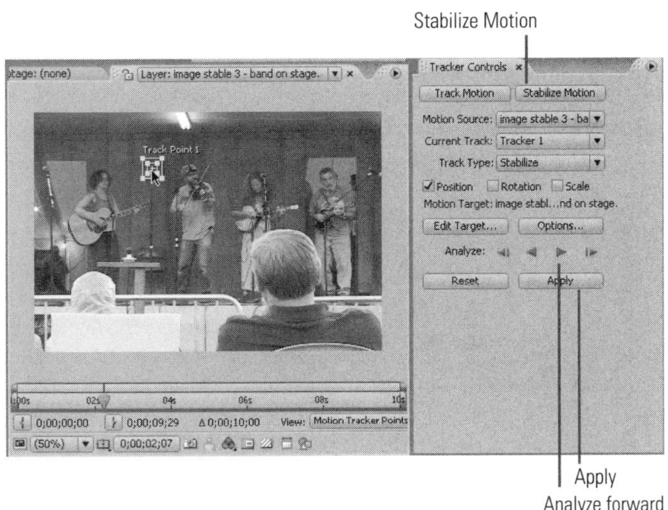

Figure 30a After Effects' Stabilize Motion tool is a subset of the Tracker Controls.

4. Drag Track Point 1 to the stable object in the frame (**Figure 30b**). In the example, I'm using the microphone.

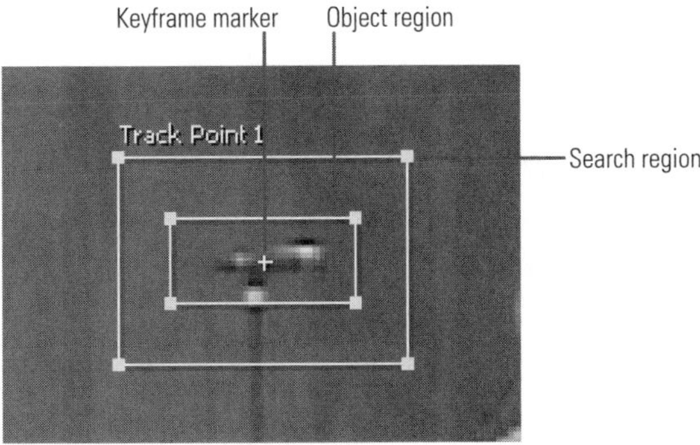

Figure 30b Drag the Keyframe marker over the object in the frame that doesn't move.

3. Click the Analyze Forward button (see Figure 30a). After Effects searches for the object and creates a keyframe in each searched frame.

continued on next page

Tracking Objects Through the Video

You can also use the Tracker controls to highlight moving objects in the video, which we'll explore in #39.

Oh Happy Day

Once you apply the Stabilize Motion effect in After Effects, you can copy and paste the clip back to a timeline in Premiere, even though there's no corresponding effect in Premiere. This makes Stabilize Motion very easy to use in instances in which SteadyMove doesn't get the job done.

Note:

If After Effects ever loses track of the object, move back to the first inaccurate frame, drag the Track point back to the correct object, and start tracking again. Repeat as necessary.

4. Once After Effects completes an accurate search, click Apply to apply the effect.
5. Choose X and Y in the Motion Tracker Apply Options, then click OK (**Figure 30c**) to apply the effect.

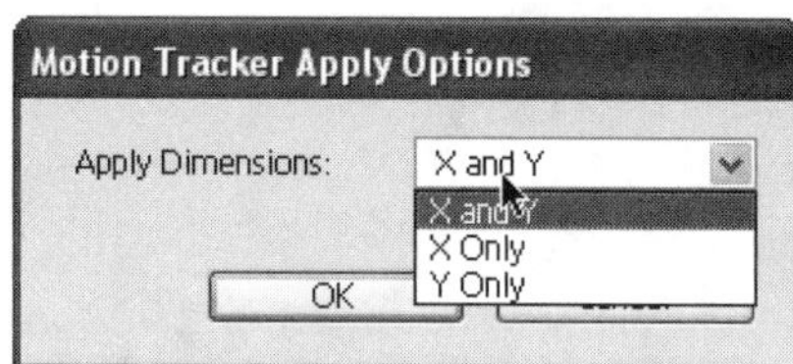

Figure 30c After Effects can adjust X (horizontal), Y (vertical), or both.

Note:

*Unlike Premiere Pro's 2d3 SteadyMove plug-in, After Effects doesn't automatically zoom the video to compensate for the video stabilization, so you'll invariably see black strips where the effect shifted the frame (**Figure 30d**). Use the scale adjustment on the timeline to enlarge the frames until all relevant black lines are gone. If you're producing for television, don't worry about the black lines until they encroach upon the safe zone. If you're producing for playback on a computer, you'll need to eliminate all the black.*

Figure 30d When After Effects shifted this frame up, it exposed a black strip on the bottom, which you can eliminate with the scale adjustment on the timeline.

#31 Pasting Effects

Once you've figured out the optimal corrective adjustments for your video, it's great to apply them efficiently to other clips on the timeline. Premiere Pro offers two options. The first option is copying and pasting effects from one clip to another. Here's how:

1. In Premiere Pro, click the corrected clip with the effects to copy.
2. Choose Edit > Copy (or press Ctrl+C)
3. Click the target clip you want to adjust.
4. Choose Edit > Paste Attributes (or press Ctrl+Alt+V) (**Figure 31**).

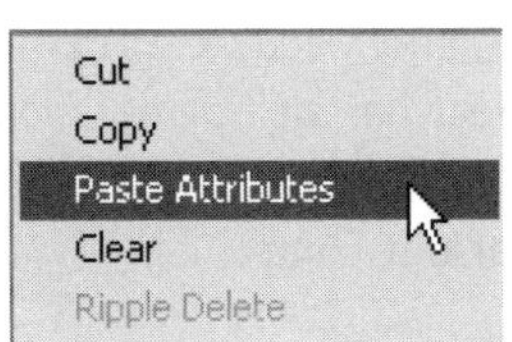

Figure 31 Use the Paste Attributes function to paste effects applied on one clip to another.

Note:
Premiere Pro will paste all effects applied to the source clip, plus any adjustments to the opacity or motion controls.

Limitations of Pasting Effects

This feature works well early in the editing process, but as you add motion, opacity, and other effects to clips, it becomes a bit of a blunt instrument because it pastes *all* effects you've applied to a clip. Consider creating a preset (#32) for repetitive adjustments.

#32 Creating Effect Presets

Trouble in River City

Note that once you apply the preset, it reverts to the name of the original effect. For example, when I apply the MC2 — Piano preset to a clip, the effect name in the Effect Controls panel is Fast Color Corrector, so there's no easy way to tell which preset you applied to a particular clip.

In projects with multiple scenes, locations, or cameras, you may find yourself applying the same corrective effects to multiple clips on the timeline. If you apply each effect from scratch, you'll waste time and produce inconsistent results. In these instances, it's most efficient to save a preset for effects applied to a particular scene, and simply drag the preset to later instances of that scene on the timeline. Here's how.

1. In Premiere Pro's Effect Controls panel, click the effect you want to preserve as a preset.
2. Right-click the effect and choose Save Preset.
3. Name the preset, and if desired, enter a description and click OK (**Figure 32a**). If your effect has keyframes, choose whether you want them scaled over the duration of the target video, or anchored to the In or Out Point.

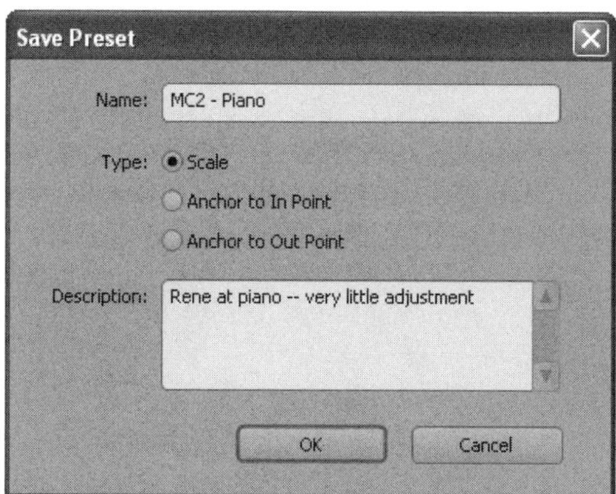

Figure 32a Here's where you name your preset.

Note:

*Premiere Pro stores the preset in the Presets folder in the Effects panel, where you can move it to different folders as necessary (**Figure 32b**).*

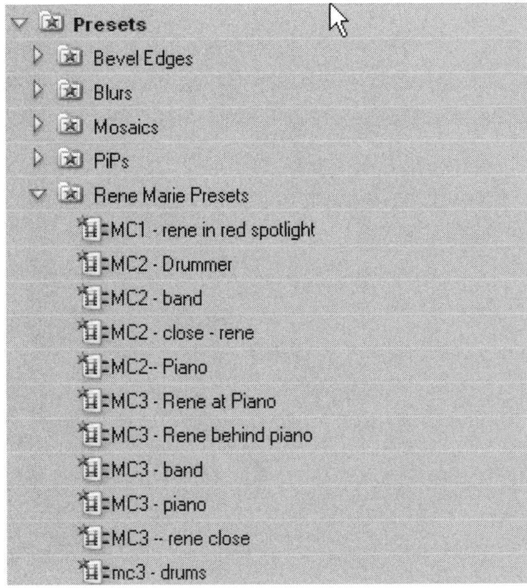

Figure 32b Here's where the preset goes after you've saved it. A funky red spotlight at the Rene Marie concert forced me to apply varying levels of color correction depending upon camera (MC1, 2, or 3) and stage position. Without presets I'd still be working on it.

4. To apply the preset, drag it to a clip on the timeline just like any other effect.

CHAPTER FIVE

Multi-Camera Production in Premiere Pro

It's great to go into post-production knowing you've captured all the footage you need in a well-orchestrated multi-camera shoot. But it can be a logistical nightmare to sort, trim, synch, color-correct, and integrate it all if your editor of choice doesn't have a tool designed to streamline the process.

Fortunately, with version 2.0, Premiere Pro has added just such a tool. This chapter covers the technical aspects of Premiere Pro's Multi-Camera editor, which, frankly, I adore. Clips are wonderfully easy to synch, Multi-Camera color correction is very efficient, operation is fast, and you have an almost unlimited ability to edit your footage after you've selected your camera angles.

At a high level, here's the workflow. You collect and synchronize your clips on one sequence, which I always name something like "piano–synch." I'll refer to this first clip as the *synch sequence* throughout this chapter.

Then you drag this synch sequence into another sequence, which I always call something like "piano-edit," where you actually make your camera selections and fine-tune your edits. As you've probably guessed, I'll call this second sequence the *edit sequence* in this chapter.

This chapter follows that workflow, and concludes with a look at how to pan and zoom within your HDV clips in a Multi-Camera edit.

Shooting Multi-Cam Events

Whether you do weddings or stage events or produce corporate training videos, shooting with multiple cameras is either a wonderful luxury or a competitive necessity. At weddings, strategically positioning two cameras on tripods while a third camera operator roams handheld getting nifty angles, has become standard operating procedure. When shooting concerts and other stage events, capturing multiple angles is essential to replicating the way such events are presented on TV and in films. As with all event production, there are no second takes.

There are two basic elements of this type of production: the Multi-Camera shoot and the editing thereof. Regarding the shoot and the artistic elements of the Multi-Camera edit, I've developed a set of rules that I follow (and share with my co-shooters on events) that you can find on this Web site: http://www.eventdv.net/Articles/ReadArticle.aspx?ArticleID=11640.

#33 Synching Clips with Markers

Synching your clips is the first and often the hardest step of the Multi-Camera editing process, precisely because it's the only step that Premiere Pro can't help you perform. It's absolutely critical to get it right for many productions, since out-of-synch video is very easy to spot, especially for musicians and vocalists who are especially attuned to the audio elements of a video production.

The high-level workflow is simple; find a common point in all video files, insert a marker at that point, and use the markers to synchronize the clips on the timeline. You can find a common point using either the audio file or video frames. Let's cover them in that order. Common audio points are loud noises that are easily visible in the waveforms produced by all cameras. This can be the music starting, the last words of the announcer, the first peal of applause, or even a loud cough. Here's what you do:

1. To find a common audio point, click the Toggle Take Audio and Video button in the Source Monitor. This brings up the audio waveform (**Figure 33a**).

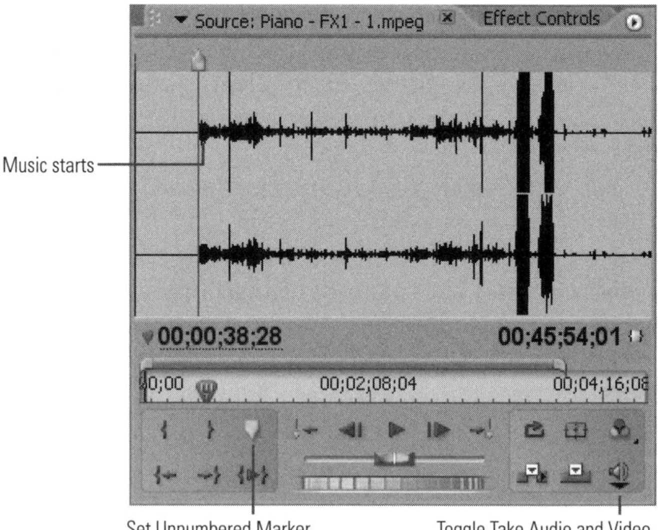

Figure 33a The audio waveform, shown here in the Source Monitor, is usually the easiest way to get your clips synchronized.

Creating and Finding a Synch Point

The easiest visual clue to synch your clips is a camera flash, but sometimes they don't appear in all cameras (they occur very fast), and often where there's one flash, there are two or three, which can complicate finding the common flash. Otherwise, you can use hand motion (the start of a clap), lip motion (someone about to talk or sing), or any other movement that's discernible at all camera angles.

Bring a Flash Camera with You

Some producers bring a flash-equipped still camera to use to help align the clips. Give the still camera to the camera operator closest to the front, and have her click a few pictures after you get your cameras rolling. For most events, however, you'll find using audio to synch your clips easier and faster.

2. Find the appropriate point and click the Set Unnumbered Marker button (**Figure 33b**).

Figure 33b It's difficult to tell from the screen capture, but there's a flash going off in this frame. I'll use this to synch the three angles from this wedding video.

3. Drag the audio and video track to the synch timeline, remembering to toggle the waveform back to both audio and video.

4. Move on to the next camera angle.

Note:

Premiere Pro has two alternatives for managing the audio from Multi-Camera angles. Audio can follow the video as you switch camera angles, or you can use one audio track throughout. To use the latter option, place the video with the desired audio. See #35 to learn to switch audio with the camera angle.

#34 Synching Clips on the Timeline

Once your Multi-Camera clips are on the timeline, here's the procedure for synchronizing them and creating the Multi-Camera sequence to edit.

1. Drag the clips so that the markers align. With Snap enabled, Premiere Pro will snap them together to ensure alignment (**Figure 34a**).

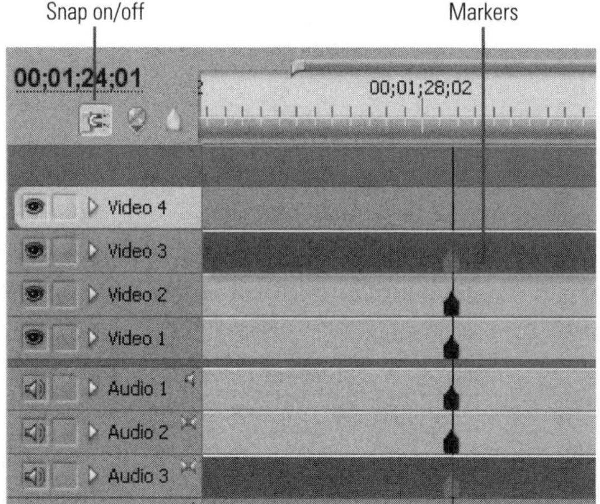

Figure 34a With Snap enabled, Premiere Pro will snap the markers together as you move the clips on the timeline, simplifying the synching process.

2. Click Play in the Program Monitor. Premiere Pro will play all videos in the synch sequence. If any videos are out of synch, the audio will sound fuzzy or you'll hear repeating sections. If this happens, go back to step 1 and re-synch.

   Note:
   *To fine-tune your clip synchronization manually, zoom in on the audio timeline (**Figure 34b**) and expand the audio waveforms to find a common event like a drumbeat or clap. Often this is the easiest technique to achieve rock-solid synch.*

3. Trim all tracks to a common beginning or ending frame to use as the synch point (see step 5).

4. Target track Video 1 by clicking the track header on the left of the timeline.

If Synchronization Is Grayed Out in the Right-Click Menu

Target a video track by clicking the header on the extreme-left side of the timeline. Technically, Premiere Pro synchronizes your clip to the target track. For example, if you choose Clip Start or Clip End as your synchronize point, Premiere Pro synchronizes the starting and ending points of *all* clips to that of the targeted track. However, sometimes it may actually shift clips around to synchronize them, which can take your carefully synchronized clips out of synch.

The best practice is to trim all clips to either a common starting or ending point so they won't shift when Premiere Pro synchs them. At this point, it doesn't matter which track you target, except that without a targeted track, Synchronize will be grayed out in your Right-Click menu (which is how you got there in the first place).

Using Clip End to Synchronize

When shooting with multiple cameras, it's not unusual for one or more cameras to start a bit late. In this instance, synchronizing on the end point is your only option, and it works just fine. When you use the Multi-Camera Monitor (#36) to choose your camera angles, clips that aren't available are blacked out. As soon as they appear in the synch timeline, they appear in the Multi-Camera Monitor.

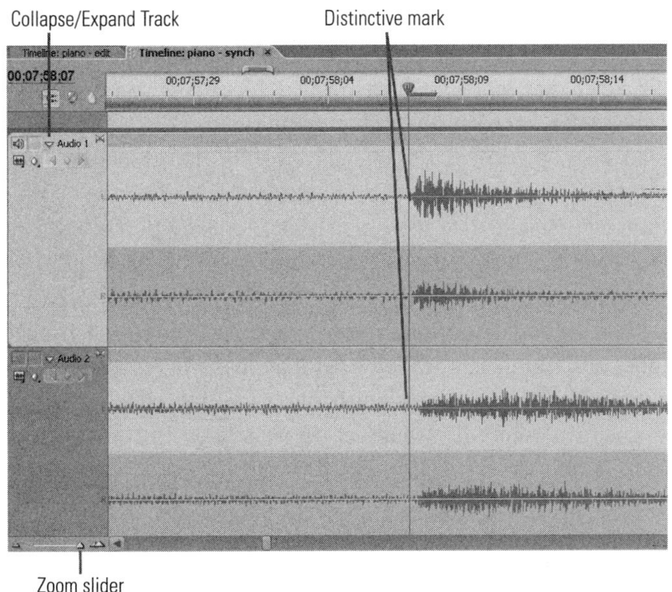

Figure 34b Zoomed in on the audio timeline, you gain significant accuracy, simplifying the synch process.

5. Select all audio and video tracks, right-click, and choose Synchronize Clips from the pop-up menu (**Figure 34c**).

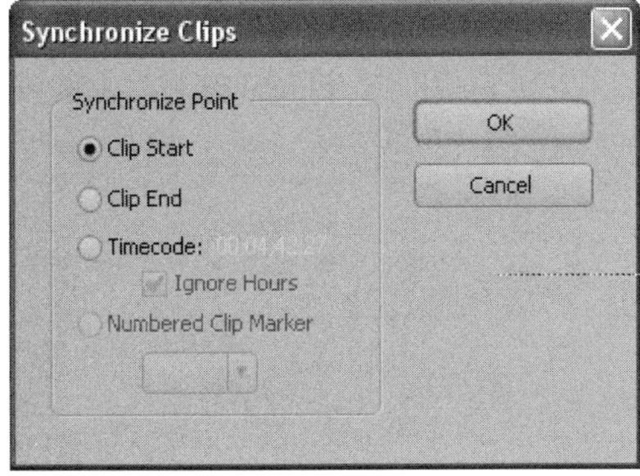

Figure 34c Premiere Pro's four Multi-Camera synchronization options.

6. In the Synchronize Clips dialog box, select the desired Synchronize Point and click OK.

#35 Perfecting Source Clips

Where Did My Color Correction Adjustment Go?

Say you've adjusted the color of one your videos in the synch sequence, and want to make a further adjustment in the edit sequence. You open the Effect Controls panel and see nothing. Where did all your meticulously applied adjustments go?

Here's the skinny. When Premiere Pro hands the synch sequence over to the edit sequence, it passes over the adjusted file with all controls zeroed out. Say, for example, you converted one of your videos to black and white in the synch sequence by applying the Black & White effect. In the edit sequence, the clip would be black and white, but you wouldn't see the effect in the Effect Controls panel—you're essentially starting from zero.

You can certainly apply any desired effects to the edit sequence, even those that were already applied to the same clip in the synch sequence. But you'll have to drag that effect onto the clip as normal, and once you do, the controls will be set to the normal preadjustment values.

Most Multi-Camera productions have color issues in one of two flavors. The most troublesome relate to on-site lighting or similar problems that rob your video of the uniform look you need. In one concert I shot recently, a stationary red spotlight distorted the lead singer's skin color as she moved about the stage, necessitating multiple corrections depending upon location. Since nonuniform adjustments like these don't apply equally to the entire clip, you have to apply them in the edit sequence to each instance of that clip.

The second issue relates to color casts, where each camera looks slightly different. Color casts are easy to resolve. If you fix the problem once in the synch sequence, the changes will flow through to your edit sequence automatically. The workflow is as follows.

1. Pick the clip with the most accurate color.
2. Click it in the Project panel to load it in the Source Monitor.
3. Work through the other clips in the synch timeline, loading each one individually in the Program Monitor.
4. Make your adjustments as described in #27, with the goal of making each clip's color match the good clip in the Source Monitor.
5. Consider opening a Reference Monitor as shown in Figure 35a. Note that you can toggle the Source Monitor to an RGB Parade scope as well, which often reveals which colors to adjust.

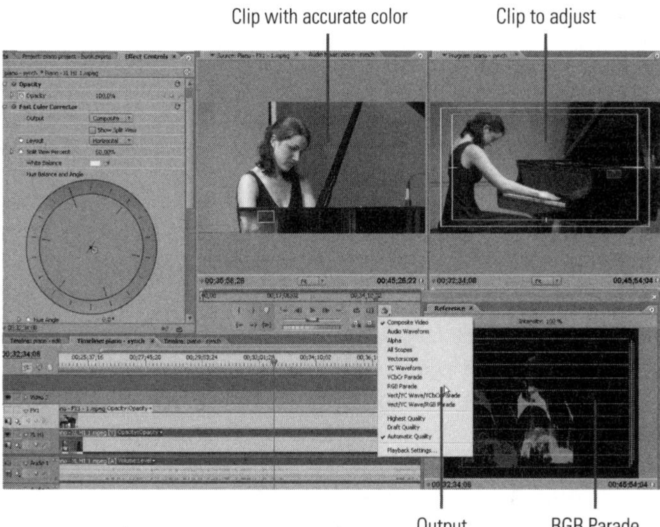

Figure 35a Place the clip with the most accurate color in the Source Monitor, and try to match all other clips to that.

6. Use the Toggle Track Output eye icon to the left of the timeline to hide and reveal the tracks as necessary. For example, in **Figure 35b**, I'm hiding the top FX1track (so named because it contains footage sourced from the Sony FX2) to load the XL H1 track in the Program Monitor for adjustment.

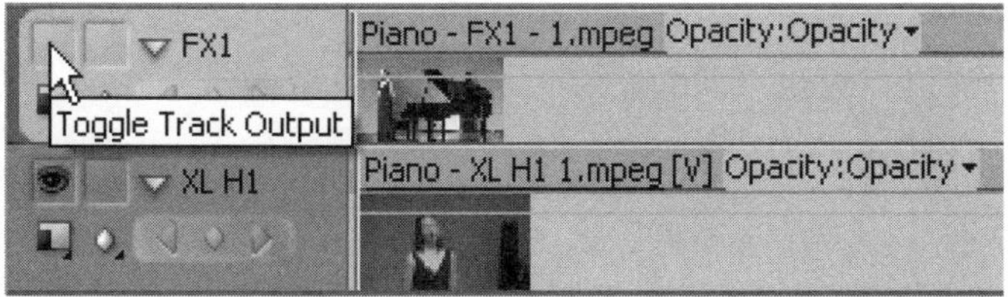

Figure 35b When you have multiple clips on the timeline, the "eye" turns the video on and off, while the speaker turns audio tracks on and off. You'll use both tools frequently with your Multi-Camera productions.

The Best Place to Assess Multi-Track Color Correction

For best color correction results when working with multiple video sources, use the Multi-Camera Monitor. Though small, it shows up to four clips simultaneously, at exactly the same point in the video. Note that you can always go back and make subsequent changes in the synch sequence, and these will automatically flow through to the edit sequence. So don't worry if you don't get it right the first time; it's usually somewhat of an iterative process.

Naming Your Timeline Tracks

In Figure 35b, you'll notice that the track names have been renamed from Video 1, Video 2 etc. to XL H1 and FX1, and that the names of the captured clips more or less match these. Oscar Wilde once said, "Consistency is the last refuge of the unimaginative." Perhaps so, but I'm guessing he never produced a Multi-Camera project in Premiere Pro, or any other editor for that matter. Wilde's dictum notwithstanding, you'll probably find it helpful to rename these tracks with simple, consistent naming conventions for easy reference to your source camera angle, and consider using the same track order within each project for different sets, acts, or however the project divides out.

To rename a track, select the track, right-click it, and choose Rename.

#36 Choosing Camera Angles with the Multi-Camera Monitor

Choosing Your Audio Track

Often in weddings and concerts you'll use an audio track that was captured by a separate device (perhaps a DAT, MP3, or MiniDisc recorder) and isn't available in any camera angles. To hear this track while performing your Multi-Camera edits, capture the audio and import it into your project, then drag this master audio file to Audio 2, and synchronize it with the waveform of the Multi-Camera clip. To hear your master audio when playing the Multi-Camera Monitor, target its audio track by clicking the track header to the left of the timeline. The Multi-Camera Monitor will play whichever audio track you target in this manner, whether it comes from one of your cameras or a discrete device.

You've synchronized and perfected your clips. Now it's time to choose camera angles. Here's how.

1. Drag your synch sequence into the Video 1 and Audio 1 tracks of your edit sequence timeline.

   Note:
   Technically, the synch sequence is called a nested *sequence, which is a great organizational and convenience feature in Premiere Pro. For example, you can build a common opening or closing video, and then simply drag the sequence into subsequent projects, rather than copying and pasting the individual assets.*

2. Target both the Audio and Video tracks by clicking the Track header on the left (**Figure 36a**).

   Note:
   For example, in the figure, both Video 1 and Audio 1 are highlighted. If you don't hear audio when playing in the Multi-Camera Monitor, it's because you haven't targeted the audio track.

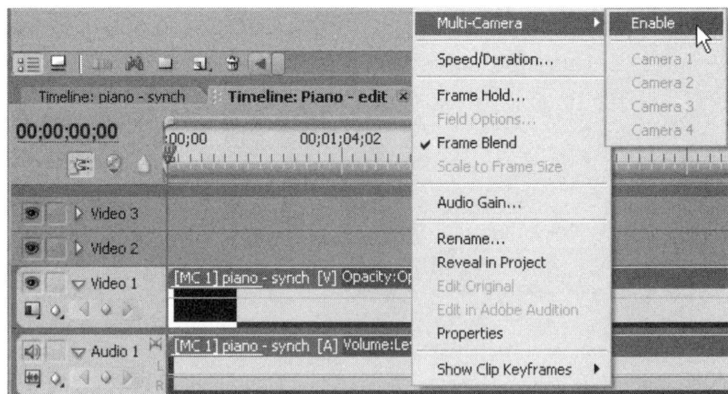

Figure 36a Right-click the synch sequence on the timeline and choose Multi-Camera > Enable to get things started. Note that both Video 1 and Audio 1 are lighter than the other tracks, meaning that they are targeted, and will appear when you play the synch sequence in the Multi-Camera Monitor.

3. Select the synch sequence on the timeline, right-click, and choose Multi-Camera > Enable (Figure 36a).

Note:

Premiere Pro seems to show at least three cameras active (black in the figure) even though this Multi-Camera sequence has only two. Don't sweat if you see the same thing; it doesn't affect operation.

4. Click the Program Monitor fly-out menu and choose Multi-Camera Monitor (**Figure 36b**).

Figure 36b To open the Multi-Camera Monitor, click the wing icon and select it from the menu that appears.

5. If desired, click the Multi-Camera Monitor fly-out menu and choose Audio Follows Video (**Figure 36c**).

Note:

If you choose this option, Premiere Pro will use the audio from the selected camera angle as you switch among them. If you don't select this, Premiere Pro will use the audio from track Audio 1 in the synch sequence.

continued on next page

Multi-Camera Workflow

If your project is longer than an hour, you'll likely have more than one tape for each camera angle. You can combine these in a long synch sequence, but the synchronization issues can get challenging because each camera will have different starting and stopping points. In these instances, consider creating separate synch and edit timelines for each act, set, or natural break point in the performance, or between the ceremony and reception at a wedding. Later, if desired, you can combine the edited sequences by copying and pasting one sequence to another. Or you can render and import them separately into Encore and combine them on one timeline.

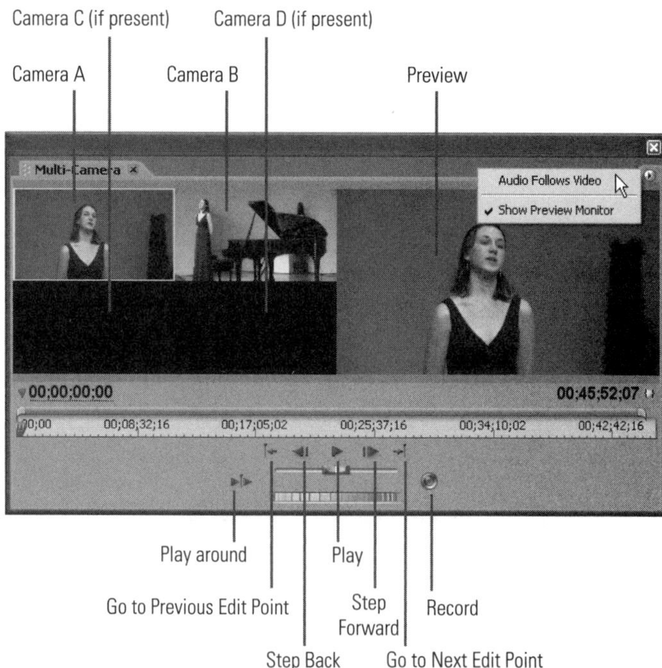

Figure 36c Here's the Multi-Camera Monitor, which works like a real-time switcher in a television station or any live-switched video shoot.

6. Click Play. Premiere Pro will render audio files as necessary (which can take awhile) and then start playing.
7. As the video plays in real time, click the desired camera.

   Note:

   You shouldn't need to use the Record button to make the Multi-Camera Monitor work. Once you click Play, you'll see a yellow box around the clip in Camera A. Technically, this means that the Monitor isn't "recording," but camera A remains the selected clip until you change it, so in effect it is *recording. Once you click another camera angle, a red box will appear around that angle (and the Record button will depress). This signifies that Premiere Pro has switched angles. If the Multi-Camera Monitor starts out on the wrong camera angle, click the desired angle before clicking Play, and it will record that angle until you choose to switch to another.*

#37 The Tao of Multi-Camera Editing

The Multi-Camera Monitor is wonderfully functional and generally intuitive, but as with any tool, you'll work more effectively with some inside tips on its use. Here's a mélange of deep thoughts on how to use it most effectively.

- During the course of the typical Multi-Camera edit, you'll open the Multi-Camera monitor many times. Consider each a separate Multi-Camera "session."
- To save the edits made in each session, click the Stop button and click the X in the upper-right corner to close the Multi-Camera Monitor. Your angle selections will appear on the timeline (**Figure 37**).

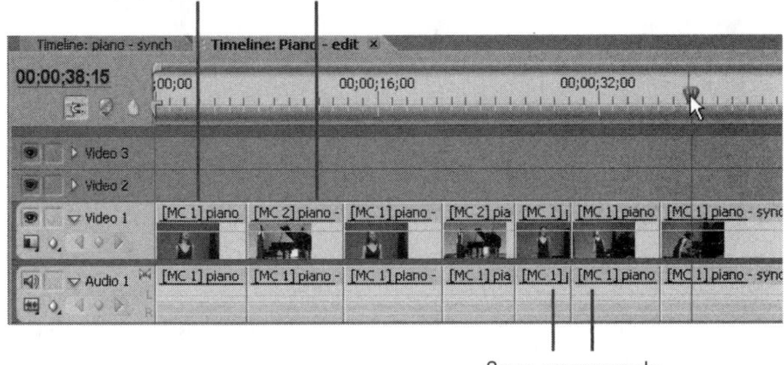

Figure 37 Here's what your edit sequence will look like after selecting clips in the Multi-Camera Monitor.

- If you click the X before clicking the Stop button, you'll lose all edits from that session. If, after closing the Multi-Camera Monitor, you click Undo before making your first edit on the timeline, you lose all edits from that session, but not from previous sessions.
- When working in the Multi-Camera Monitor, your goal should be to get within one or two seconds of the desired switching point, then perfect the edit on the timeline, in which you'll find better tools for doing so.

Adjacent Clips from the Same Camera Angle

It's okay to have adjacent clips from the same camera angle on your edit timeline, but it adds work when you're applying effects separately to each instance of a camera angle, and can lead to errors when applying transitions between clips. Don't sweat about this when using the Multi-Camera Monitor, but consider fixing these on the timeline as described in #38.

Fixing Your Multi-Cam Mistakes

If you make a big mistake in the Multi-Camera Monitor (like switching when you really didn't want to switch or switching to the wrong angle), there's an easy way to fix it. When you catch the error in preview, click the Stop button, then the Go to Previous Edit Point button, and then click the desired camera angle (even if it's the same angle as the previous segment). As you can see in Figure 37, you can have the same camera angle lying sequentially on the timeline and Premiere Pro will play right through the sequential video (and all angles) without a break.

#38 Editing a Multi-Camera Sequence on the Timeline

After selecting clips with the Multi-Camera Monitor, you can edit the clips on the timeline as normal. Here are the three most common edits you'll make.

1. To change camera angles in a clip in the edit sequence, select the clip, right-click, and choose Multi-Camera and the desired camera from the pop-up menu (**Figure 38a**).

Figure 38a Change audio or video tracks on the timeline using this right-click control.

Note:

- *Note that this will change the audio track to that of the selected clip unless you unlink the audio and video files (select the clip, right-click, and choose Unlink).*

2. To fine-tune the timing of the camera-angle switch, use the Rolling Edit tool, as shown in **Figure 38b**. This tool displays the last frame of the first clip and the first frame of the second clip in the Program Monitor in real time as you change the edit point between the two clips.

Adding Transitions Quickly

Sometimes you'll want to add transitions to smooth the flow between camera angles or for artistic effect. A killer keystroke combination for this is the Page Down (PgDn) key for moving from cut to cut, followed by the Ctrl+D combination to insert the default transition. Choose the default transition by right-clicking the transition in the Effects panel, and set the default duration by choosing Edit > Preferences > General.

Program
Last frame of first clip Monitor First frame of second clip

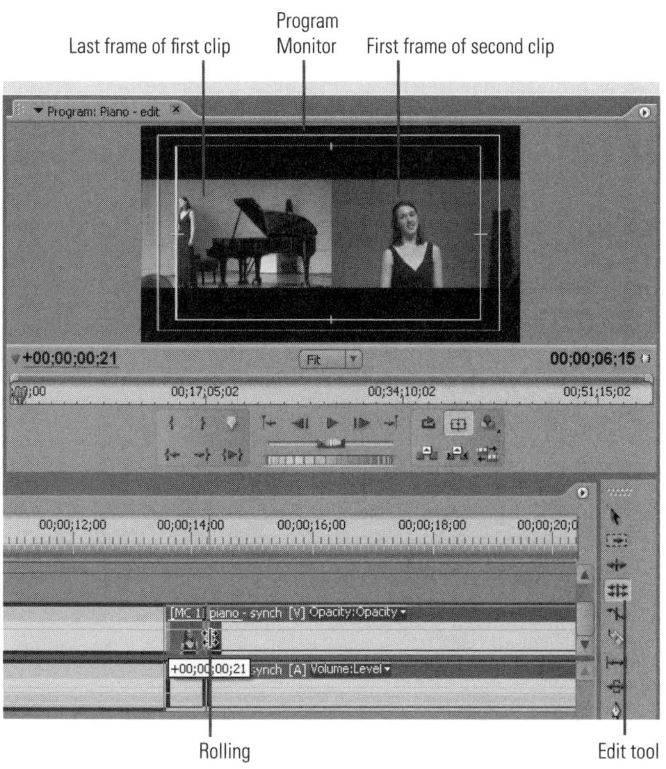

Rolling Edit tool

Figure 38b Premiere Pro has great tools for finalizing the timing of your camera-angle switches.

3. You can also delete any clip on the edit timeline and drag the adjacent clip across to close the gap (**Figure 38c**). Premiere Pro does a marvelous job of maintaining synch. (Have I mentioned that I really like this tool?)

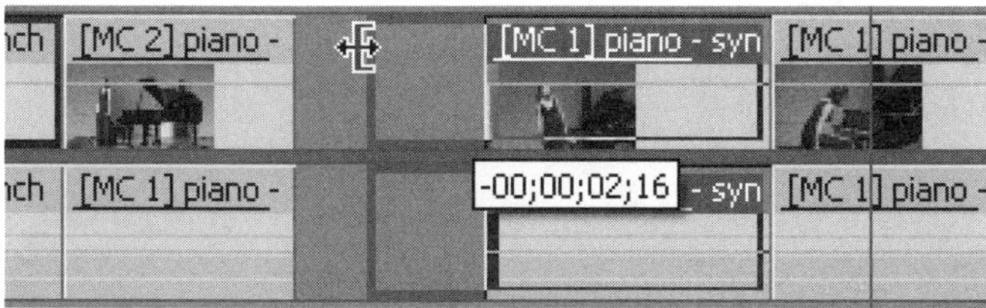

Figure 38c You can delete clips on the timeline and drag across the adjacent clip without losing synchronization.

Audio Waveform

When editing a concert or similar event, sometimes the audio waveform provides better clues to the optimal timing of camera-angle switches than the frames in the Program Monitor. To use the waveform as a guide, twirl the Collapse/Expand track triangle in the track header of your audio track to reveal the waveform, and drag the track down to expand it.

#39 Setting Up Overlay Effects with the Multi-Camera Tool

Be Careful When Moving Clips

If you click and drag either clip in this exercise, you'll lose synchronization. Think about it like this: you're not moving the clip to a new location; you're exposing another camera angle at the same location on a higher track to produce the overlay effect.

All Dressed Up and Nowhere to Go?

Now that you're all set up for picture-in-picture and overlay effects, perhaps you'd like some help in implementing them. If so, see #42 and # 45.

While switching back and forth between camera angles adds a lovely professional touch, adding multiple layers and picture-in-picture effects can convert your edits to pure art. For example, how else could we show a close-up of the concert pianist's face and her hands playing, as shown in **Figure 39a**?

Figure 39a An example of a layered effect you can easily create using the Multi-Camera tool in Premiere Pro.

To create any overlay effect, you need to place one track on top of the other, without loss of audio synchronization, of course. Here's how to get that done.

1. Identify the target clips for the overlay effect on the timeline.
2. Drag the target top clip to Video 2 and Audio 2, as shown in **Figure 39b**.

   Note:
   If your layered effect includes more than two clips, drag each clip one track higher (or lower, for audio) on the timeline.

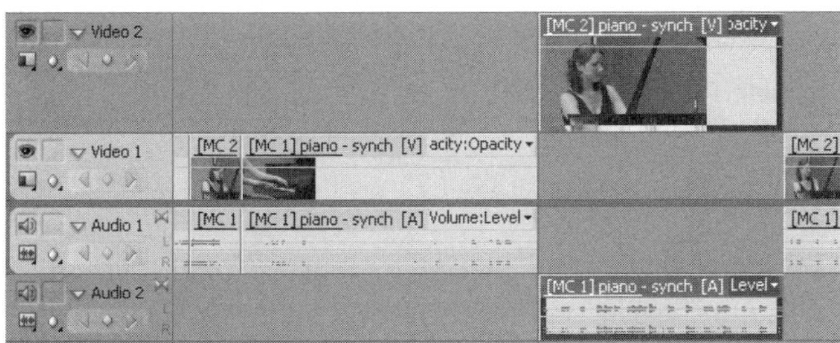

Figure 39b You have to drag both the Video and Audio clips to different tracks in order to layer the two clips.

3. Use the Trim tool to fill the Gap in Video 1 and pull Video 2 over the target region for the effect (**Figure 39c**).

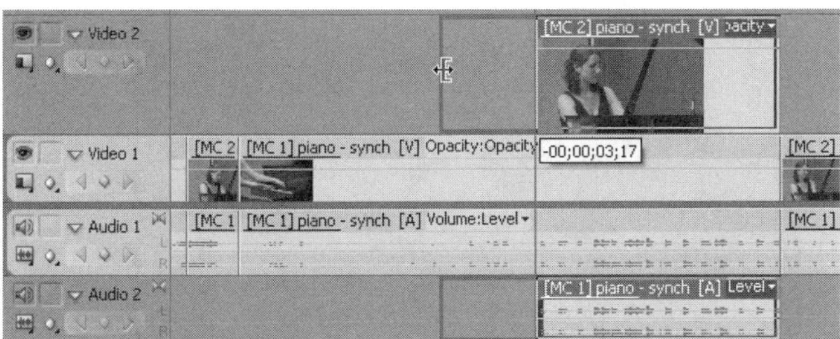

Figure 39c Use the Trim tool to close the gap in the lower track and drag the upper clip(s) to create the layers.

4. Apply the desired effect.

#40 HDV and Multi-Camera Editing, Part I

One of the joys of shooting in HDV for SD delivery is the ability to pan and zoom around the HDV clip with little or no loss in quality. When editing HDV outside of the Multi-Camera environment, Premiere Pro's motion tools make this a snap. However, when you use the Multi-Camera tool, you lose some flexibility.

In essence, when you drag your synch sequence into the edit sequence, you're dragging over a 720x480 frame, not the original 1440x1080 frame. If you want to zoom in to the image while editing in the edit sequence, Premiere Pro doesn't go back to the original HDV video for additional detail; it zooms in to the 720x480 image. This can result in pixelation and suboptimal quality.

If you zoom in to your HDV video in the synch sequence and then try to pan across the image, you'll see a black strip in the video frame like that shown in **Figure 40**, even if the HDV video has image detail in the original HDV frame.

Figure 40 Premiere Pro truncates the HDV frame to a 720x480 resolution when you nest the synch sequence in an SD edit sequence. Even though there's additional detail on the left in the original HDV frame, you can't access it in the edit sequence; instead you'll see the black bar on the left.

If pan and zoom is critical to your project, #41 describes a procedure that lets you work around this issue, and it works perfectly for occasional adjustments in a project. However, if you're planning to pan and zoom around your HDV footage extensively, you may want to consider foregoing Premiere Pro's Multi-Camera tool and performing the task manually.

Which Preset Should You Use?

Which preset should you use when producing a Multi-Camera project with HDV video? As discussed more fully in #1, you should always use the preset that matches your target output, which for most producers is 16:9 SD resolution video.

#41 HDV and Multi-Camera Editing, Part II

This tip leverages two features of Premiere Pro. First is the ability to jump from the edit sequence to the same point in the synch sequence by pressing Shift+T. With this keystroke combination, you can jump from any nested sequence to the same point in the original sequence.

Second is the ability to set keyframes to "Hold," so they don't change until manually adjusted later in the project. As you may know, the default behavior for keyframes is to interpolate their values from one position to the next (see #60 for a description of keyframe operation).

Essentially, these two features allow you to pan and zoom in the synch sequence and have the effects flow through to the edit sequence. Here's how it works.

1. Create your synch and edit sequences and select your camera angles as normal.
2. In the synch sequence, click the Toggle animation clock to the left of the Position and Scale properties to add keyframes to the start of each HDV clip you intend to pan and zoom.
3. Right-click the Position keyframe and choose Temporal Interpolation > Hold from the menu (**Figure 41a**).

continued on next page

Can You Mix HDV and DV in the Same Multi-Camera project?

Absolutely. If your target is SD, you'll have to downconvert the HDV video down to about 46% to fit perfectly in the 16:9 SD window. If your target is HDV, consider upconverting your DV video to HDV in After Effects, which produces better quality than Premiere Pro during this process.

Real Panning and Zooming

The procedures described in this tip let you change the static position of your HDV video from keyframe to keyframe. You could produce actual pan-and-zoom motion within the clips by choosing the linear interpolation method between sets of key frames, which is in the same menus described in steps 3 and 4. Just remember to reset your last key frame values to the desired position, and the interpolation technique to Hold to reset all subsequent uses of that clip to the desired position in the edit sequence.

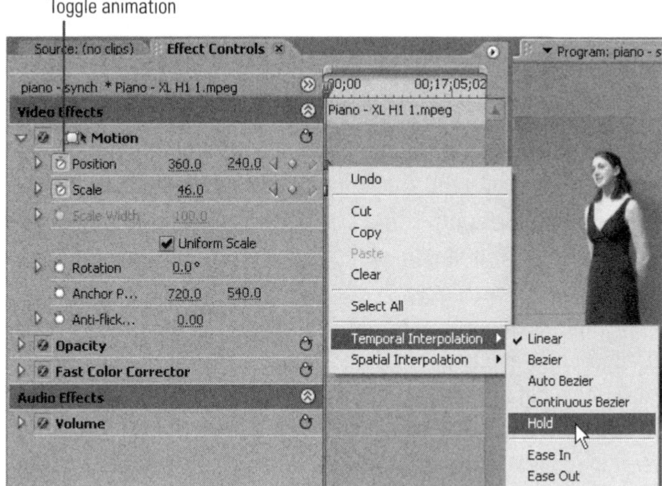

Figure 41a In essence, if this keyframe was a dog, selecting Hold is like telling it to "stay." In other words, don't move until the editor manually adjusts the setting.

4. Right-click the Scale keyframe and choose Hold from the pop-up menu that appears.
5. In the edit sequence, navigate to the first target frame for a pan-and-zoom effect.
6. Press Shift+T. Premiere Pro takes you to that frame in the synch sequence.
7. Click the Add/Remove Keyframe button to add the necessary keyframes in the Position and Scale properties at that location. Note the current values for those properties because you'll restore them in step 12 (**Figure 41b**).

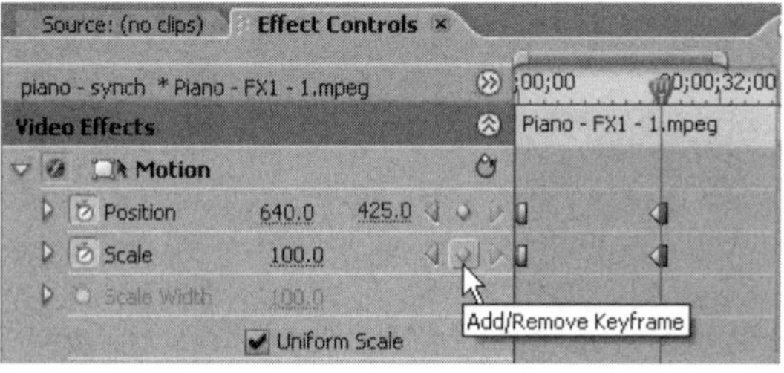

Figure 41b Use subsequent keyframes to create the desired pan and/or zoom effect.

8. Use the Position and/or Scale properties to pan and zoom around the clip as desired.

Note:
Setting these keyframes adjusts the position and scale of the clips from that point forward, affecting all subsequent uses of that clip in the edit sequence. You'll reverse that in the next few steps.

9. In the edit sequence, navigate to the last target frame for the pan-and-zoom effect.
10. Press Shift+T. Premiere Pro takes you to that frame in the synch sequence.
11. Click the Add/Remove Keyframe button to add the necessary keyframes in the Position and Scale properties at that location.
12. Adjust the values back to the settings before the adjustments made in step 7.

Note:
Just in case you forgot to write them down, the default settings for Position on an SD timeline are 360x240. Most of the time, to make 1080i video fit in a 16:9 DV SD frame, you'll scale it to 46% of the original.

CHAPTER SIX

Applying Cool Special Effects

It would be impossible to count the effects and effect variations offered by the potent combination of Premiere Pro and After Effects, and it would be beyond the scope or the purpose of this book to try to cover them all. This chapter provides a sampling of some of the coolest.

It starts with a look at overlay effects, including layering, split-screen, picture-in-picture, and chroma key, and then takes a look at creating and applying masks in Premiere Pro.

The final two techniques use After Effects to track motion in a video file and then apply the tracking data to animate a layer in the composition.

#42 Producing Overlay Effects

Premiere Pro Takes a Top-Down Approach

When you have multiple clips on the timeline, Premiere Pro displays the top clip first, and only shows clips under it if you've adjusted the opacity of the top clip, applied a chroma key effect to eliminate a blue or green background (see #48 and #49), or reduced the resolution of the top clip so that it fits in a small window in the background video (also called a picture-in-picture effect). This is why you have to place titles and logos *above* the video track over which you plan to display them; otherwise the video tracks will obscure them.

The 1990 movie *Ghost*, starring Patrick Swayze and Demi Moore, is a great example of an overlay effect used in a movie. As you may recall, Swayze faded in and out of the video several times during the movie, which (in the words of one reviewer at www.imdb.com) "launched the era of new special effect techniques."

This effect is simple to produce and useful in many common productions, including weddings, concerts, and even plays or ballets. Technically, it's an "overlay" effect because you start by placing one track of video over another. But it's also called "layering" since it involves more than one layer of video. Whatever you call it, here's how to produce it:

1. In Premiere Pro, place two clips at the same location on the timeline, one on Video 1 and the ,other on Video 2 (**Figure 42a**). In this example, I'm combining a close-up of the hands of a pianist over a long shot of her playing.

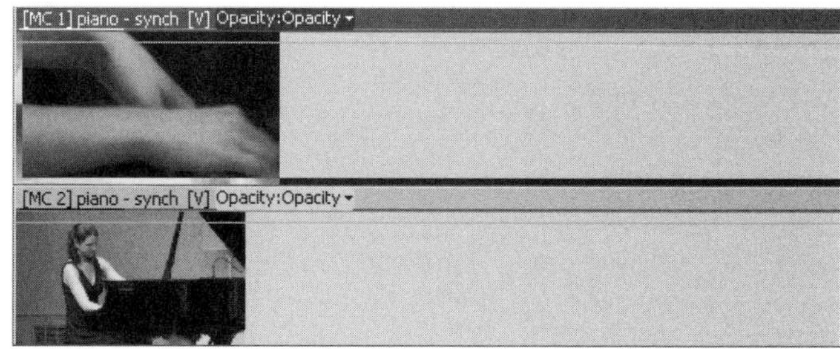

Figure 42a Here's the basic setup for the overlay effect: one clip on top of the other.

2. Select the top clip, and open the Effect Controls panel.
3. Twirl the triangle next to the Opacity property to open the control (**Figure 42b**). Adjust the value to 50% to start; you should see the two images blending together in the Program Monitor. Customize the value to get the desired look.

Note:

You can adjust the Opacity property (and most other Premiere Pro effect properties) in three ways. You can drag your pointer over the number to increase or reduce it; click the number and type a different value; or twirl the triangle to the left of the property to reveal a slider you can drag as desired. You can also adjust Opacity directly on the timeline by selecting the clip you want to adjust, hovering the mouse over the bar that runs across it (similar to the volume bar in an audio track), and dragging the bar up and down. But you can perform much more precise adjustments in the Effect Controls panel.

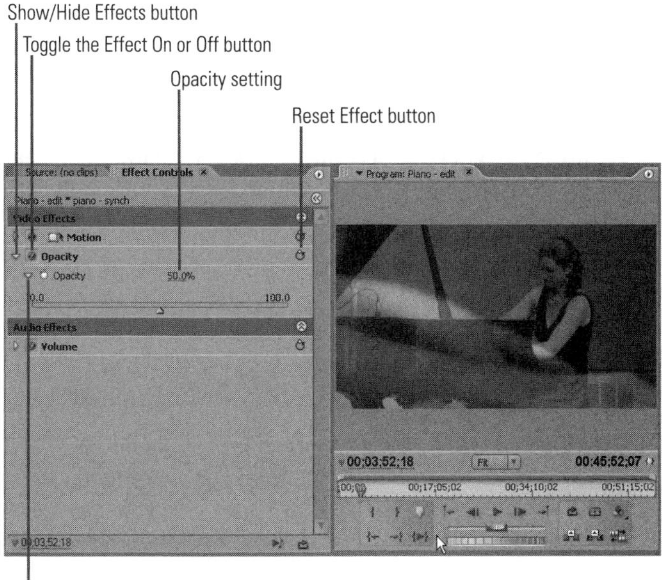

Figure 42b Adjust the opacity of the top clip so that the bottom clip shows through.

Sourcing Your Overlay Footage

Overlays are a natural when shooting with multiple cameras; see #39 to learn how to manipulate one clip on top of another with projects built in the Multi-Camera editor. You can also use a B-Roll shot after or during the event in an overlay effect, or a related clip from any other source.

Watch Your Brightness

Sometimes an overlay effect will darken the bottom clip. To offset this, apply the Brightness & Contrast effect to the top clip until the overall brightness of the clip approximates what it was before you applied the overlay.

#43 Customizing Effects with Keyframes

Almost Limitless Customizability

You can add a keyframe per frame for any applied effect, which translates to near-limitless customizability over the duration of even a short project.

Using Dissolves to Fade Effects

You could also fade the effect in by dragging a dissolve transition to the start of the overlay clip. I like the additional control that keyframes provide, however, and prefer to do it this way.

Keyframes allow you to adjust the value of an effect over time, enhancing your ability to customize your productions. By placing a keyframe on the main timeline or on the timeline within the Effect Controls panel, you're essentially identifying a *key frame* at which Premiere Pro (or After Effects) will apply or modify an effect. By setting successive keyframes, you can chart the exact points in a clip at which the values of an effect will change, such as with a fade in or fade out.

Here are two techniques that enable you to fade in an overlay effect with keyframes. To perform the basic overlay effect described in #42, you'll need to start with two clips on the timeline, one on Video 1 and the other on Video 2 (see Figure 42a).

1. In Premiere Pro, select the top clip in the Timeline, and click the Effect Controls panel.
2. In the Effects Controls panel, click the Show/Hide Timeline view button to open the timeline video (**Figure 43a**).

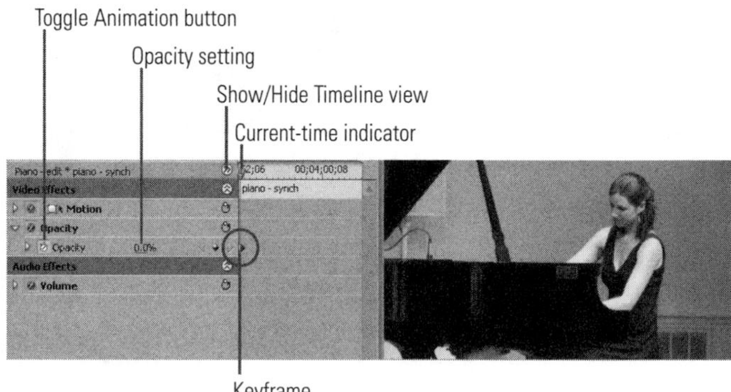

Figure 43a Set the initial keyframe with a value of zero so the overlay clip doesn't appear.

3. Drag the current-time indicator all the way to the left to ensure that you're at the first frame of the clip.
4. Click the Toggle Animation button to set a keyframe at the first frame.
5. Set the Opacity value to 0%.

Note:

At 0%, the clip should be totally transparent, and you shouldn't see the overlay clip of the pianist's hands. Next, you'll fade that in.

6. Drag the current-time indicator approximately 1 second to the right.
7. Set the Opacity value to 50% (or whatever value works for your production). Premiere Pro automatically creates a new keyframe (**Figure 43b**).

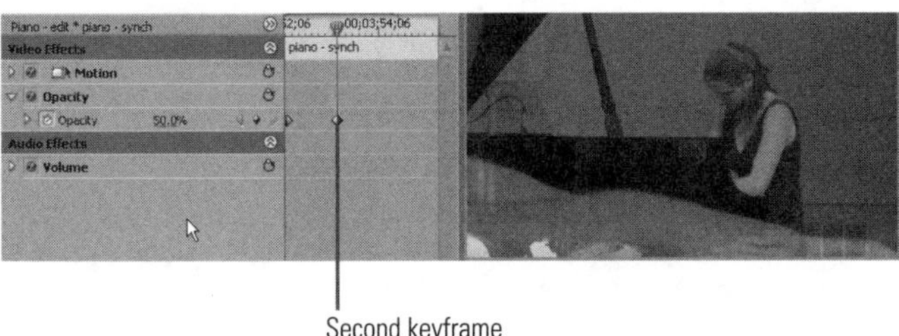

Second keyframe

Figure 43b Place the second keyframe where you want the overlay effect to appear at its final value (here 50%).

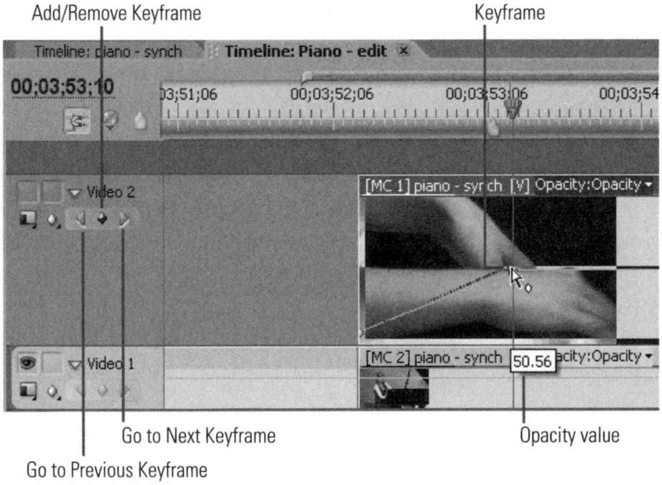

Add/Remove Keyframe

Keyframe

Timeline: piano - synch

Timeline: Piano - edit

00;03;53;10

Video 2

[MC 1] piano - synch [V] Opacity:Opacity

Video 1

[MC 2] piano - synch

50.56

Go to Next Keyframe

Opacity value

Go to Previous Keyframe

Figure 43c Premiere Pro also has Opacity controls on the timeline, which are very useful for making final adjustments to crossfades and other effects.

Rubber Band Controls

You can set and adjust keyframes for audio the exact same way you adjusted the Opacity controls in Figure 43. These types of controls are commonly called *rubber band controls.*

More on Customizing Effects with Keyframes

Once you set the keyframes, Premiere Pro will automatically create all frames necessary to smoothly fade the overlay effect in from a value of zero to a value of 50%.

Each time you apply an effect, Premiere Pro allows you to adjust it on the timeline, as with the Opacity controls shown in **Figure 43c**. As above, drag the current-time indicator to the desired keyframe location, then click the Add/Remove Keyframe button to add (or remove) a keyframe. Then drag the keyframe up or down to achieve the desired effect.

#44 Going Split Screen—Diagonal

Layering is one way to show two videos in the same screen, as discussed above. Let's explore another—a diagonal split screen (**Figure 44a**)—that you create by applying a "garbage matte" effect to one clip that exposes the clip in the track under it. Here's how it works.

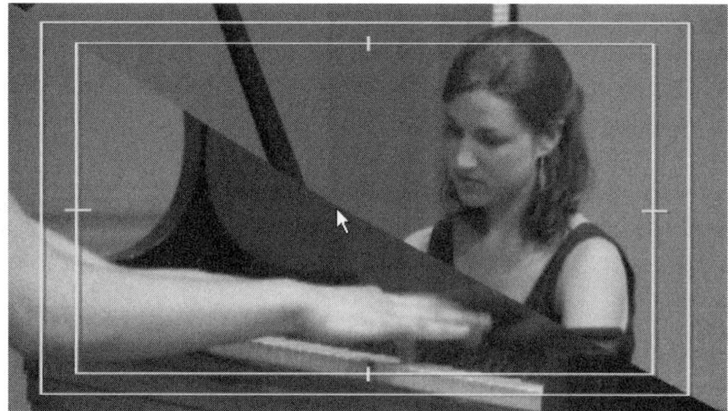

Figure 44a Here we see the upper-left corner of one clip and the bottom-right corner of another. This effect is a natural for this concert.

1. In Premiere Pro, place two clips at the same location on the timeline, one on Video 1 and the other on Video 2 (see Figure 42a). In this example, I'm combining a close-up of the hands of a pianist over a long shot of her playing.
2. Apply the Four-Point Garbage Matte to the top clip (Video Effects > Keying Folder).
3. In the Effect Controls panel, click the Four-Point Garbage Matte effect to make it active. You should see circular positioning handles on each corner (**Figure 44b**).

Garbage Mattes

The garbage matte is a free-form trapezoid that you draw around a section of your video or video layer. Once the garbage matte is in place, the editor discards everything outside the matte in that layer, like, well, garbage. Garbage mattes are most commonly used with chroma key effects to exclude edge detritus, but they also play a useful general-purpose role any time you want to exclude portions of a frame. Premiere Pro has Four-, Eight-, and Sixteen-Point garbage mattes.

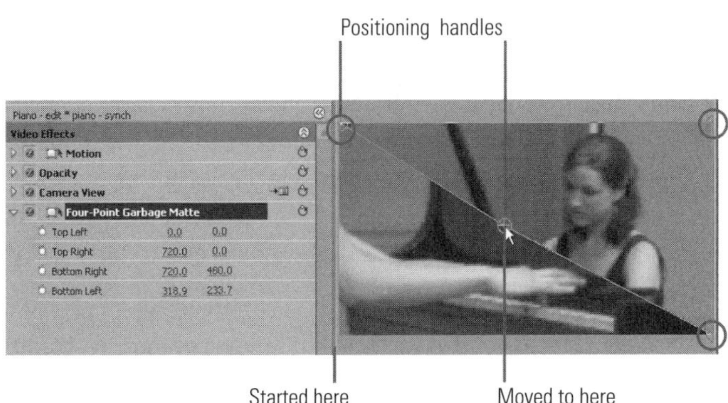

Figure 44b Premiere Pro hides regions outside the garbage matte, revealing the clip under it. To create this effect, drag the handle from the lower-left corner until it forms a straight line.

4. In the Program Monitor, grab the lower-left corner of the garbage matte and drag it toward the center until there's a straight line from the upper-left corner to the lower-right corner. This obscures the lower-left portion of the top clip, letting the bottom clip show through.

#45 Producing a Picture-in-Picture Effect

Picture-in-picture (P-i-P) is an overlay effect that starts with two clips at the same location on the timeline, one on top of the other. It's an effect that you'll use for performances, interviews, or any time you'd like to show footage from one video interacting with another.

At a high level, you'll use Premiere Pro's Motion controls to resize the top clip, and then move it around to the desired location on the bottom clip. Then, optionally, you'll dress up the P-i-P with beveled edges and a drop shadow.

1. Select the top clip in the Timeline, and open the Effect Controls panel (**Figure 45a**).

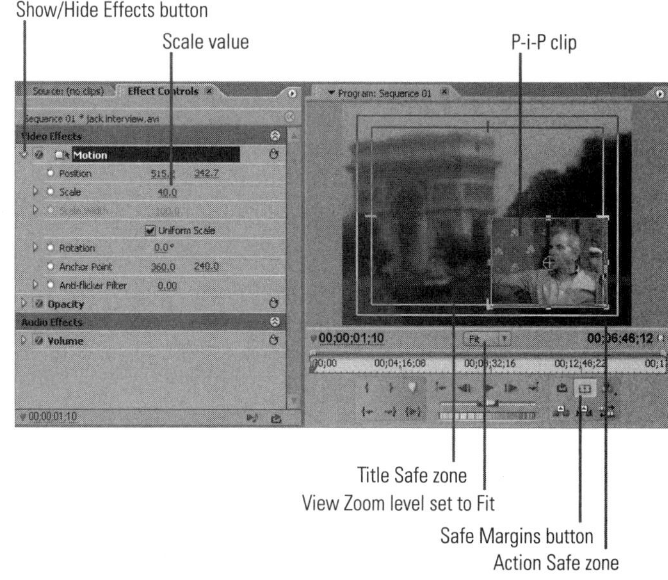

Figure 45a After shrinking the top clip, drag it to the desired location on the larger frame. Be sure most of your P-i-P clip is inside the Title Safe zone. With the View Zoom level set to Fit, I'm showing the entire frame so you can see the P-i-P in action.

2. Twirl the Show/Hide Effects button to expose the motion controls.

3. Change the Scale value to 40.

4. Drag the smaller window to the desired location within the larger frame. In the example, the P-i-P is in the lower-right corner. Your P-i-P is set; now let's dress it up.

Fading the P-i-P In and Out

Consider adding a short dissolve transition of 7-15 frames to the start and end of the P-i-P to smooth its appearance and disappearance.

Standardizing with Presets

When using repetitive P-i-P effects, create presets to standardize the size, positioning, and other attributes of your P-i-P effect once you've adjusted the settings to your liking or to the requirements of your project. Otherwise, each will appear slightly different, detracting from the professional look of your video.

Note:

If you're producing a DVD or other project for display on a 4:3 NTSC television, note that the outer 10-15% of the video may be excluded as "overscan." For this reason, click the Safe Margins button in the Program Monitor to expose the Title Safe zone (inner box) and Action Safe zone (outer box), and make sure the edges of your P-i-P are well within the Action Safe zone.

5. In the Effects Panel, click the Presets folder to open it, then select the Bevel Edges folder (**Figure 45b**).

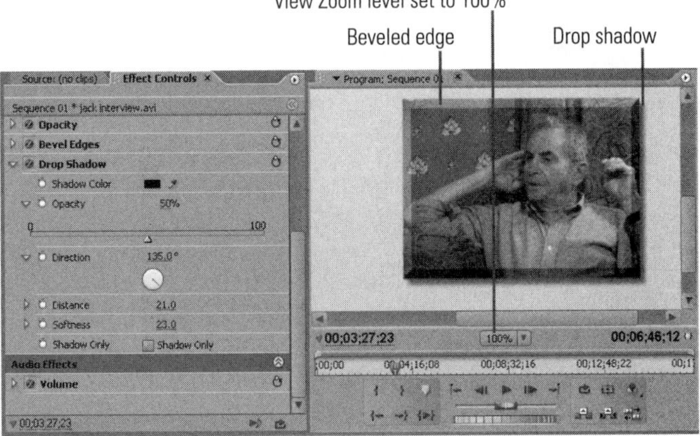

Figure 45b The P-i-P dressed up with beveled edges and a drop shadow. With the View Zoom set to 100%, I'm zoomed into the bottom-right corner of the frame so you can see the detail in the P-i-P. I also moved away from the Arc de Triomphe to provide a better background for seeing the P-i-P.

6. Drag the Bevel Edges Thin preset onto the top track. Accept the presets.

7. Click the Video Effects panel, select the Perspective folder, click the Drop Shadow effect, and drag it onto the top track. In the example shown in Figure 45b, I've adjusted the default setting to reveal the shadow to the bottom right of the P-i-P—now displayed over another scene from the trip—and zoomed in so you can see the details of the P-i-P with Safe Margins turned off.

Note:

Obviously, neither the beveled edges nor the drop shadows are required (and you can customize the parameters to suit your taste), but they add a nice touch of polish to the P-i-P.

Using the Title Tool to Create a Frame

Say you wanted a blue frame around your P-i-P. What would you do? Premiere Pro doesn't allow you to create and paint edges around your video, but you can create a blue box in the title tool, place it under the P-i-P, and achieve the same result.

#46 Converting Clips to Sepia in Premiere Pro

Working from an Example

Though we tend to think of sepia as a single color value, different programs produce it as anywhere from light tan to dark orange. When attempting to generate a sepia look, it helps to have an example with the exact tone of sepia that you're trying to match. For example, if you're using sepia titles or DVD menus in your project, create a prototype menu first, then attempt to match the video to that prototype.

Fading the Sepia Effect In and Out

It's easy to transition from Sepia to full color; just set keyframes for the Amount to Tint value, setting it at 100% for full sepia, and 0% for full color. See #43 for more on keyframes, and #47 for how to transition in from Black & White to color.

Converting your video to sepia is a great look for weddings and many other videos intended to convey a sense of nostalgia. Unfortunately, Premiere Pro doesn't have a turnkey sepia effect, so you'll have to create your own. Here's how to do it:

1. Apply the Tint Effect (Video Effects panel > Image Control folder) to your clip.
2. Open the Effect Controls panel and twirl the Tint Effect button (**Figure 46a**).

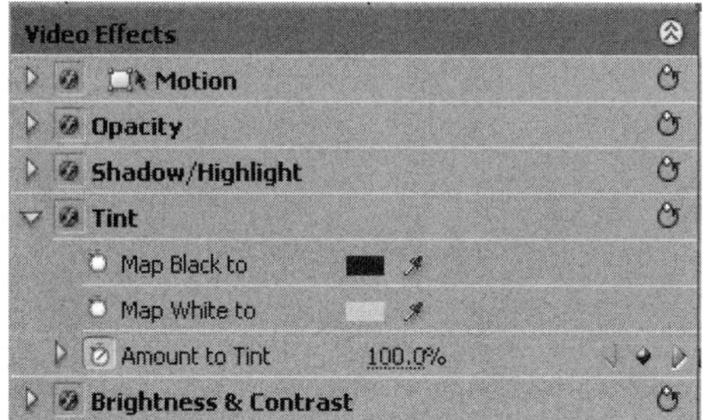

Figure 46a Creating a sepia look with the Tint Effect (in concert with others).

3. Click the Map White to chip to open the Color Picker dialog box (**Figure 46b**). Adjust the RGB values to Red = 224, Green = 212, and Blue = 195.
4. Click the Map Black to chip to open the Color Picker dialog box. Adjust the RGB values to Red = 66, Green = 39, and Blue = 2.
5. Set the Amount to Tint value to 100%.

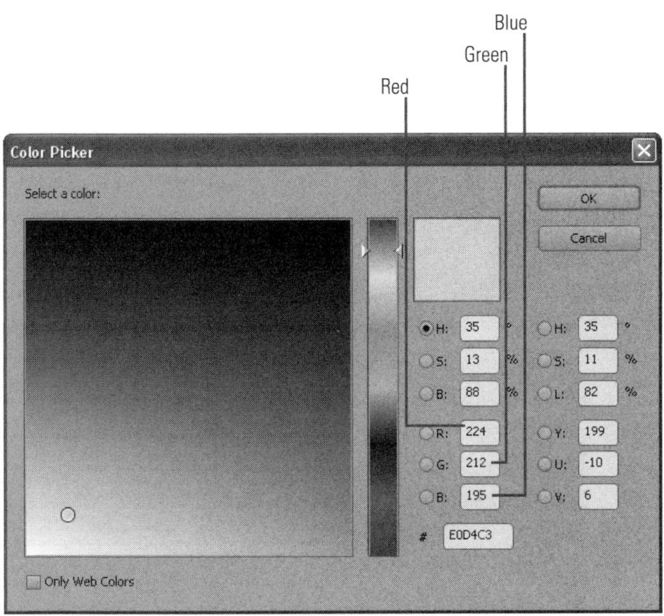

Figure 46b Here's where you set the RGB values for the white pixels in the image (and on a screen just like this for the black pixels). After setting the values, the color should approximate tan, which you can adjust as you like.

6. If the video is too dark after applying the Tint, drag the Brightness & Contrast effect (Video Effects > Adjust folder) and lighten the clip as desired. The Shadow/Highlight tool is also useful for heightening the drama of the effect.

Third-Party Sepia Plug-ins

There are several third-party plug-ins that provide a sepia-look, with lots more fine-tuning controls than you'll find in Premiere Pro. I'm most familiar with the Magic Bullet series from Red Giant Software (www.redgiantsoftware.com). If your videos tend to include lots of old "looks," you'll find the series very helpful.

Using After Effects' Sepia Effect

After Effects has a Sepia effect, which is excellent (though a touch orange for my taste), and works well when you want to convert an entire clip to sepia. However, it's very labor-intensive to transition from sepia to full color in After Effects and bring the effect into Premiere Pro. So if you have lots of clips to convert to sepia and plan to transition full-color video in and out, you're better off creating your sepia look in Premiere Pro.

#47 Transitioning from Black and White to Full Color

One technique frequently used for a dramatic effect in wedding video and similar productions is to transition black-and-white video to full-color. Here's how it works in Premiere Pro:

1. Apply the Color Balance (HLS) effect (Video Effects > Image Control folder) onto the target clip (**Figure 47**).

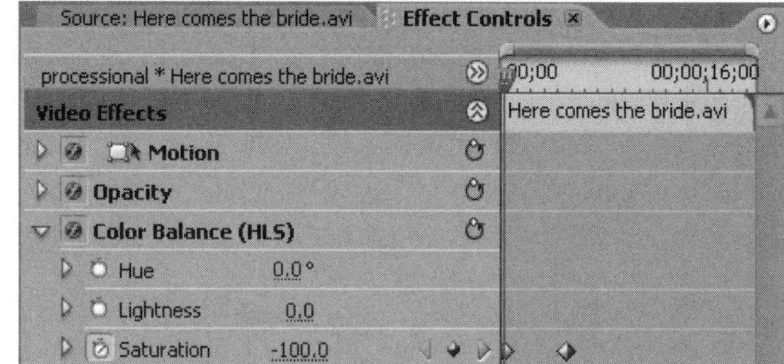

Figure 47 You'll use the Color Balance (HLS) effect to create your black-and-white clip, then use keyframes to transition from black and white (–100 Saturation) to full color (0 Saturation).

2. Set a keyframe for Saturation approximately 5 seconds into the video with a value of 0 (which is the default, meaning full color).

3. Set another keyframe on the first frame of the clip, with a value of –100, which means absolutely no color (Figure 47). Premiere Pro will transition from black and white at the start of the clip to full color at the 5-second mark. Obviously, you can adjust the duration to fit your content.

Why Not Use the Black & White Filter?

Premiere Pro has a Black & White filter, but it has no configurable controls, so it can't be used to create a smooth transition from black and white to full color. Use it when you want a clip to become black and white and stay that way from start to finish.

#48 Perfecting Chroma Key in Premiere Pro

If you have After Effects Professional, use the Keylight plug-in (#49) to perform your chroma key effects. (Chroma key, briefly, is the process of selecting a "key" color in a video layer and rendering it transparent, revealing elements of underlying layers. A typical example of chroma key would be shooting a reporter in front of a green screen in a studio, keying out the green background, and replacing it with the scene she's reporting on for an "on-location" effect.) If you don't have After Effects Professional, here's how to get the best possible results in Premiere Pro:

1. Place your background clip on Video 1 and the chroma key clip on Video 2 (or the track immediately above the background clip).
2. Apply the Chroma Key effect (Video Effects > Keying folder) to the clip containing the chroma key video. This effect produces better results than the Blue Screen, Green Screen, or Color Key effects.
3. Click the eyedropper icon to the right of the chip next to the Color control (**Figure 48a**). Press and hold the Ctrl key, then click the area of the background where the light is about average value.

   Note:
   When you hold down the Ctrl key, Premiere Pro samples an area of 5x5 pixels, further averaging the color values.

continued on next page

Blur the Background Clip

You can improve the perceived quality of your chroma key video by blurring the background slightly, using the Fast Blur filter (Video Effects > Blur & Sharpen folder) with a blurriness value set to 5 (or adjusted to suit your content). This helps smooth the edges between the chroma key clip and background, and makes the subject of the chroma key video look much more distinctive.

Apply Additional Effects under the Chroma Key Effect

Premiere Pro applies effects from the top down. If you apply any effects above the Chroma Key effect, Premiere Pro may adjust the color values of the chroma key clip, potentially destroying your clean key. Any effects applied below the Chroma Key effect will affect only the cleanly keyed subject.

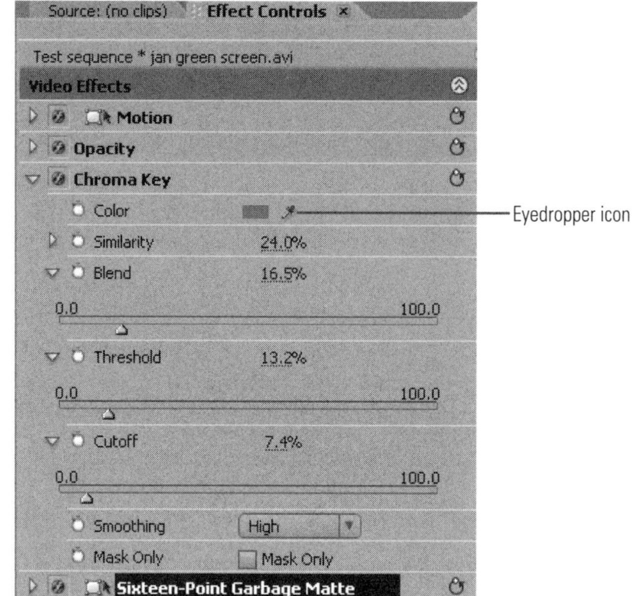

Figure 48a The business end of the Chroma Key filter.

4. Adjust the Similarity property first, then Blend, Threshold, and Cutoff. Basically, you're looking for settings that eliminate the background color without eating into the subject of the chroma key clip.
5. Click the drop-down menu next to the Smoothing control and set it to High.
6. While adjusting your settings, use the View Zoom Level adjustment under the Program Monitor to zoom in to the image and check edges between the chroma key clip and background (**Figure 48b**).

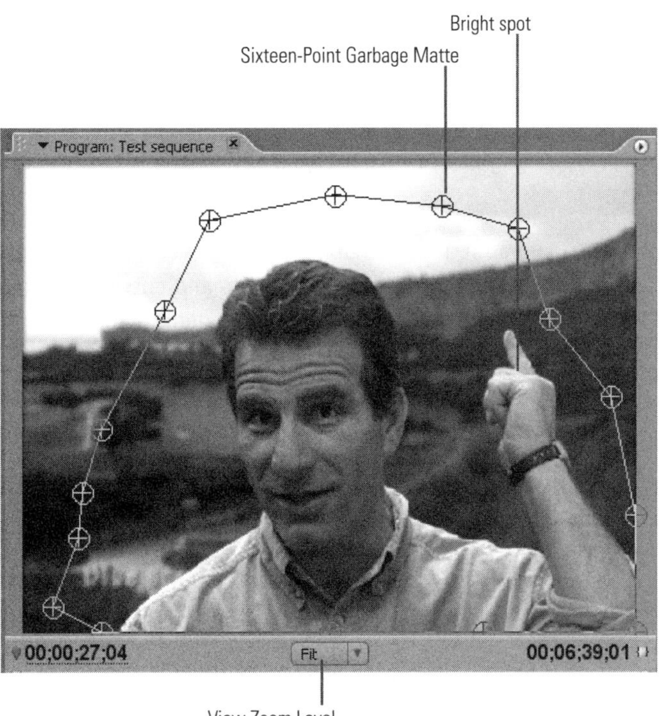

Figure 48b Here's the chroma key clip neatly keyed out over the background. Note the Sixteen-Point Garbage Matte eliminating edge residue.

7. Check the entire video before finalizing your settings. Often there will be one or two problem spots, perhaps a bright light shining against a forehead or hand (like that seen in Figure 48b) or a similar anomaly that could distort the effect. If necessary, use keyframes to vary Chroma Key values over the duration of the clip.

8. If the edges around the video frame are a problem, consider applying a Garbage Matte (Video Effects > Keying Folder), which eliminates any pixels outside the matte. In Figure 48b, you can see the Sixteen-Point Garbage Matte surrounding the speaker. Simply grab each positioning handle and move it inward to hide the edge residue. Be sure that arm, head, or other motions don't extend beyond the matte; otherwise, they will be excluded as well.

continued on next page

If Possible, Preview on an NTSC Monitor

Televisions are generally more forgiving than computer monitors, and you can drive yourself nuts attempting to fix chroma key issues that appear on your monitor but won't show up on your television. So, if you're producing for television (or for a DVD to be viewed on one), preview on a television.

9. As a further check, select the Mask Only checkbox at the bottom of the Chroma Key effect. All edges should be clean, and there should be no residue within the white mask. If there is, your settings are eating into the chroma key subject and need to be adjusted.

10. Finally, click the chroma key clip in the Program Monitor and drag it about 30 pixels to the right. Compare the background under the chroma key clip and outside the chroma key clip to ensure that the effect didn't darken the background (**Figure 48c**).

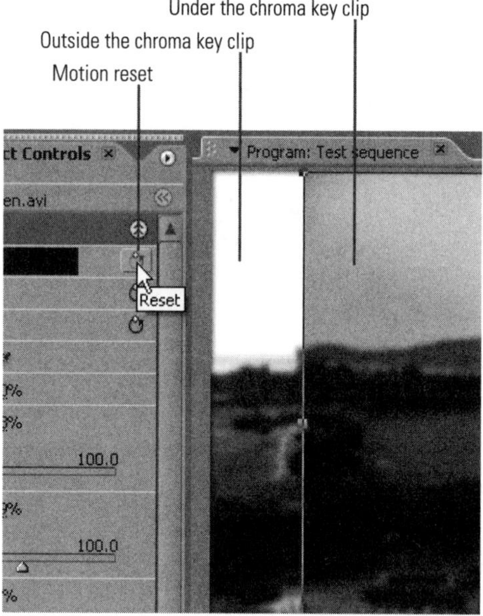

Figure 48c Shifting the chroma key video to the right makes it easy to see that the Chroma Key effect darkened the background clip (which you'll have to fix by adjusting the settings). Don't forget to click Reset to shift the chroma key clip back into position.

11. Click the Motion Reset icon to shift the chroma key clip back into the original position.

#49 Using After Effects' Keylight Plug-in

The Keylight Effect is simple to use, and one of the most effective chroma key tools available in any product. It's included with the Professional version of After Effects, though you'll have to install it separately.

Assuming that you're producing your video in Premiere Pro, the simplest workflow is to start an After Effects composition in Premiere Pro (see #20), copy and paste the background and chroma key clips into the After Effects composition, apply the filter, and save the composition. It will then appear in your Premiere Pro project panel, where you can deploy it as you wish.

Once you've created your After Effects composition, here's what you do to apply the Keylight effect in After Effects.

1. In the timeline, click to select the chroma key clip.
2. Choose Effect > Keying > Keylight to apply the Keylight effect.
3. Click the eyedropper icon to the right of the chip next to the Screen Colour control (**Figure 49a**). Press and hold the Ctrl key, then click an area of the background where the light is about average value.

Note:

When you hold down the Ctrl key, After Effects samples an area of 5x5 pixels, further averaging the color values.

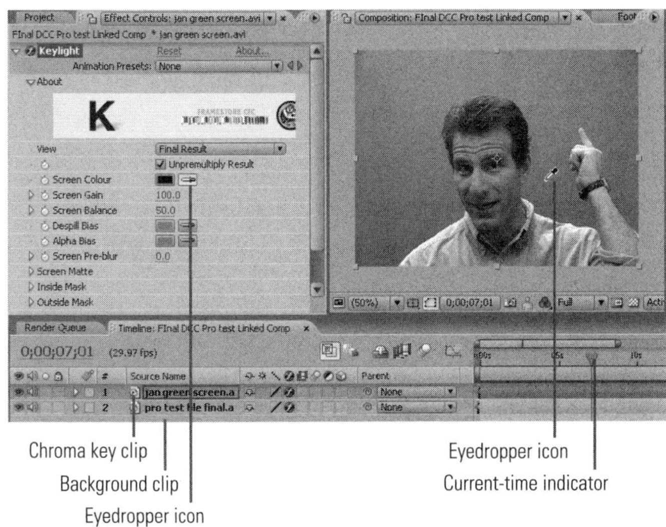

Figure 49a Applying the Keylight filter with Adobe After Effects.

continued on next page

Keylight Not Installed?

Although Keylight ships with After Effects, it's included as a third-party plug-in from a British company called The Foundry (www.thefoundry.co.uk). Like other plug-ins, it doesn't install automatically with the software. To install Keylight, insert the first Adobe Production Studio DVD into your DVD-ROM drive. When you arrive at the main installation screen, click Install Third Party Plug-Ins. You can install Keylight from there.

More Help with Keylight

The Keylight effect has more dials and gauges than we can describe here, but if you have further questions, you'll find a very helpful PDF User Guide in your Windows Start menu at Start > Programs >The Foundry > Keylight 1.1 for After Effects 7.0 > Keylight 1.1 for After Effects 7.0 Documentation.

4. Click the View list menu and choose Status (**Figure 49b**).

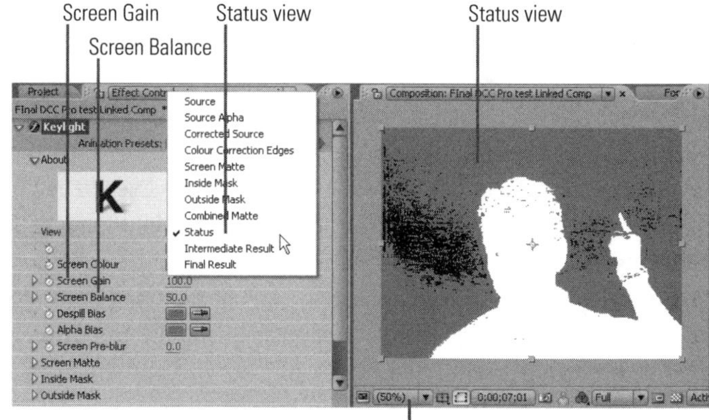

Figure 49b The Status view shows how "clean" the key is. We've still got some residue here.

5. Adjust the Screen Gain control until the background is predominantly black save for a gray edge around the foreground subject.
6. Adjust the Screen Balance control until the foreground subject is predominantly white.
7. Click the View list menu and choose Final Result. Inspect the results by zooming in to the image using the Magnification ratio pop-up menu to check the edges between the foreground and background videos, and dragging the current-time indicator through the entire clip to check for rough spots.

#50 Working with Mattes in Premiere Pro

I recently shot a country wedding on the banks of the North Fork River in North Carolina. All DVD menus and titles were sepia-toned, as was the start and end of each component clip. We got a great side shot of the bride walking to the altar, and I applied the sepia filter to this shot as well, save for a small, full-color circle surrounding the bride and her father. Of course, you can't see the sepia tone in the grayscale image in this book, but I've darkened the video surrounding them in **Figure 50a**, which should give you some sense of the effect I created.

Figure 50a In the real video, the oval surrounding the father was full color, and the background sepia, but that doesn't show in grayscale book images, so I've darkened the background video.

Though this application may sound a bit campy, the concept of highlighting regions of video within a video is incredibly powerful. It's CNN showing a missile zooming in from the left, the evening news inserting a blur filter over the face of an underage offender, or ESPN SportsCenter focusing on the middle linebacker making a play.

The next three techniques (#51, #52, and #53) describe the individual steps of producing a highlighting effect. First, you'll create a matte in Premiere Pro's Titler, then apply the matte with the Track Matte key, then animate the matte to follow the bride (or other focal point of your video) using motion controls.

Start with two tracks of the exact same video, shown here on Video 1 and Video 2 (**Figure 50b**). The bottom track is the background track, which in the example is tinted sepia (see #46), but could easily be black and white or even normal, if you're applying a blur filter over a face.

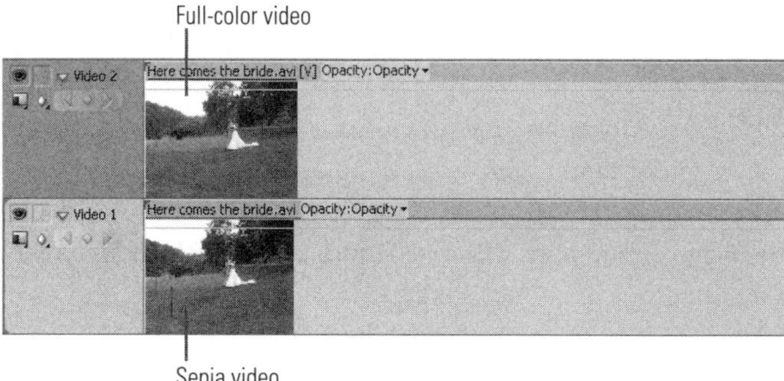

Figure 50b Start with the same identical video on two adjacent tracks, here Video 1 and Video 2. The bottom track is the background track, and the top track is the video that will show through after you create and apply the matte.

The top track is the original video. Using the approach discussed in the next three techniques, you'll identify and modify a region in that video that will display over the background video. In the example, I'll create an oval around the bride and father, showing them in full color, but blocking out the rest of the full-color clip, allowing the sepia background to show through.

#51 Creating Mattes in Premiere Pro

The easiest way to create a matte in Premiere Pro is to use the design primitives in its Titler. Here's how:

1. In the timeline, move the current-time indicator to the start of the clips. This will allow you to see the clips in the Titler while you're creating your matte, which is critical for precise positioning.
2. Choose File > New > Title to open the Title editor. Name the title something memorable like "oval matte."
3. In the Titler, be sure that the Show Video checkbox is selected so the video shows through (**Figure 51a**).

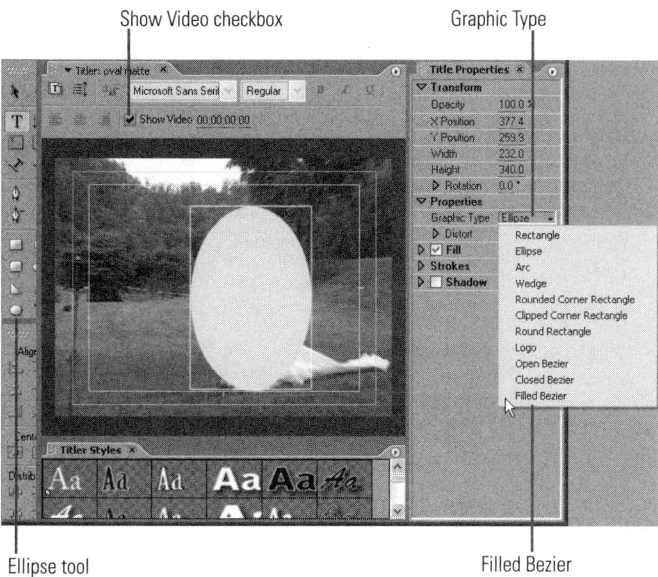

Figure 51a Creating a Closed Bezier to define the regions of your video-within-a-video.

4. Click the Ellipse tool and drag an ellipse around the subject of the video.
5. Select the Graphic Type pull-down menu and choose Closed Bezier.

continued on next page

Premiere Pro's Design Primitives

One key strength of Premiere Pro's titling utility is the ability to create rectangles, ovals, squares and other shapes, which are called generically "design primitives." These are explored in detail in #59.

Using Other Design Primitives

You can use other design primitives, including the Pen tool, to create completely custom shapes, as long as you end up with a Closed Bezier graphic.

Make 'em in Photoshop

You can also make your mattes in Photoshop. Create your shapes over a transparent background and save the file as a grayscale PSD file. After applying the Track Matte Key, the transparent area will block the background and the video will flow through the shape in the Photoshop file.

Note:

At this point, you have an ellipse with a hard edge, which is fine if you're applying a mosaic or blur filter to hide someone, but doesn't look great in a vignette-like application like this one. The next step will soften the edge, creating the blurry line seen around the ellipse in Figure 50a.

6. Select the Shadow checkbox and twirl the triangle to reveal the properties. The critical properties here are color (which must be white so it doesn't degrade the quality of the matte effect) and angle (which must be zero so it doesn't look lopsided). You can experiment with Opacity, Size, and Spread, but start with the values in **Figure 51b**.

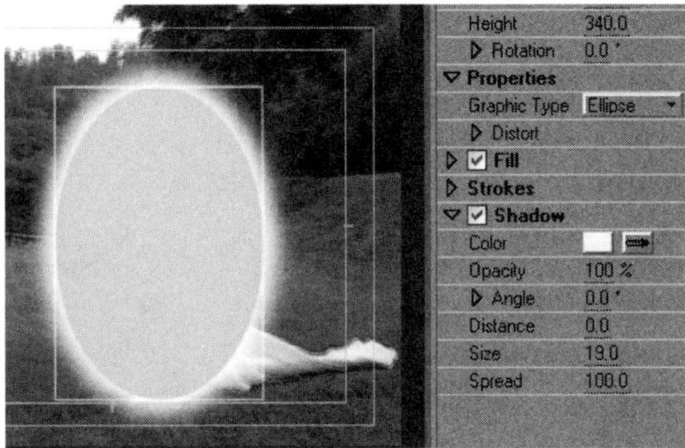

Figure 51b You can customize your drop shadow by experimenting with the Opacity, Size, and Spread values.

7. Close the Titler.

#52 Applying the Track Matte Key

Once you have the timeline set up (#50) and the matte created (#51), it's time to apply the Track Matte Key and complete the highlight effect. Here's how.

1. Drag the new title to Video 3 directly above the two other clips.
2. Apply the Track Matte Key (Video Effects > Keying folder) to the top video clip (Video 2 in the example), not the new matte.
3. Select the clip on Video 2, and open the Effect Controls panel.
4. In the Track Matte Key controls, click the Matte: drop-down menu and choose the track containing the matte. In this example, it's Video 3 (**Figure 52**).

Figure 52 Once you choose the track containing your matte, Premiere Pro should apply the effect, showing the result in the Program Monitor.

5. Leave all other controls at their default settings. You should see the video from Video 2 (in the example, full-color video) showing through the matte, with video from Video 1 (in the example, the darkened video) elsewhere in the frame.

Troubleshooting

This technique is binary; if you've got everything set up correctly, it should work; if not, it won't. If you're using a Premiere Pro title as the matte, the most common mistake is forgetting to save the file as a Closed Bezier (see #51). If you're working with a matte you imported from Photoshop, check to make sure that you saved the file as a grayscale image and left the background transparent.

Applying a Blur or Mosaic Filter

Let's say you want to blur out the face of someone on the video. How would you do it? Use the same procedures described in the last three techniques, and apply a blur or mosaic video to the video on Video 2. The matte will limit its application to the defined region, blurring the face and showing the rest of the video in full detail.

#53 Animating Clips in Premiere Pro

Add Rotation to the Mix

If you feel the urge to rotate your logo or other graphic element, use the Rotation parameter shown in Figures 53a and 53c. Click Toggle animation to make it active, and use keyframes to control speed and positioning. To rotate one revolution clockwise, enter 360 (which Premiere Pro will convert to 1x0^{0}). To rotate one revolution counterclockwise, enter –360, which Premiere Pro will convert to –1x0^{0}).

We insert a lot of static objects into Premiere Pro, such as masks, titles, arrows, and other graphics. At times, we need them to adjust to the background video. For example, you may want a graphic arrow to remain pointing at a moving object, or a blur filter over someone whose identity you're attempting to hide. Or, to follow through with the example from the last three techniques (#50, #51, and #52), to keep the bride and her father in full color.

You'll use the same basic toolset—Premiere Pro's Motion Controls and keyframes—for all of these tasks. Here's how:

1. Click the clip containing the matte to activate it (on Video 3 in our example).
2. Make sure the current-time indicator is set to the initial frame of the clip.
3. Open the Video Effects panel, and click the Show/Hide Effects button next to the Motion controls to reveal its configurable parameters (**Figure 53a**).

Figure 53a The positioning on the first frame. Everything looks perfect.

4. Click the Show/Hide Timeline View to open the timeline to the right.

5. Click the Toggle animation buttons next to the Position and Scale parameters to set your starting keyframes.

   Note:
   If you created your matte using the Premiere Pro titler on the first frame of the video, you shouldn't have to adjust the matte at the first keyframe. If you created it over a latter frame in the video, or in Photoshop, you may have to adjust the settings for the initial frame.

6. Drag the current-time indicator to the right until the shape no longer covers the targets in the background. In the example, at 10 frames in, the ellipse is too small (**Figure 53b**) and a bit too far forward.

Figure 53b Ten frames in, the oval is too small.

7. To make the oval larger, drag over the scale value of 100 to the right (**Figure 53c**). To adjust positioning, drag over the Position X and Y values (default values are 360 and 240).

   Note:
   You don't need to create keyframes manually. If you move the video to a different frame and adjust any parameter with Toggle animation enabled, Premiere Pro will create the keyframe for you.

continued on next page

Go 3D

If you want to move your image in 3D space, apply the Camera View effect (Video Effects > Transform folder), which lets you spin along the longitudinal or latitudinal axis. As with Premiere Pro's motion controls, all parameters are individually keyframeable for ultimate control.

Smooth Motion

When you preview your clip, the motion should be smooth from keyframe to keyframe. If not, right-click the keyframes and check the Interpolation methods used from keyframe to keyframe. Linear should work well, but if you've selected Hold, the motion will be very abrupt at each keyframe.

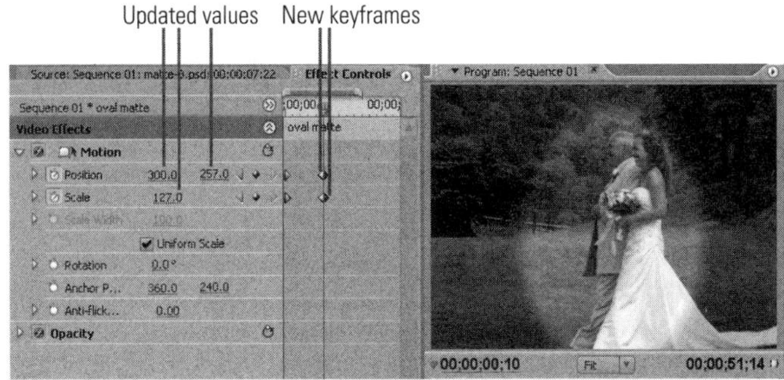

Figure 53c Back on track. Instead of moving 10 frames at a time, you can also just drag the current-time indicator to the first frame where you lose alignment.

8. Repeat as necessary throughout the effect to keep the object and background video aligned.

#54 Motion Tracking in After Effects

In #30, you learned how to use After Effects' Tracker feature to stabilize video. Here, you'll learn how to use it to track a moving object within a video and attach that tracking data to another object. Specifically, you'll track a person walking through a park in Washington, DC and then attach that motion to an arrow that follows him through the walk. You can imagine the commentary on the evening news: "Here's DC power broker Jon Seagull in a secret meeting with Congressman Mike Smith in July."

In addition to applying the tracking data to other objects in the composition, you can apply it to an effect already applied to a clip—say, automatically tracking lens flare effect to the shiny bumper of a car. This makes it a truly useful tool, albeit one available only with After Effects Professional.

In this technique, you'll learn how to track an object within a video; in #55, you'll learn to attach the tracking data to another layer in the composition (in this case, the arrow pointer).

After Effects' Tracker Controls are as follows:

- + sign—This marks the exact spot of the keyframe stored during the motion tracking. Drag this to the middle of the object you're attempting to track, which is also called the "Feature region."
- Feature region—This is the inner box; drag it to and around the object that you're tracking.
- Search region—This outer box defines the area that After Effects will track. It needs to be large enough to contain the frame-to-frame motion of the object, but if it's too large, it will slow the search process.

Here's a simple step-by-step example to get you started with motion tracking in After Effects.

1. Import the video file and create a new composition (#18)
2. Make sure the Tracker controls are showing by choosing Window > Tracker Controls.
3. Click the Track Motion button (**Figure 54a**).

continued on next page

Take a Deep Breath...

For me, the Track Motion effect either works smoothly, saving oodles of time, or things get ugly quickly. Track Motion is a highly functional effect, but you may have to experiment with it a bit (and study the manual) to get it working smoothly.

To State the Obvious...

Motion tracking works best with distinct shapes and colors. If the selected tracking point lacks detail, you probably won't get a good result without lots of manual adjustments.

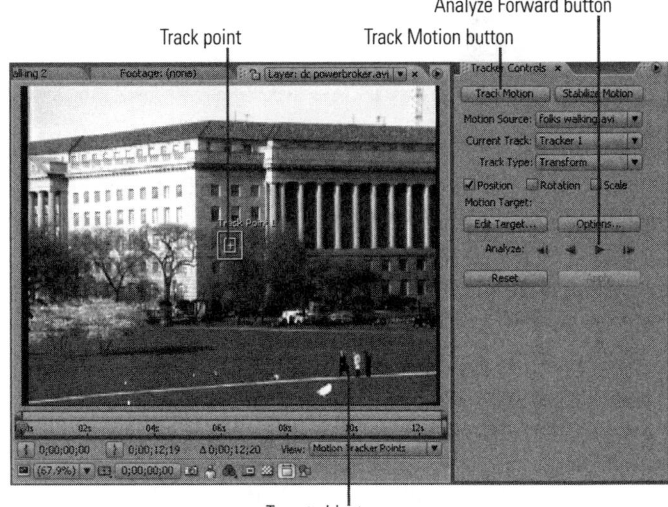

Figure 54a We're going to use the Tracker controls to track the man in the black overcoat walking in the lower-right corner (the guy on the extreme left).

4. Drag Track Point 1 (the plus sign in the middle of the two boxes) to the object, in this case the man's head (**Figure 54b**).

Figure 54b First drag the Track Point, then the Feature Region and Search Region over the object you're tracking. This image is in the bottom-right corner of the screen, showing the Feature Region zoomed in to the head of the man you're tracking.

5. Drag the Feature Region and Search Region boxes over the object. After Effects zooms the view to assist your precision-tuning.

6. Click the Analyze Forward button (see Figure 54a). After Effects tracks the object and creates a keyframe in each searched frame.

   Note:

   If After Effects ever loses track of the object, move back to the first inaccurate frame, drag the track point back to the correct object, and start tracking again. Repeat as necessary.

#55 Applying Motion-Tracking Data

Using Tracking Data in Premiere Pro

Since After Effects translates the tracking data to keyframes and similar coordinates, you can copy and paste the results of your work directly into Premiere Pro. Or, if you think you will be making further changes to the After Effects composition, you can import the composition into Premiere Pro via Dynamic Link. See #20 for more details.

In #54, you learned how to create tracking data; in this technique, you'll learn how to apply it to another layer in your After Effects composition. Specifically, in #54 you learned to track a man as he walked through a park. Now you'll apply an arrow to highlight the man's journey. Here's how:

1. In After Effects, drag the object (in this case the arrow) to the composition, placing it above the video with the tracked data.

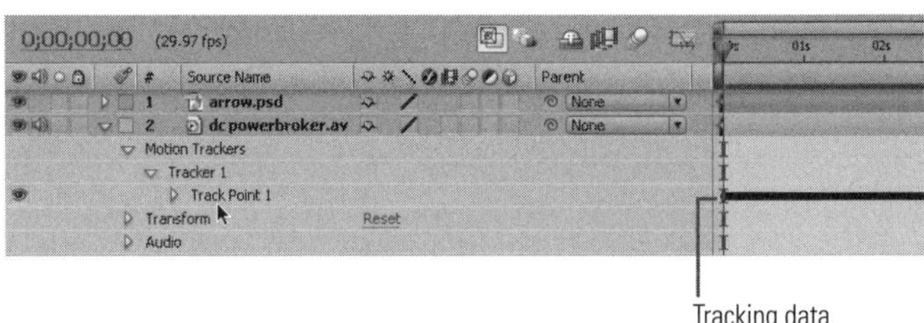

Figure 55a Arrow.psd contains the arrow, while dc powerbroker.avi contains the tracking data from Track Point 1.

2. In the Tracker Controls dialog box (**Figure 55b**), click the Motion Source drop-down menu and choose the file with the tracking data (dc powerbroker.avi).

Figure 55b The Motion Source is the file with the tracking data, the Current Track is the track with the data, and the Target is the track to which you'll apply the data.

3. In the Current Track drop-down menu, choose the track with the tracking data (Tracker 1).
4. In the Track Type drop-down menu, choose Transform.
5. In the Tracker Controls dialog box, select the Position checkbox.
6. Click Edit Target. After Effects opens the Motion Target window (**Figure 55c**).

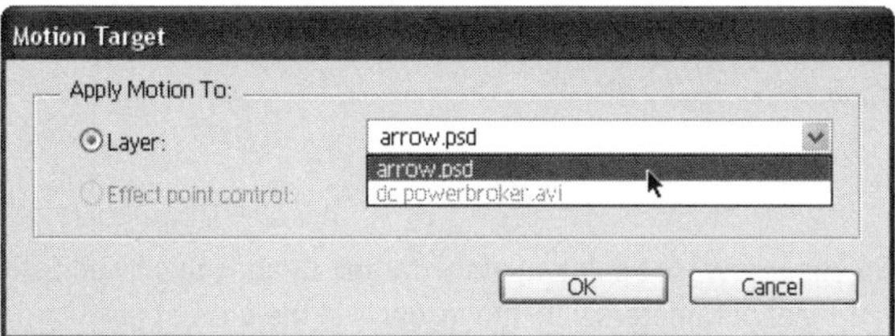

Figure 55c Here's where you choose the layer to which you'll apply the tracking data.

7. Click OK to close the Tracker Controls dialog box.
8. After Effects opens the Motion Tracker Apply Options dialog box. Choose X and Y (the default option) and click OK. After Effects applies the effect.

   Note:
   After Effects will apply the tracking data to the Anchor Point in the target file, which is usually in the middle of the file. This is why the arrow in the upper frame of ***Figure 55d*** *is over the target's head, not pointing at it. Fix this on the timeline by twirling the Transform parameters for the target object and changing the Anchor Point parameters. For example, the arrow is pointing at the target in the bottom frame after adjusting the Anchor point from 38.5, 27.5 to 77.5, 27.5, by dragging over the first (horizontal) property until the arrow was in the proper position. Don't drag the arrow to the right position in the image, as this will change the Position parameters, not the Anchor Point.*

continued on next page

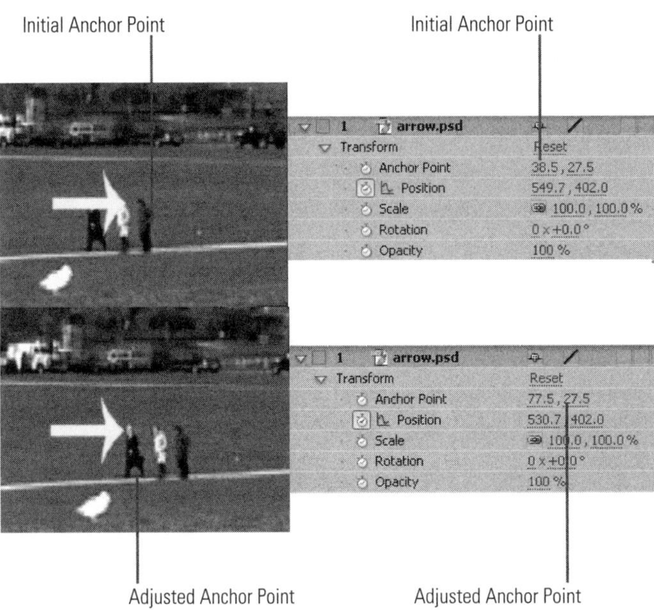

Figure 55d The arrow isn't pointing at the target. Change this by adjusting the Anchor Point parameters until the arrow is in the correct position.

CHAPTER SEVEN

Transitions and Titles

Applying transitions is one of the simplest functions in Premiere Pro; you simply drag them from their folder to the timeline. So our discussion of transitions will be limited to a short list of details about transitions that you may not know.

Producing titles can be more complex. You can create them from templates, you can design your own in Premiere Pro, or you can make them scroll or crawl. You can also integrate content from Photoshop, Illustrator, and After Effects. For these reasons, we'll devote the bulk of this chapter to addressing these title-related topics.

#56 Five Things You Don't Know About Premiere Pro Transitions

Anywhere, Anytime

You can apply transitions to any object in any video track, including still images, titles, videos, animations, and masks. You don't need to apply them to the intersection of two clips; you can apply them to the start and end of any content on the timeline. For example, to create a smooth transition in or out of a Picture-in-Picture effect, you can drag a dissolve transition to the front and/or back of the P-i-P clip.

If you scan this section, you'll notice that there are actually 11 concepts covered (9 numbered topics and 2 sidebars), but I'll assume that you know at least several of them. Hence, the "five" in the title. On to the techniques, starting with choosing a default transition for your project, or for the remaining portion or next section of your project.

- Set the default transition by right-clicking the target transition in the Effect bin.
- Set the default transition duration in the General section of the Preferences screen (Edit > Preferences).
- The default transition duration affects only transitions inserted *after* you change the duration, not those previously inserted.
- Default transition duration matters in (at least) two scenarios: when using the Automate to Sequence feature (#10) to insert multiple still images or videos into the timeline, and when using the Ctrl+D keystroke to insert the default transition at the default duration. When combined with the Page Dn keystroke to move to the next edit point on the timeline, Ctrl+D is a killer timesaver with Multi-Camera productions, or any time you decide to insert transitions as the last step in a production.

  If you study the transition in **Figure 56a**, you'll notice that it extends over both clips. The portion of the transition to the left of the cut uses frames from the second clip (typically called *heads*) combined with frames from the first clip. The transition portion to the right of the cut requires frames from the first clip (typically called *tails*) combined with frames from the second clip.

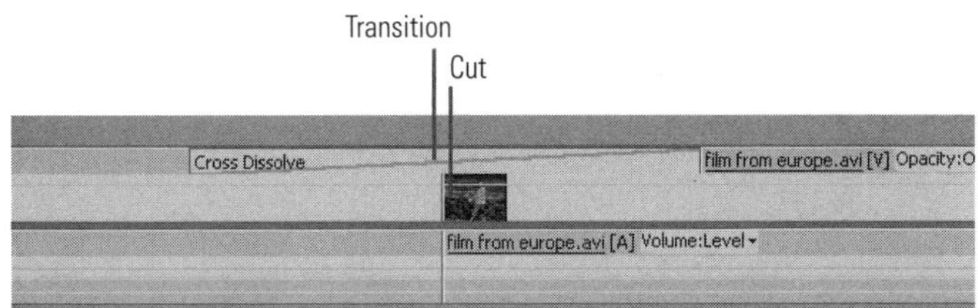

Figure 56a A transition extends over both clips.

- When you add a transition to an edit point on the timeline and neither clip has the required heads or tails to support the transition, Premiere Pro will insert it and display a window with the message "Insufficient media. This transition will contain repeated frames." If the clips contain lots of action, this could produce a short but noticeable stuttering effect. You can fix the problem by trimming the clips to create the necessary heads and tails to support the transition.
- When you add a transition to an edit point on the timeline, if one of the clips has sufficient heads or tails and the other doesn't, Premiere Pro won't let you insert the transition at the cut line between the clips. Instead, it forces you to insert it on the side with sufficient frames to support it. Most viewers won't notice the difference, but if you must change the alignment, double-click the transition to open it in the Effect Controls panel (**Figure 56b**), and adjust the transition's parameters.

  As you can see in Figure 56b, you can change the alignment to Center at Cut, Start at Cut, or End at Cut, but if there are no sufficient heads or tails to support the alignment, Premiere Pro will display the zebra pattern shown in **Figure 56c**. Again, this could produce a stuttering effect that you can fix by trimming the first clip to create a sufficient tail, or by clicking the Alignment drop-down menu and choosing End at Cut.

continued on next page

Fading to and from Black

Applying a dissolve transition to the first clip in your movie is the fastest way to create a fade in from black effect. Applying a dissolve transition to the last clip in your movie is the fastest way to fade to black.

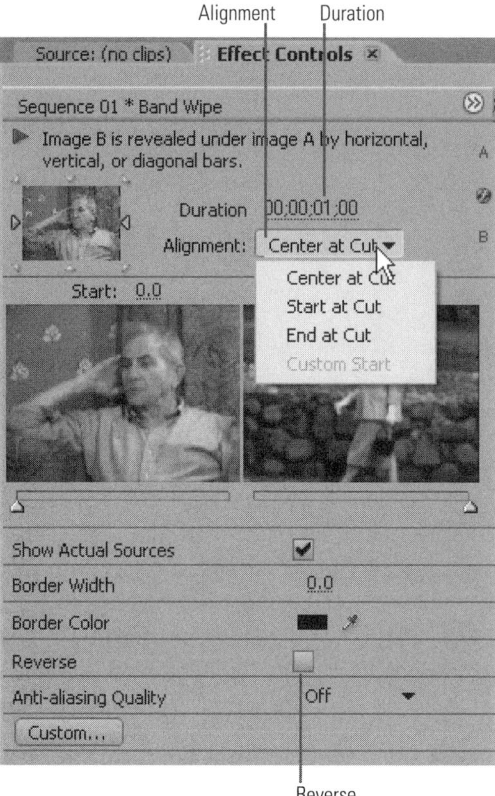

Figure 56b Double-click the transition to open it in the Effect Controls panel. Adjustments will vary by transition.

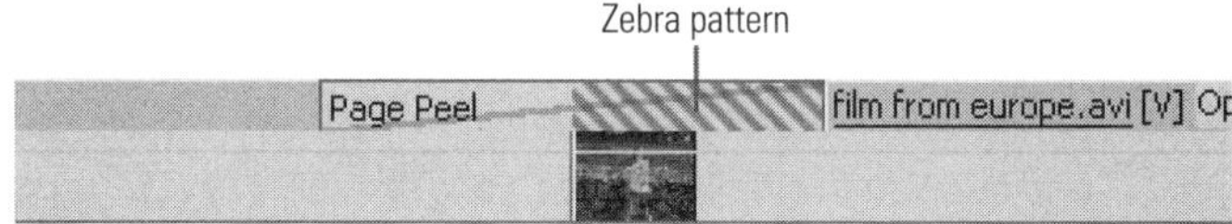

Figure 56c The zebra pattern warns you that you have insufficient media to support the transition.

- To change the duration of a transition, drag either edge or both to the desired length, or enter a new duration in the Effect Controls panel.
- Many Premiere Pro transitions offer customization options accessed in the Effect Controls panel (see Figure 56b). For the Band Wipe transition shown in Figure 56b, for example, you can change the width and color of the Wipe border, reverse the effect, adjust the Anti-aliasing Quality, and (via the Custom button on the bottom) change the number of bands included in the wipe.

#57 Synch Your Titles and DVD Menus

One great way to make your productions look more professional is to create a common look for DVD menus and the titles used in your movies. While Premiere Pro has some outstanding titles, Encore has some awesome menu templates that you can easily customize for your own use. For many projects, you should peruse and choose DVD templates before creating your titles.

For example, consider the wedding template in **Figure 57a**, which is the NTSC_Bride Menu.psd from Encore's menu library. If you bring that into Photoshop, you can easily strip away all the layers of text and button highlights and create a perfect menu background for your wedding titles.

Figure 57a What a beautiful DVD menu template! The arrow symbol is a "drop zone" you can customize with your own image.

For a recent project, I created the background images for all Premiere Pro titles in Encore, removing the text in this title and dragging in images for each major section in the project (**Figure 57b**). Then I captured each screen and added it to Premiere Pro, using the same font as Encore to create a neat, consistent appearance. The other way to go, of course, is to borrow backgrounds and other design elements from Premiere Pro title templates to build your DVD menus.

Choose Your Fonts Well

However you design your titles, remember that simple fonts work better on television, DVDs, and streaming video clips than complex and (especially) skinny, artsy fonts. When designing for television display, keep your text at 20-point or larger, since smaller font sizes can be difficult to read.

Designing for Streaming

When producing streaming video, test your font and font size choices by rendering small portions of video with a title using Premiere Pro's Render Workspace function to assess their readability. Try to avoid scaling your text down during rendering, since this can distort text appearance. For example, when producing for 320x240 output, use a 320x240 preset.

Figure 57b Look familiar? This is a title (with faces blurred out) used in the actual wedding video.

Whether you crib Encore's menus, base your DVD menus on Premiere Pro title templates, or create your own from scratch, if you're producing a DVD, consider designing your titles so that they appear similar to your DVD menus.

#58 Working with Premiere Pro Title Templates

Premiere Pro includes a highly useful collection of title templates, which generally include at least four variants on a theme, and often many more. For example, **Figure 58a** reveals four variations of medical titles; here's what each category represents:

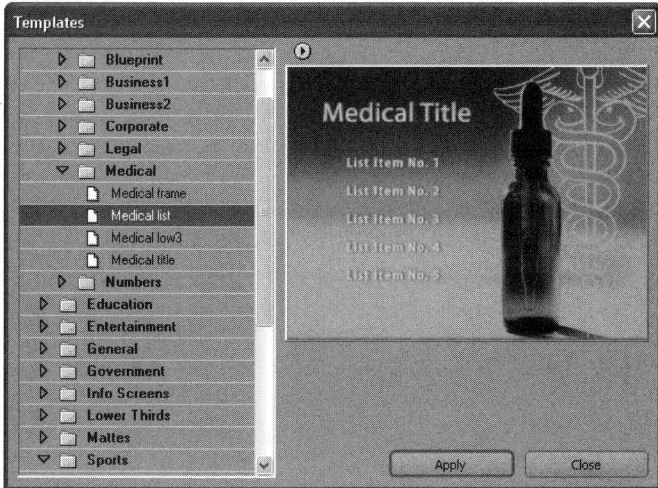

Figure 58a Premiere Pro includes lots of useful templates you can use as is or customize to your liking.

- Frame—content on the top and bottom, with video showing through in the middle. Side frames have content on either or both sides, with video showing through on the other side.
- List—a full-screen title with a list field appropriate for a discussion list or meeting agenda.
- Low3—a lower-third title, which appears on the lower third of the video screen, with video playing above it. This is a good choice for supplying the name and title of the person in the video.
- Title—a full-screen title appropriate for the opening and/or closing title of a movie.

Some templates have "HD" variations for high-definition productions, and "wide" variations for widescreen video.

Where Are Titles Stored?

Unlike previous versions of Premiere Pro, version 2.0 stores all titles in the project file, not as separate files on your hard drive. You can import titles created in previous versions just like any other asset; just choose File > Import and browse until you find the file.

You Don't Have to Save Titles Anymore

Premiere Pro automatically saves every edit made to a title, so you can exit the Titler and you won't lose your most recent edits. The flip side is that if you decide you don't like your edits, you can't close the file and exit without saving; you have to manually undo.

You can save your own templates via the Template fly-out menu shown in **Figure 58b.** After saving, the template appears in the User Templates section, and you can choose it as the Default Still menu in the same menu. Thereafter, you can easily create new titles with that template in Premiere Pro's main menu by choosing Title > New Title > Default Still.

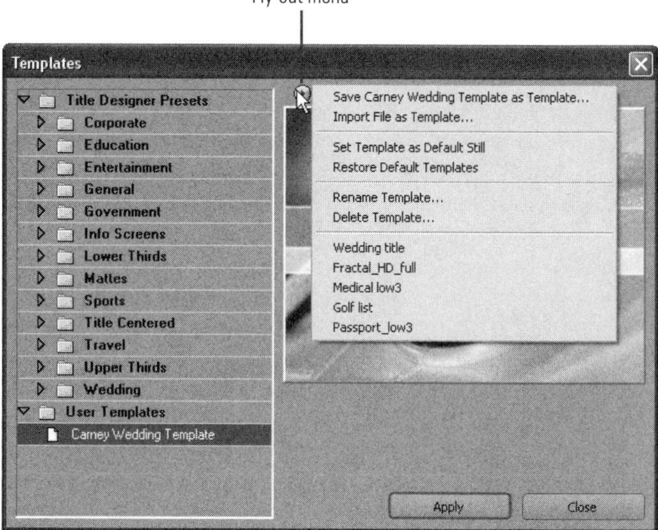

Figure 58b Use the Template fly-out menu to create and store your own templates.

#59 Designing with the Titler's Design Primitives

In Premiere Pro, one of the Titler's most useful functions is the set of design primitives—such as circles, rectangles and ellipses—you can use to create backgrounds that make your text titles readable irrespective of the video playing behind them. At a high level, you have to draw the shape, make it a color that highlights your font color, and if desired, make it translucent so it interferes with the background video as little as possible.

Here's how you build titles using primitives.

1. In the Timeline, place the current-time indicator at the start location for the title you're producing.
2. Open the Titler by pressing F9 or by choosing File > New > Title.
3. In the middle-left section of the Titler, click the desired shape for your background object (**Figure 59a**). The example uses a rectangle.
4. Draw the shape in the desired location. In the example it's a rectangle under the Congressman, placed within the title safe region, of course.
5. To adjust the color in the Title Properties panel (in the example, the white title font needs a dark background behind it), click the color chip under the Fill property.
6. In the Color Picker window, drag the selection circle to a dark gray color. Close the window.
7. In the Title Properties panel, set the Opacity property under the Fill property to 50%.
8. Add your text in the selected font, color, and size.
9. Adjust your background to fit the text. Close the Titler window and your new or modified title will save automatically (**Figure 59b**).

Cut Your Design Time

The new tool "New Title Based on Current Title" in the upper-left corner of the Titler is a great way to create multiple titles with the same look. Click the button to create a new title, which Premiere Pro will force you to name, then make your changes and move to the next.

Vertical Text? Diagonal Too?

Spend some time experimenting with the text tools in the upper-left corner of the Titler, which supply great options for diagonal and vertical text. Ditto for the Fill, Strokes, and Shadow options in the Title Properties panel in the upper-right corner. You'll learn that the Titler is an incredibly functional tool.

Import Logos into the Titler

If you're creating a title around a logo, you can import the logo into the Titler by right-clicking inside the Design window and choosing Logo > Insert Logo. If you use your logo frequently, you can save the title as a template as described in #58.

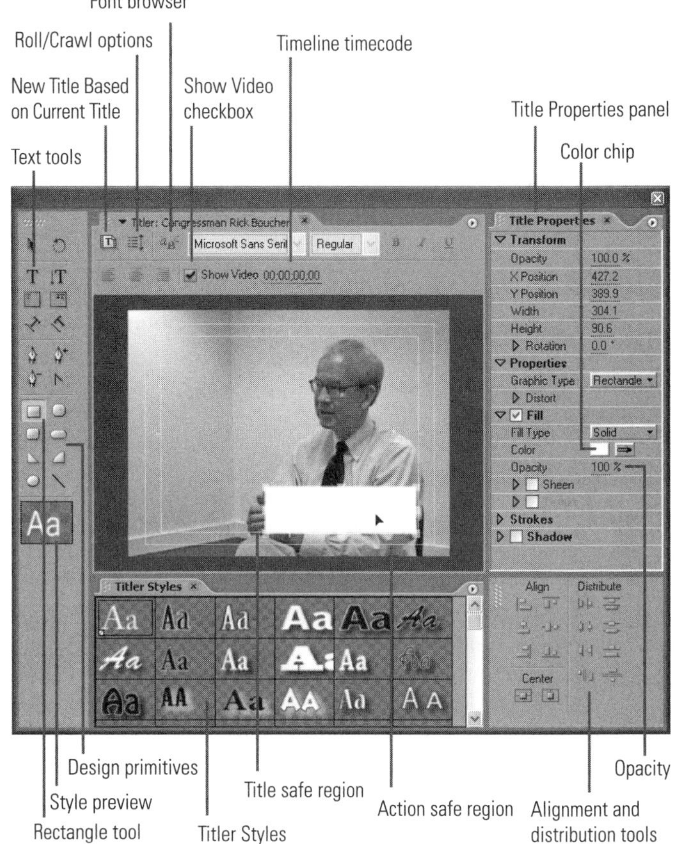

Figure 59a Here's the Titler in all its glory. Note the white rectangle under the Congressman. Note also that you can drag panels around, which is how the Alignment panels ended up on the right.

Figure 59b Here's the title—fast, easy, and highly readable, courtesy of the dark, translucent background.

#60 Producing Rolling Credits

Most television shows and movies end with rolling credits. Let's go through the basics of creating rolling credits in Premiere Pro, assuming that you have the Titler open and are ready to type.

1. Click the Type Tool and start typing your credits. Press Enter on your keyboard to add additional lines, and use the scrollbars to move the Design window with the text (**Figure 60a**).

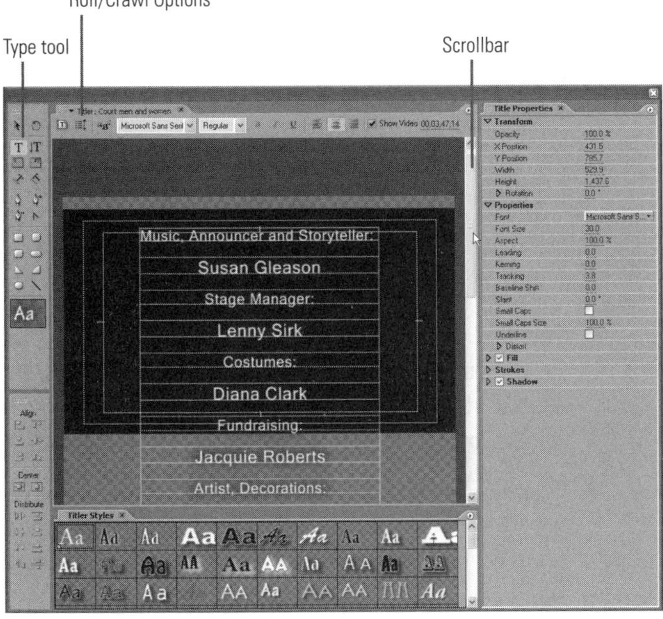

Figure 60a Here's the list of credits to scroll. Note how they extend below the Titler's visible area; use the scrollbar to read or edit the names.

2. Click the Roll/Crawl Options button. Premiere Pro opens the dialog (**Figure 60b**).

continued on next page

Preview with Transitions Inserted

If you're adding transitions to the beginning and end of your rolling or crawling credits, remember that these transitions can affect what's viewable in your title. If you add a transition and don't specify a sufficient Preroll or Ease-In duration, the transition may obscure the first few names or items in your credits.

To Produce Crawls

Click Crawl in the Title Type section of the Roll/Crawl Options dialog, and choose the desired direction. Beyond that, the process is identical to producing rolls.

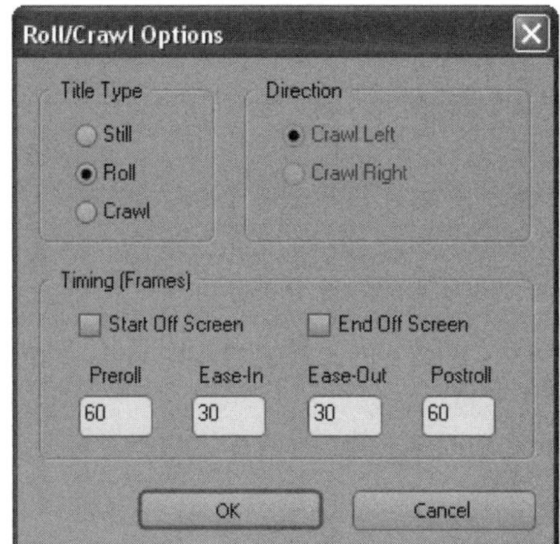

Figure 60b The Roll/Crawl Options dialog has lots of great options.

3. In the Title Type section, choose Roll.
4. In the Direction section, choose Crawl Left.
5. In the Timing (Frames) section, choose among the following options.
   - Start Off Screen/End Off Screen—Select these checkboxes to start or end the title with text completely off screen. If you elect to start off screen, the Preroll option is grayed out; if you end off screen, the Postroll option is grayed out.
   - Preroll—This specifies the number of frames during which the title appears on screen before starting the movement. It's a useful option when you're dissolving into the title and don't want to obscure the initial frames.
   - Ease-In—This specifies the number of frames during which the title slowly accelerates to full rolling speed.
   - Ease-Out—This specifies the number of frames during which the title slowly decelerates from full rolling speed.
   - Postroll—This specifies the number of frames during which the title stays on screen after the rolling stops. It's useful when you have "THE END" as the final text in your rolling credits and want to keep that on screen for a few extra moments before fading to a dramatic close.

5. After making your selections, click OK to close the Roll/Crawl Options dialog.
6. Click the X in the upper-right corner to close the Titler.
7. Drag the title to the timeline. Rolling speed is set by the duration of the title on the timeline. That is, if you drag the title over a 20-second duration on the timeline, it will roll faster than if you set it for a 30-second duration.

Use Motion Controls for Other Motion

The controls in the Roll/Crawl Options dialog make rolls and crawls very easy to implement. You can also add motion to your text via the Motion Controls that Premiere Pro assigns to each clip on the timeline. See #53 for details on how to animate a track matte.

#61 Creating Titles in Photoshop

You Can Always Edit the Entire PSD File in Photoshop

Irrespective of whether you import the PSD file as a sequence, footage, or individual layer, you can always access the entire PSD file, layers and all, by right-clicking and choosing Edit in Adobe Photoshop.

Here are seven high-level concepts that you'll need to know to design titles (and other content) in Photoshop for use in Premiere Pro.

- You create your Photoshop file from within Premiere Pro (File > New > Photoshop File). This ensures that the file is the proper format, size, and aspect ratio to use on your timeline.
- Transparent areas in Photoshop will be transparent in Premiere Pro.
- Changes made to a Photoshop file that has been imported into Premiere Pro will automatically appear in Premiere Pro each time you save the file.
- To edit a PSD file imported into Premiere Pro, select the file in the Project panel or timeline, right-click it, and choose Edit in Photoshop.
- When you create your Photoshop file in Premiere Pro (as described in the first item on this list), Premiere Pro merges all layers in the PSD file, so you can't access individual layers to animate them or apply other effects.
- To access the layers, you have two alternatives. The fastest and easiest is to reimport the file (File > Import) and choose Sequence from the drop-down menu in the Import Layered File dialog (**Figure 61a**).

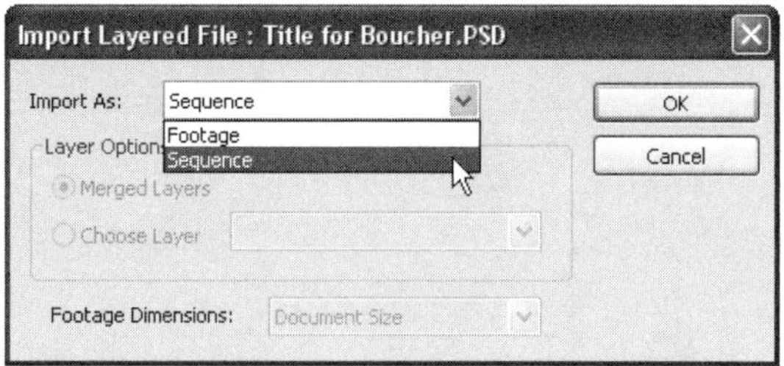

Figure 61a When Premiere Pro imports a Photoshop file as a sequence, you can edit and animate the individual layers.

When you import the PSD file as a sequence, Premiere Pro creates a sequence (essentially a separate timeline) and inserts all layers separately on that sequence. This is shown in the Project panel in **Figure 61b** and on the timeline in **Figure 61c**.

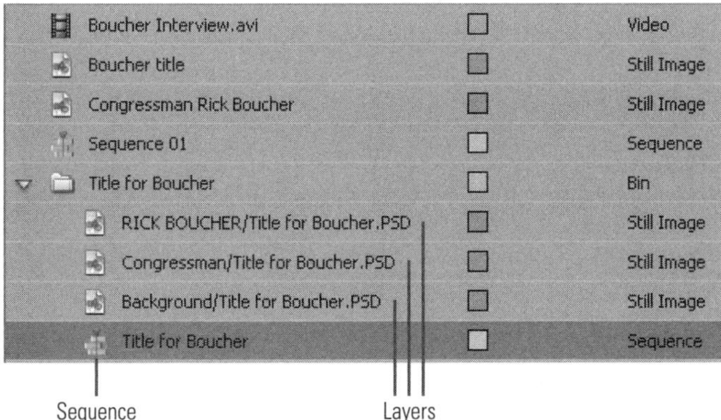

Figure 61b Here are the layers in the Project panel.

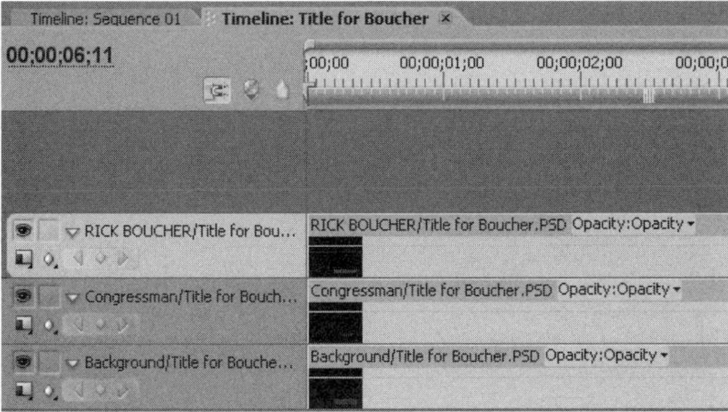

Figure 61c Here are the layers in the Sequence open on the timeline.

Since each layer is preserved separately in the sequence, you can animate or edit each layer as desired. To deploy the title, drag the *sequence* (rather than an individual layer) to the timeline to the target location. Once applied, the title sequence is

continued on next page

called a *nested sequence*. You can access the nested sequence by double-clicking the sequence on the timeline or in the Project panel.

- The second alternative for importing a layer is to choose Footage from the drop-down menu in the Import Layered File dialog, and choose the desired layer. This imports just that layer as a separate piece of content. This is useful if you want to apply just one layer, or if you want to import each layer separately and work with the layers as regular image content, rather than a nested sequence.

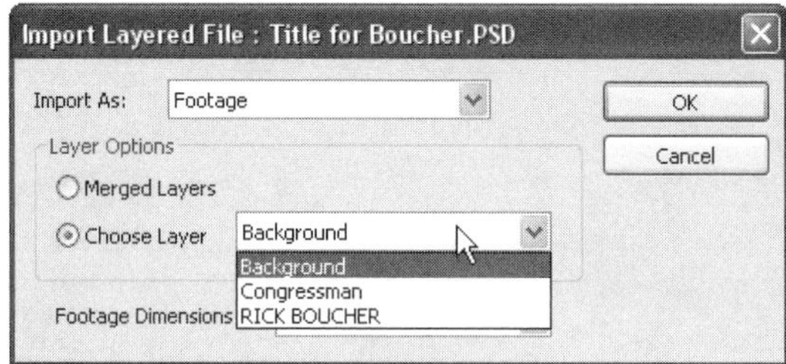

Figure 61d Import one layer at a time if you want to work with them as ordinary image content.

#62 Creating Titles in Illustrator

Here are five high-level concepts that you'll need to know to design titles (and other content) in Illustrator for use in Premiere Pro.

- There is no option for creating an Adobe Illustrator (.ai) file in Premiere Pro (as there is with Photoshop and After Effects). Remember that most standard-definition video has a resolution of 720x480. Though Premiere Pro can scale Illustrator's vector-based artwork upward or downward, if you design at too high a resolution, some detail may be lost when scaling down for Premiere Pro.
- Transparent areas in Illustrator will be transparent in Premiere Pro.
- To edit an .ai file in Illustrator, select the file in the Project panel or on the timeline, right-click it, and choose Edit Original.
- When you import your .ai file, Premiere Pro merges all layers.
- As a workaround, you can import a layered .ai file into After Effects as a composition, which gives you access to all layers (**Figure 62**).

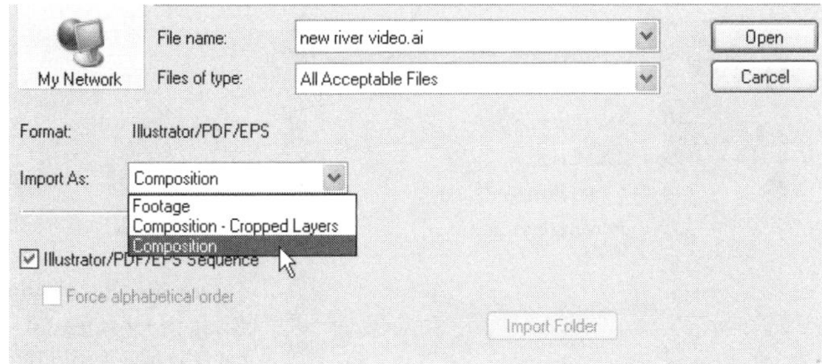

Figure 62 Though Premiere Pro can't import an Illustrator file with layers, After Effects can import it as a composition, providing access to all layers.

Why Illustrator?

Adobe Illustrator is a great tool for creating vector-based drawings that can scale to any resolution, which is one reason why so many logos are designed in Illustrator. Importing an .ai file, rather than a raster image, lets you scale the image in Premiere Pro without loss in quality.

#63 Producing Title Backgrounds in After Effects

The next two techniques describe how to use two key features of After Effects to spice up your titles in nothing flat. You'll also learn how to use Adobe Bridge to browse for and mine After Effects' capacious stores of content.

Let's assume that you're creating a video in Premiere Pro and will use Dynamic Link to import the titles you create in After Effects. Here's how to find, import, and modify a moving background to give your title a compelling, dynamic look.

1. In Premiere Pro, choose File > Adobe Dynamic Link > New After Effects Composition. This creates the After Effects composition and runs After Effects.

2. Press Alt+Tab to access After Effects.

3. On the extreme-right side of the After Effects interface, click the fly-out menu in the Effects & Presets panel and choose Browse Presets (**Figure 63a**) to open Adobe Bridge. If the panel isn't open, choose Window > Effects & Presets to open it.

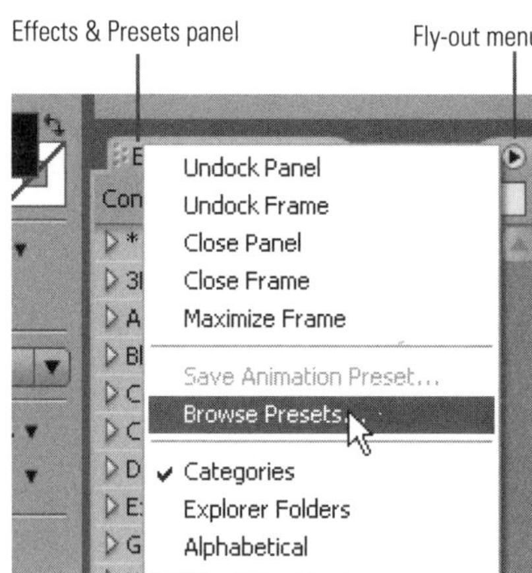

Figure 63a One of Adobe Bridge's most useful roles is helping you find After Effects content. Of course, first you have to find Adobe Bridge.

The Rest of the Story

Once you save the composition, Premiere Pro updates it in the Project panel. From there, you can use it like any other clip; just drag it to the timeline and trim or otherwise edit as desired.

Changing the Duration

After Effects defaults to a 30-second duration for new compositions, including those created from Premiere Pro. If you need a background with a longer duration, change the Composition duration in the Composition Settings dialog (Composition > Composition Settings) before inserting the background.

4. Click the Backgrounds folder to view the background presets. Click a background to play it in the Preview window (**Figure 63b**).

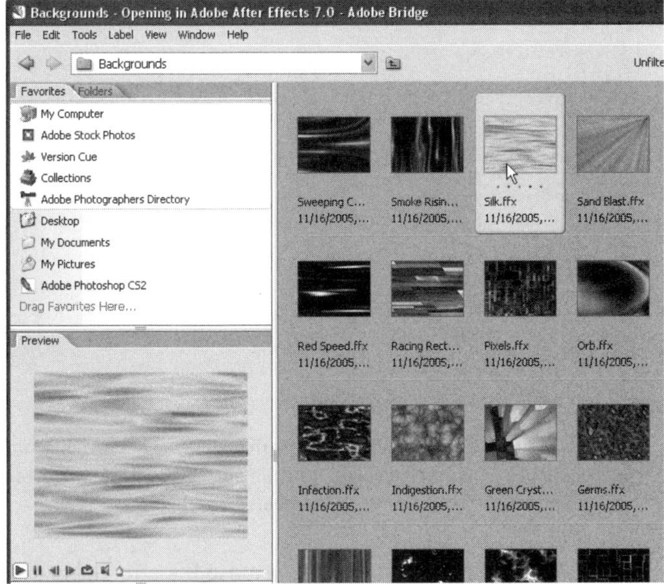

Figure 63b Here are Adobe Bridge's and After Effects' motion background presets. I like the feel of silk!

5. After selecting a background, double-click it to insert it into the composition timeline (**Figure 63c**). You don't need to create a layer to accept the background; After Effects will do that for you, creating a layer that extends for the entire duration of the composition.

continued on next page

Motion Menu Backgrounds

You can use the same workflow from within Adobe Encore DVD to create motion backgrounds for your DVD menus.

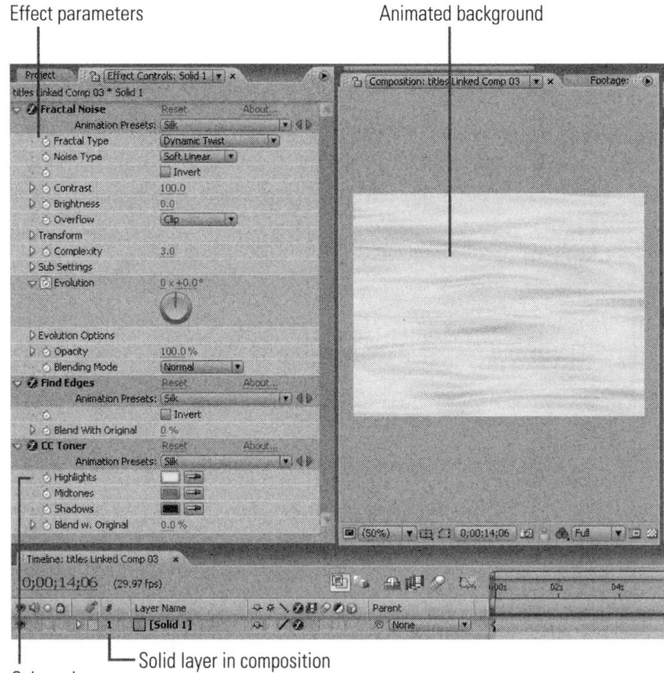

Figure 63c After you've selected and inserted a motion background into After Effects' composition timeline, you can adjust the effect parameters to customize your background to your heart's desire.

6. Click the Effect Controls tab to expose the effect parameters. As you can see, After Effects creates the background using three effects: Fractal Noise, Find Edges, and CC toner. To customize the background, you can change any parameter in any effect, including Fractal Type, which will change the look and motion. You can also change the colors of the Highlights, Midtones, and Shadows.

#64 Creating Simple Text Animations in After Effects

One of After Effects' strongest features is its ability to animate text, which you'll learn how to access here. This technique uses the background created in #63, but this is not a prerequisite. If you're starting from scratch, just remember to create your After Effects composition from within Premiere Pro using Dynamic Link (#63).

1. Click the Horizontal Type tool on the Adobe After Effects toolbar and type the desired text in the Composition window. You don't need to create a separate layer for text; After Effects will create it for you (**Figure 64a**).

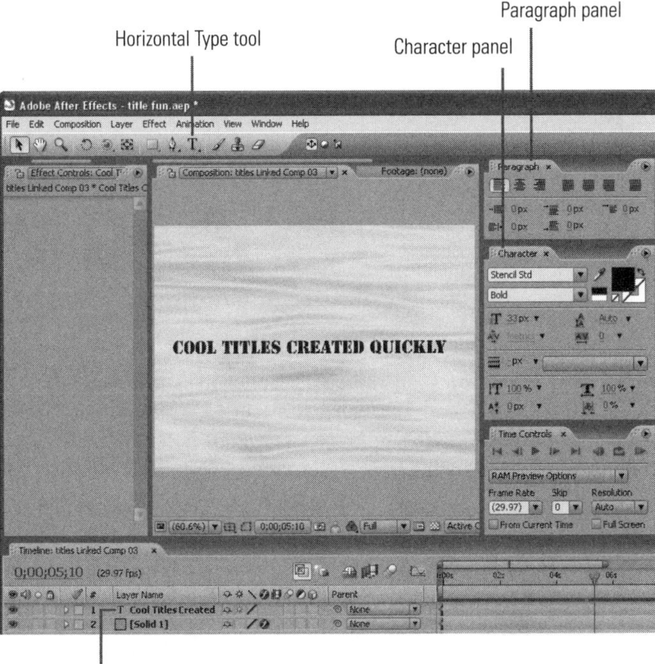

Figure 64a Here's After Effects' text-creation toolset. No need to create a layer; just start typing.

continued on next page

Dynamic Link Only

You can't copy and paste text animated in this fashion from After Effects into Premiere Pro, since Premiere Pro doesn't have this animated text effect. Instead, you'll need to render the animated text file or use Dynamic Link to import it into Premiere Pro.

2. To access text font, color, or size options in the Character and Paragraph panels (if they're not open already), choose Window > Character or choose Window > Paragraph. Modify these elements of your title as desired.

3. Click the text layer in the composition to select it. Otherwise, After Effects may apply the selected animation to another layer.

4. On the extreme-right side of the After Effects interface, click the fly-out menu in the Effects & Presets panel and choose Browse Presets (see Figure 63a). If the panel isn't open, choose Window > Effects & Presets to open it.

5. In the Effects and Presets panel, click the Text folder to view the text-animation categories, then click a subfolder to view the animations. The example uses the Animate In folder. Click an animation preset to view it in the Preview window on the left (**Figure 64b**).

Figure 64b I struggled with the mixed metaphor inherent to using a stenciled font with a typewriter-style animation, but ultimately decided to go with it. I hope the critics take it easy on me.

6. Double-click the selected animation preset to add it to the text layer.

7. To customize duration for your composition so it matches your chosen animation, twirl the text layer, then the Animator 1 properties, then Range Selector 1 (**Figure 64c**). To make the animation shorter and faster, drag the keyframes closer together; to make it slower and longer, drag the keyframes further apart.

8. Once you've completed your composition, save it and return to Premiere Pro where you should be able to deploy it immediately.

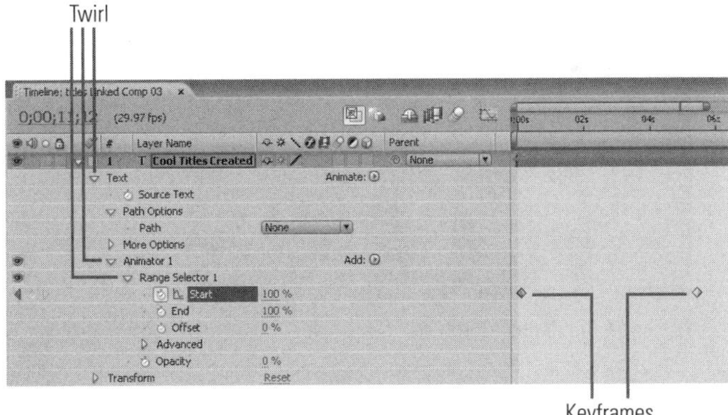

Figure 64c You have to dig deep in the text layer to edit the Animator 1 keyframes, but that's the only way to change effect duration.

#65 Producing Matte Effects with Titles

This one is kind of a gimme, but it's such a fun effect that it deserves its own space. **Figure 65** shows a title used as a matte to reveal the river in the background video through the text.

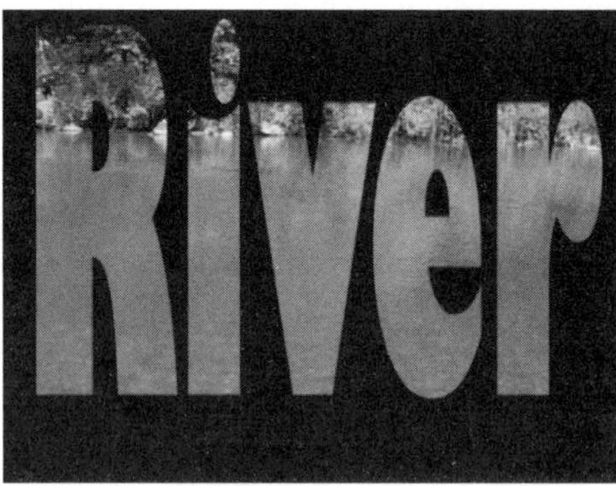

Figure 65 I love this effect!

To create the effect in Premiere Pro, do the following:

1. Build your title in a font with wide letters (Gill Sans Ultra Bold in the example). If the font color is white, the text will be completely translucent; darkening the text to darker shades of gray reduces the transparency (the example uses white text).
2. Save the title as normal, and drag it over the desired background video.
3. Follow the instruction described in #52 to produce the keying effect.

CHAPTER EIGHT

Creating Slide Shows in Premiere Pro

Adobe Production Studio has two basic approaches for producing slide shows from digital images, like those from a digital camera or inputted from a scanner. If your goal is a highly customized production with pans, zooms, and narration à la the two well-known Ken Burns productions, *Baseball* and *The Civil War,* you should produce your slide show in Premiere Pro.

No matter which program you use, you may want to preprocess your images in Photoshop, and you'll need an understanding of how Premiere Pro handles the display of square-pixel images in rectangular pixel videos in order to produce images that will import into Premiere Pro as you want them to appear.

This chapter covers these two topics first, and then describes how to produce slide shows in Premiere Pro. It concludes with a look at the Frame Hold function in Premiere Pro, which is great way to convert video to a still frame for credits or other overlays.

#66 Preprocessing Images for Premiere Pro in Photoshop

Never Change the Aspect Ratio

If you do resize in Photoshop, don't change the aspect ratio of the image, which can visually distort the picture. For example, if you're resizing an image to 720x480, make sure that the Constrain Proportions checkbox is selected. If Photoshop won't let you produce the desired image size, this means that your camera is using a different aspect ratio from Premiere Pro. If so, make sure that the resolution you ultimately select is as large (or larger) than your target on both the horizontal and vertical axes. That is, if your target is 720x480, 720x540 is okay, but 620x480 is not.

There are four types of edits you can perform on images: resizing, reframing, corrective, and artistic. Premiere Pro can perform all four, which in many instances makes preprocessing your images in Photoshop a choice rather than a necessity.

There are some notable exceptions. Premiere Pro can't import an image larger than 4096x4096 in resolution, so you'll have to use Photoshop to resize larger images down to that size or smaller to import them in Premiere Pro. You'll also have to work in Photoshop to access filters that Premiere Pro doesn't share, especially red-eye reduction and other image-centric effects.

But if you're working with 6–7 megapixel images, you can skip Photoshop, as Premiere Pro is quite adept at working with large images. In addition, if you plan to apply pan-and-zoom effects to an image, you'll produce better results with the original image, because Premiere Pro can access all the original pixels during zooming. In contrast, if you resize the image in Photoshop down to 720x480 resolution and then apply a pan-and-zoom effect, Premiere Pro will have to make pixels up to create the zoom, which can lead to distortion or pixelation.

On the other hand, if you're creating a slide show with 100 images, all of which you plan to process identically, Photoshop has automation features that are superior to Premiere Pro's in this regard, and they will save you a great deal of time. When preprocessing in Photoshop—especially when you're working with a large number of images—keep two rather obvious (but still worth mentioning) thoughts in mind. First, before batch processing all of your images, process one image, import it into Premiere Pro, and preview the result to check your adjustments (measure twice, cut once). Second, always resize to a copy of the image, and never overwrite the original image.

Finally, if you're importing single-layer Photoshop files into Premiere Pro (or After Effects), import them as Footage, not as a Sequence (**Figure 66**). For a discussion of these issues, see #61.

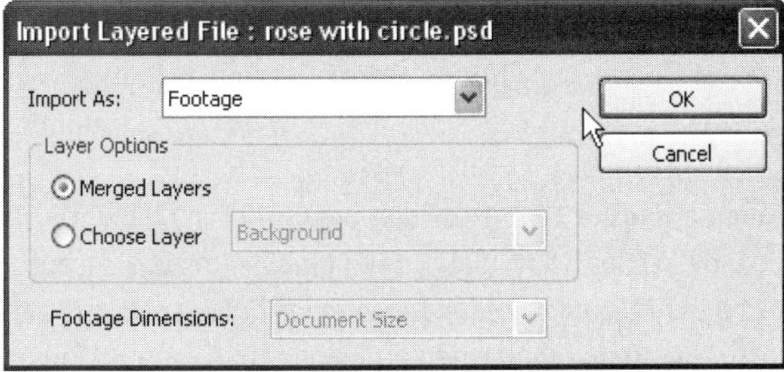

Figure 66 When importing single-layer Photoshop files into Premiere Pro, be sure Footage is selected from the Import As pull-down.

#67 Understanding Square Pixels

Sometimes a little knowledge is a dangerous thing. For example, you probably know that your digital camera captures pictures in square-pixel format, but that your television displays images and video using rectangular pixels. So you might expect to have to adjust your pictures to make them look right when producing a slide show for TV viewing. Not to worry—Premiere Pro knows the aspect ratio of your digital images, and how TV video is supposed to look, and adjusts images automatically.

For example, **Figure 67a** is a video preview of my daughter Rose surrounded by circles that look convincingly circular. I shot the image with a digital camera, added the circles in Photoshop (holding down the Shift key) and imported the image into a 16:9 DV Premiere Pro project. As you can see from the preview, Premiere Pro knew the image was square-pixel and that I wanted the circles to stay circular, and it automatically made all the adjustments.

Figure 67a Circular circles, evidence that Premiere Pro automatically adjusted square-pixel input for 16:9 rectangular-pixel output.

Notice the black bars to the left and right of the image. Premiere Pro produced these rather than stretching the image to fill the video frame, which would distort the image. In this situation, you can fill the screen (and eliminate the bars) by zooming in to the image using Motion controls in the Effect Controls panel.

Supported Formats

Premiere Pro can import images in the following formats: Adobe Illustrator (AI), Adobe Photoshop (PSD), Bitmap (BMP, DIB, RLE), EPS, GIF, ICO, JPE, JPG, JFIF, PCX, PICT, PIC, PCT, Portable Network Graphics (PNG), PTL, PRTL (Adobe Title Designer), Targa (TGA, ICB, VDA, VST), TIFF, and PSQ.

Figure 67b illustrates the one scenario in which Premiere Pro seems to lose its footing, specifically when you grab a video frame from a 16:9 video as described in #79. After importing this frame back into Premiere Pro, the circles are decidedly uncircular.

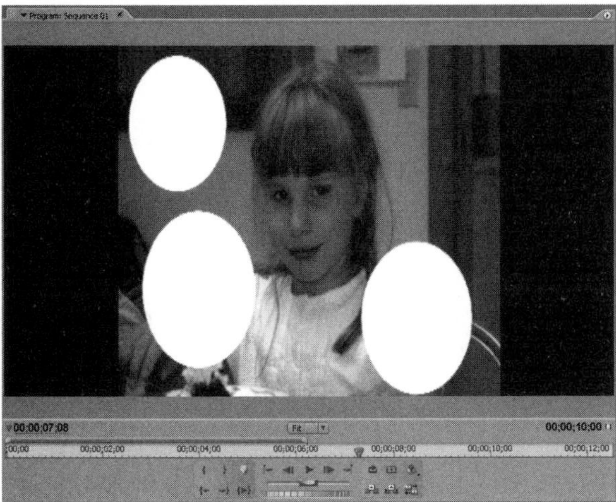

Figure 67b Our circles just turned into ovals. We definitely have an aspect-ratio misunderstanding.

To fix this or any instance in which Premiere Pro appears to have selected the wrong pixel aspect ratio for video or still images, do the following:

1. Right-click the asset in the Project panel.
2. In the pop-up menu that appears, select Interpret Footage.

continued on next page

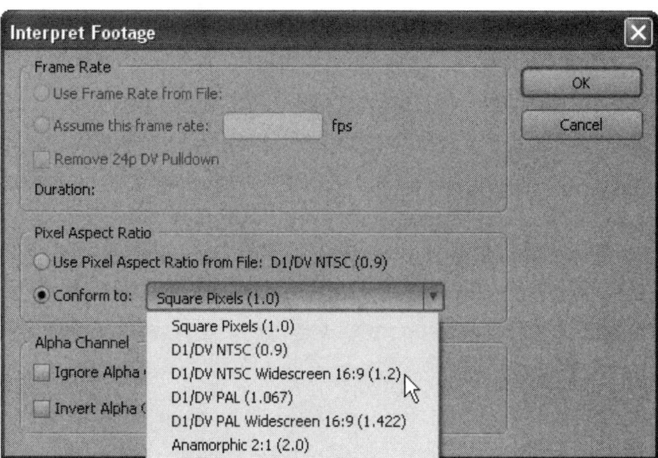

Figure 67c This tells Premiere Pro the correct pixel aspect ratio of the image. You may never need this control, but if you do, it's nice to know where it is.

3. In the Interpret Footage dialog box, click the Conform to drop-down menu and select the correct pixel aspect ratio for the image source; this should resolve the problem (**Figure 67c**).

#68 Managing Images in Premiere Pro

Premiere Pro does an excellent job managing images, but unless you know what the program is doing behind the scenes, sometimes it can be confusing. For example, **Figure 68a** is a 3072x2048 resolution picture of my daughter Whatley, but it looks like it's about 640x480 resolution with the full image displayed in Premiere Pro's Program Monitor (in this 16:9 project).

Figure 68a Premiere Pro automatically scales imported images to the project frame size, which can be confusing.

A quick check of the Motion controls reveals that the image is at 100% scale (**Figure 68b**)! Where did the rest of the image go? Well, when Premiere Pro imports an image, it automatically scales it to the current video frame size—in this case, 720x480. This works well if you're quickly creating a simple slide show, but can be confusing if you're planning extensive panning and zooming in the image.

Copy and Paste Effects

As described in #31, Premiere Pro can copy and paste attributes from clip to clip, including images. The attributes can include motion, resizing, and color and brightness effects. To make repetitive adjustments on multiple images, edit one image to the desired parameters, then copy and paste the attributes to the other images in the slide show.

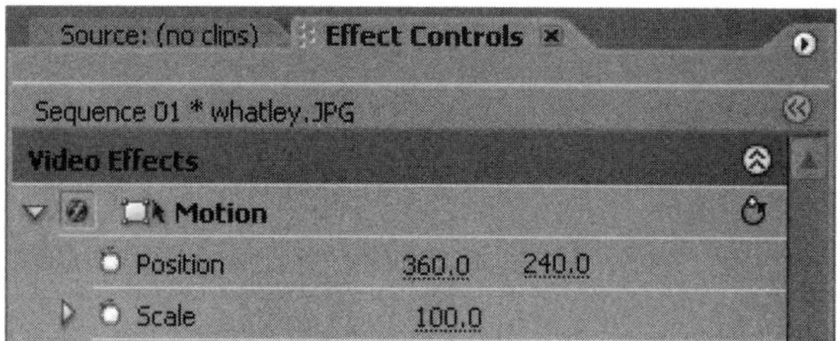

Figure 68b Based on the parameters we have set in the Motion controls, it looks like this image is displayed at full resolution. Where did the rest of the pixels go?

To reverse this default, right-click the image and click Scale to Frame Size to de-select it, which displays the image at 100% resolution (**Figure 68c**).

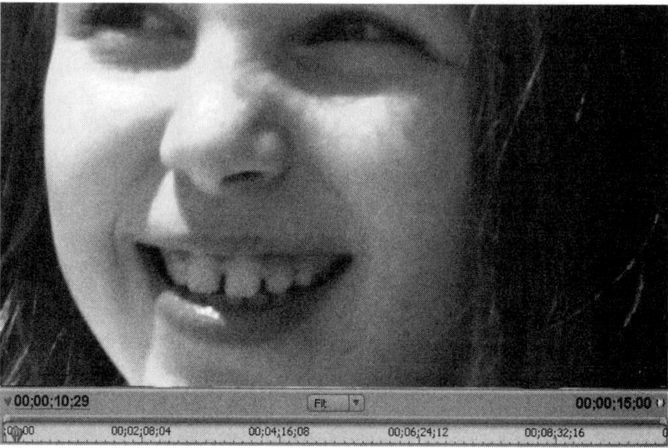

Figure 68c After deselecting Scale to Frame Size, you see that it's actually a much larger image—too big, as you would expect, to be fully displayed in the Program Monitor in a 16:9 DV project.

There are a few other points to consider. First, Premiere Pro sets image duration when you drag an image to the timeline. You can change this in the General Preferences dialog (Edit > Preferences), but this is prospective only, and won't affect images already on the timeline. Once on the timeline, of course, you can click the edge of an image and drag it to any length.

In addition, while Premiere Pro doesn't have a formal storyboard feature, you can use the Project panel to arrange your images, and even send them to the timeline with frame overlap and a transition inserted. See #10 for details. Finally, you can apply effects and transitions to images on the timeline, just as you do with video.

#69 Producing Pan-and-Zoom Effects in Premiere Pro

Figure 69a is a black-and-white sideline shot from a college football game, a bit later in time but similar to the shots used in Ken Burns' *Baseball*. In the noble Burns tradition, let's create a dramatic pan-and-zoom effect, starting from the wide shot, then zooming in to the individual players. Here's how it works:

1. In the timeline, click the clip to activate it.
2. Click the Video Effects panel, and click the Show/Hide Effects button next to the Motion controls to reveal its configurable parameters (**Figure 69a**).

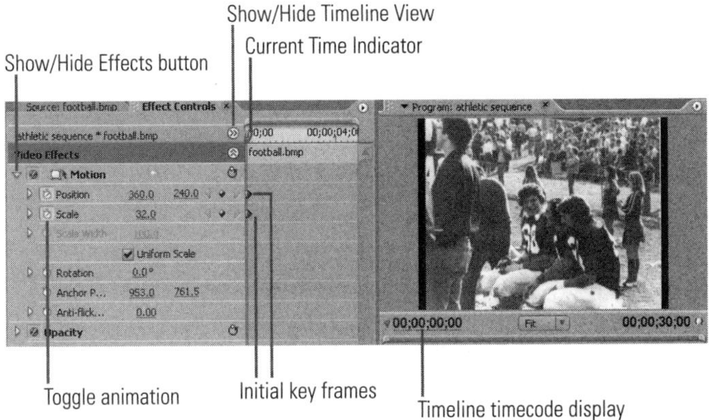

Figure 69a Here's the positioning on the first frame. This is the big picture view, with the desired framing.

3. Make sure the current-time indicator is set to the initial frame of the clip (drag it all the way to the left).
4. Click the Show/Hide Timeline View button to open the Timeline to the right.
5. Click the Toggle Animation buttons next to the Position and Scale parameters to set your starting keyframes.
6. Drag the current-time indicator to the frame where you want the initial close up. In the example, it's three seconds in (**Figure 69b**).

continued on next page

Using the Timeline Timecode Display

The Timeline Timecode Display (Figure 69a) is not just a passive number; it's a useful navigational tool. For example, to travel to a specific point on the timeline (such as when the client reports a glitch at 22;18;12), just click the display to make it active and type the numbers (no semicolons are required). Press Enter and you'll go right to the frame.

Note that you'll need to enter all the numbers for min:sec: frames, or you won't get to the desired spot. For example, if you just entered 2218, Premiere Pro would take you to 22 seconds, 18 frames.

You can also enter instructions like +15 and press Enter, and Premiere Pro will take you 15 frames to the right. Get hip to the lingo, however, to get the best results. For example, entering +300 won't take you 300 frames to the right; it will take you 3 seconds and no frames to the right. Note that the displays in After Effects and Encore DVD have similar features, which can be great timesavers.

Apply Transitions Last

If you insert transitions before producing your pan-and-zoom effects, the transitions can obscure the view at the start and end of the clip. So, pan and zoom first, keeping in mind that your transitions will obscure the first and last few frames, then insert transitions. Remember the killer timesaver keystroke combination, Page Dn to move to the next edit, and Ctrl+D to insert the default transition.

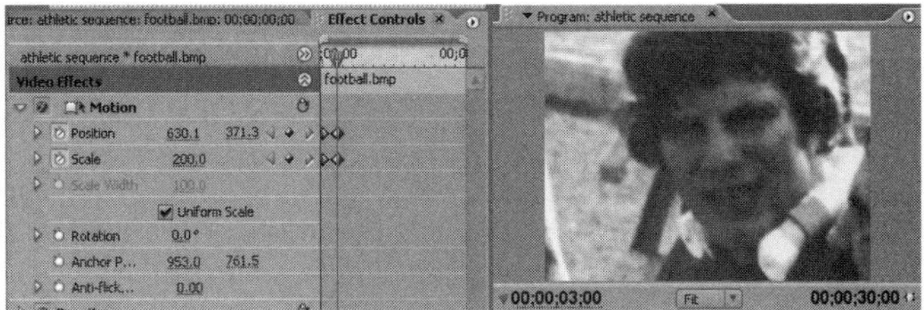

Figure 69b Three seconds in—the first close-up.

7. To zoom in to the image, increase the Scale value (to 200 in the figure).
8. To pan across the image, click and drag the image in the Program Monitor to the desired framing, or adjust the positioning with the horizontal and vertical positioning parameters (630.1 and 371.3 in the figure).

   Note

   - *You don't need to create keyframes manually. If you move the current-time indicator to a different frame and adjust any parameter with Toggle Animation enabled, Premiere Pro will create the keyframe for you.*

9. Repeat as necessary to produce the desired effect.

#70 Creating a Still Frame with Frame Hold Control

Suppose you wanted to display rolling credits over a single frame in the video; how would you create that still frame? Well, you have two options. You can export the still frame as described in #79, or use the Frame Hold control, which is faster and simpler. Frame Hold applies to an entire clip, so it's easiest to apply when you isolate a short clip, even perhaps of a single frame, and apply the Frame Hold to that frame.

For example, **Figure 70a** is a frame of a pianist bowing after her performance. It's not the last frame in the video, but it's appropriate for the scrolling credits. Here's how to freeze that frame.

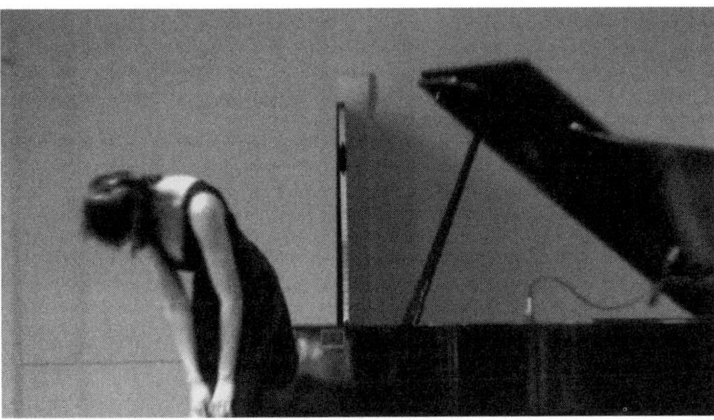

Figure 70a Here's the frame we want to freeze.

1. Zoom in to the timeline with the Zoom tool until you can see each individual frame.
2. Move the current-time indicator to the frame on which you want to hold.
3. Using the Razor tool, split the final frame from the rest of the clip (**Figure 70b**).

continued on next page

Just Like a Regular Still Image

After applying the Frame Hold, you can drag the clip to any length and apply effects or transitions, just as you would with a regular still image.

Figure 70b Use the Razor tool to separate out the final frame.

4. Right-click the final frame, and choose Frame Hold. The Frame Hold Options dialog appears.
5. In the Frame Hold Options dialog, select all the checkboxes, and choose In Point in the drop-down menu (**Figure 70c**).

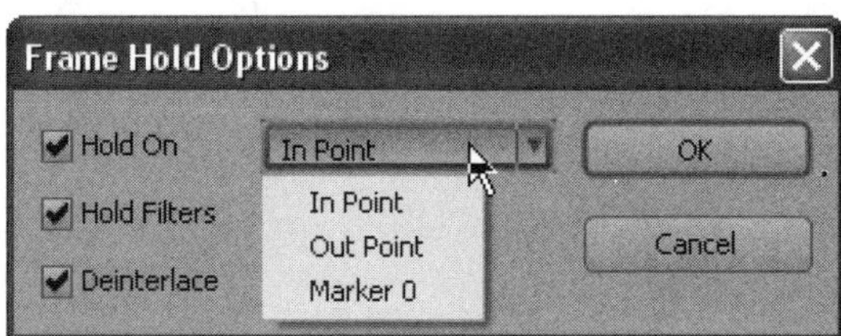

Figure 70c Conform your settings to these.

Notes

- *Selecting Hold On creates the freeze frame; otherwise, if you stretched the clip to the right, the frames in the original clip would appear rather than the freeze frame.*
- *Selecting Hold Filters keeps the filters applied at the current level; otherwise, if you had keyframed in variable settings, they might change as you dragged the clip to the right.*
- *Selecting Deinterlace helps reduce flicker in the rendered clip.*

6. Click OK to close the Frame Hold Options dialog.

#71 Creating Slide Shows in Premiere Pro

OK, let's pull it all together and create a slide show. Here's a comprehensive list of tasks to consider or perform when creating your slide show.

1. Pre-process your images in Photoshop as required (#66). Two obvious issues to correct are rotating images shot in landscape mode to portrait, when appropriate, and correcting red-eye.
2. Import your images into Premiere Pro as Footage, not as a Sequence (#66).
3. Open your General Preferences (Edit > Preferences > General) and set default still image and transition duration (**Figure 71a**). You can also uncheck the Default scale to frame size checkbox if you want Premiere to display the images at their full resolution (#68).

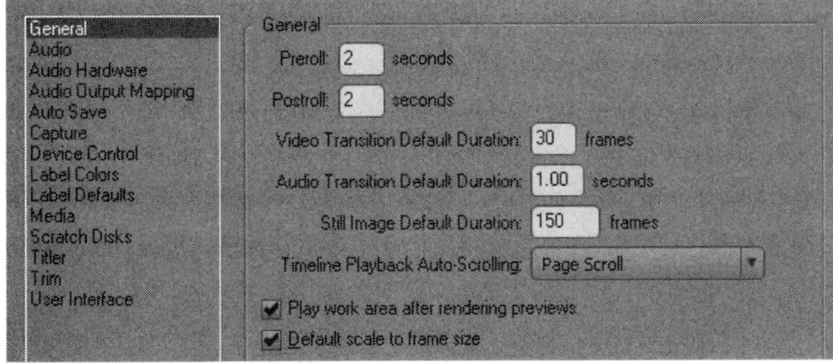

Figure 71a Set default still image and transition durations here, and choose whether to display the image at full resolution or frame size (Default scale to frame size checkbox).

4. Set the default transition in the Effects panel by right-clicking the target transition and choosing Set Selected as Default Transition.
5. Arrange the images in the desired order in the Project panel (**#10**).

continued on next page

Spread Your Transition Wings with Slide Shows

I'm a straight cut-or-dissolve kind of guy when it comes to most video transitions, but have been known to get a bit wiggy when choosing transitions for slide shows. My favorites are the Page Peel transitions in the Video Transitions folder in the Effects panel, which simulates the feel of a scrapbook, and the Clock Wipe (Effects > Video Transitions > Wipe > Clock Wipe) that simulates the passing of time.

Watch for Flicker

When you apply pan-and-zoom effects to still images with lots of fine detail, you may see flicker or shimmering in the video Premiere Pro produces. If so, right-click the image and choose Field Options to open that dialog box. Then choose Flicker Removal in that dialog box and click OK to close it. Flicker removal blurs the image slightly, but should reduce or eliminate the flicker. If this doesn't work, or if the image is too blurry, try clicking Always Deinterlace in the Field Options dialog box then click OK to close it. For more details on deinterlacing, see #83.

6. In the bottom toolbar of the Project panel, click Automate to Sequence (**#10**). Premiere Pro opens the Automate to Sequence dialog box (**Figure 71b**). After choosing the desired parameters, click OK to close the dialog box.

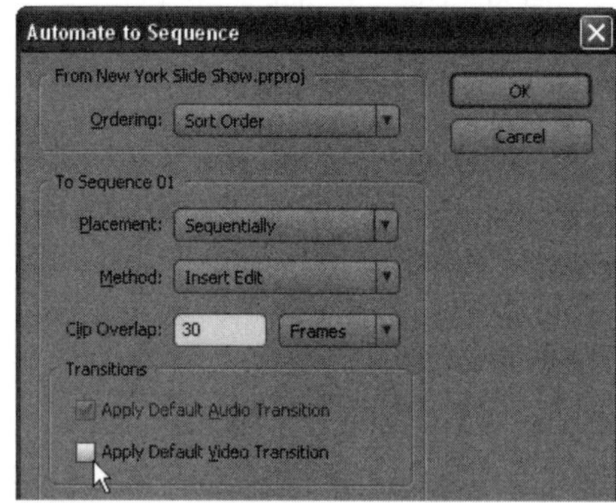

Figure 71b You can set the clip overlap (in frames) here, and choose whether or not to apply the Default Video transition.

Note

- *If you plan to apply pan-and-zoom effects to your still images, uncheck the Apply Default Video Transition checkbox in the Automate to Sequence dialog box. If you don't, then leave the box checked.*

7. If desired, apply pan-and-zoom effects to your clips (#69).
8. If you haven't applied transitions to your still images, apply them quickly by pressing the Page Down key to move from cut to cut and Ctrl+D to insert the default transition.

CHAPTER NINE

Working with Audio

Most experienced producers will tell you that audio quality is at least as important as video, and in many situations—like a concert or even a wedding with softly whispered vows—absolutely critical. Often, the easiest way to differentiate the work of a professional videographer from what an enthusiastic uncle or other amateur might produce is the clarity of the sound mix. Fortunately, the audio components of the Adobe Production Studio, in addition to being very competent overall, do two things exceptionally well.

The first relates to access. If you right-click any audio file in Premiere Pro and then choose Edit in Adobe Audition, Premiere Pro will create a temporary audio file and load it into Audition. As soon as you save the file in Audition, Premiere Pro will substitute the edited (and newly saved) file for the original, making it fast and easy to access Audition's comprehensive feature set.

Second, Audition does an excellent job cleaning up your audio. As you probably know, you'll typically encounter two types of audio problems: consistent background noises like hums or whines from air conditioners or AC ground noise, and random noises like pops or clicks. Audition's noise-removal tool is top notch for the first, while its Repair Transient function is simply the best available for eliminating random noises.

Of course, Audition and Premiere Pro also do a great job at day-to-day blocking and tackling functions like volume adjustment, normalization, and mixing, so we'll start there.

#72 Working with Audio in Premiere Pro

Let's say you've shot an interview and plan to add soft background music for a professional touch. You'll need to control the music's volume to ensure that it doesn't interfere with the voices. **Figure 72** shows the audio at the beginning of the video, and illustrates the key features in Premiere Pro's audio controls.

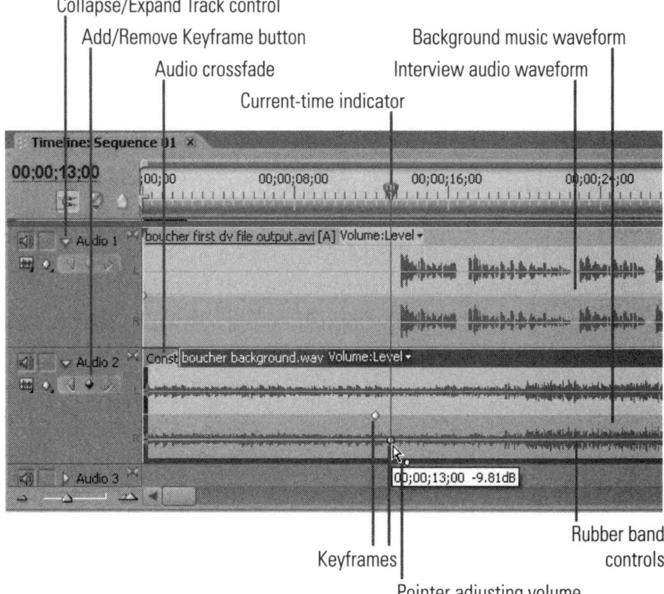

Figure 72 Manually mixing the volume from two audio tracks, one containing an interview (Audio 1) and the other containing background music (Audio 2).

The beginning of the video contains several titles, and the discussion doesn't begin for about 13 seconds (Audio 1). The first audio that the viewer hears is the background music, which quickly fades in to full volume then drops down just before the interview begins.

Here are the highlights of the audio features shown in Figure 72.

- Collapse/Expand Track—Expands the track so you can see and edit the waveform. Click the triangle to expand the track.

Adjusting Clip Gain

Right-click any audio clip in Premiere Pro and select Audio Gain from the pop-up menu that appears to access the Clip Gain control, where you can manually insert a decibel (dB) level to adjust audio volume, essentially accomplishing the same thing as dragging the rubber band controls up and down on the track itself. The Clip Gain control also provides access to Premiere Pro's Normalize function, discussed in #74.

Keyframing in the Effect Controls Panel

You can also adjust volume with keyframes using the timeline found in the Effect Controls panel, but it's typically easier on the main timeline where you can see the waveforms.

- Audio transitions—Premiere Pro has two crossfade transitions (Effects > Audio Transitions > Crossfade), Constant Gain, and Constant Power. Constant Gain, analogous to a video dissolve, provides the smoother effect of the two, and is the default audio transition used when you apply a video transition between two clips. You can apply either type of crossfade to the beginning of a track to fade the audio in (or at the end to fade the audio out). As with video transitions, just click and drag the transition to the target track. Obviously, you can also use the Crossfade transition between songs like any transition.
- Volume adjustment—Premiere Pro allows you to click and drag the yellow line (gray in Figure 72) in an audio track in the timeline up or down to adjust volume. This adjustment affects the entire track unless you add a keyframe. These types of keyframeable adjustments are frequently referred to as rubber band controls (#43).
- Add/Remove Keyframe—Keyframes (#43) let you customize audio volume for various regions of the audio track. In Figure 72, the volume of the background music is adjusted downward so that it doesn't interfere with the interview. To add a keyframe, move the current-time indicator to the target location and click Add/Remove Keyframe in the track header on the left. As you can see in Figure 72, you typically have to add two keyframes, one to maintain the previous volume level, and the other to set the new volume.

The Audio Mixer

You can also use Premiere Pro's audio mixer to perform the operation described above. The mixer is best used for constant multi-track mixing throughout a project, while manually adjusting volume via keyframes and crossfades is more efficient for simpler projects with a few volume adjustments spaced over the entire duration. Check out the Premiere Pro manual on page 229 for more detail on the Audio Mixer.

Looking for Royalty-Free Background Music?

SmartSound (www.smartsound.com) is an excellent source of background music that's royalty-free and easy to search, download, and apply. It's also easy to customize the length of the track to fit your clip and still retain the feel of a complete track. You can sample their entire libraries online. If you don't find what you're looking for, also consider Digital Juice's BackTraxx music library (www.digitaljuice.com) and Sony's Cinescore (www.sonymediasoftware.com).

#73 Getting Started in Audition

Importing Video Files

Audition can import a full range of audio files (WAV, CDA, MP3, AIF, WMA, and PCM) and import audio from many video files (AVI, MPEG, MP2, M2T, WMV, and MOV). The most notable exception is the inability to import RealAudio files.

For more advanced audio editing functions like Noise Reduction, Audition is your tool of choice. Let's review Audition's interface, then get to work. **Figure 73** shows Audition in Edit mode, which you'll use for all techniques shown here. In the middle of the upper panel, you'll find buttons that open the Multitrack View, where you can mix multiple audio tracks, and the CD View, a simple and effective way to combine different audio tracks into a CD-Audio disc.

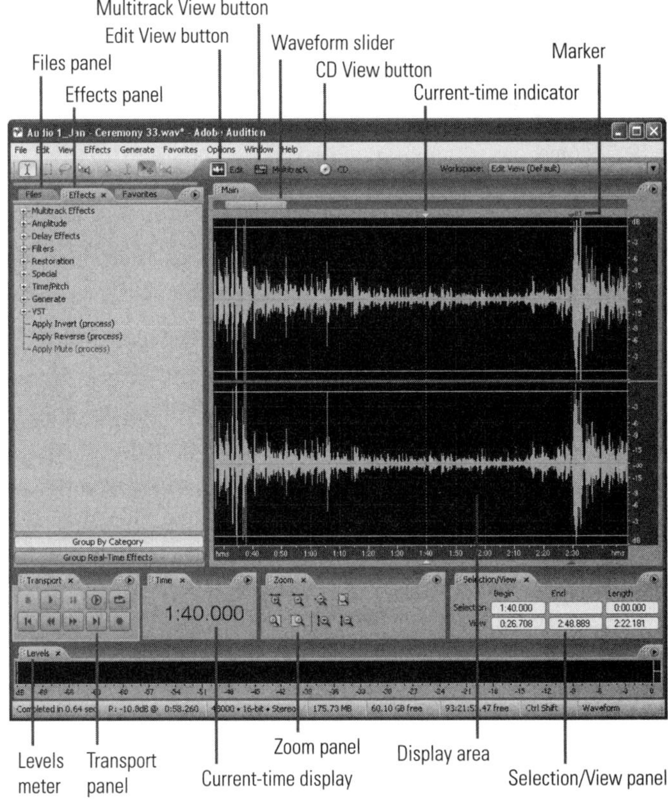

Figure 73 In Edit mode, Adobe Audition resembles most WAV editing tools, with a big work area and easy-to-use supporting tools.

Operation in Edit mode is similar to Premiere Pro and After Effects. You import files into the program, and Audition stores them in the Files panel. Once selected, the audio waveform appears in the Display area, where you can apply effects from the Effects panel or Effects menu item.

You play the file using controls in the Transport panel. Select the portion of the file to be edited by clicking and dragging the current-time indicator in the Display area, and adjust the view with controls in the Zoom panel. These controls allow you to display the entire file for a big-picture view, or zoom in to specific regions for fine-tuning. If you are zoomed in, you'll find the Waveform slider in the upper Display area the fastest way to navigate through the audio file.

If you're using the program on a standalone basis, you'll typically import a WAV file, perform your edits, and then export in your distribution format of choice. If you access Audition by right-clicking an audio clip on the Premiere Pro timeline and selecting "Edit in Adobe Audition" from the pop-up menu that appears, the originating file in Premiere Pro is automatically updated once you save the edited file in Audition.

Exporting Streaming Audio

In addition to WAV and many other uncompressed formats, Audition can output MP3 and WMA audio, with extensive output options for both. Again, the most notable exception is RealAudio support.

#74 Normalizing Audio in Premiere Pro and Audition

Typically, you normalize audio volume so your entire production will have similar levels and your viewers won't have to adjust the volume from scene to scene. Technically, however, normalization increases the amplitude of the audio to a target level, usually 100%, which is maximum volume available without distortion.

What's critical to realize is that normalization affects the entire file equally. So if you have a file (or region in a file) with loud segments, but also with low segments, normalizing the entire file will probably not increase the volume of the low points.

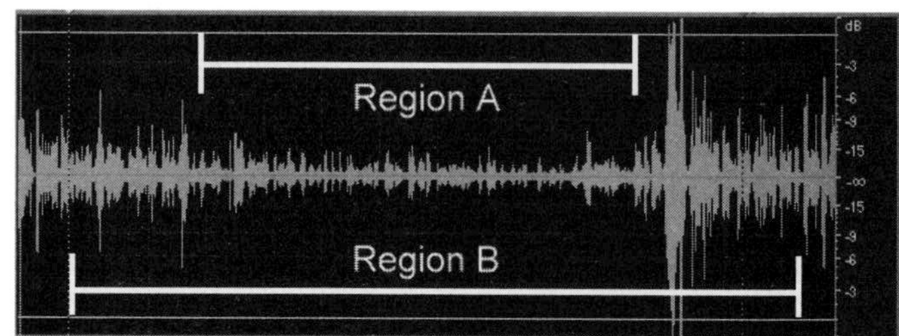

Figure 74a Normalizing Region A will produce a different result from normalizing region B. This is a stereo file, but I'm showing only the upper track for clarity.

Consider the two regions defined in **Figure 74a**. Region A has consistently low volume, while Region B has both high and low points. If you normalized Region A, you would increase the volume of the low points to much higher levels. However, if you normalized Region B, Audition might even reduce the volume a bit, making the low-volume portions even harder to hear.

If Figure 74a was a piece that was supposed to have high and low regions (say, the 1812 Overture), normalizing Region B, or even the entire song, would produce the desired result—a piece rendered at maximum volume with the desired highs and lows without distortion. In this case, you could safely use Premiere Pro's Normalization tool, accessed by right-clicking the Audio clip and choosing Clip Gain from the pop-up menu that appears, and then clicking the Normalize button (**Figure 74b**).

Audition Will Drive You Crazy if You Don't Know This One

Got your attention, didn't I? Audition grays out most effect controls, including Normalization, when you pause rather than stop audio playback. To make the controls active, click the black "Stop" button in the upper-left corner of the Transport panel (grayed out in Figure 73).

Still Not Loud Enough?

If normalizing the low-volume regions doesn't boost volumes to the required level, try increasing the volume using the Amplify effect (Effects > Amplitude > Amplify). As long as the waveform doesn't flatten out at the top or exceed the 0 dB levels, you shouldn't introduce any distortion into the audio.

Audio Getting Noisy?

Boosting volume through the Normalization or Amplify effects invariably seems to introduce noise into the audio. If you're experiencing this problem, check out #75.

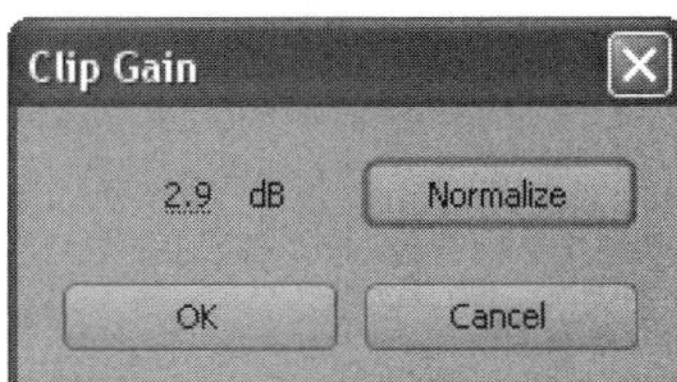

Figure 74b You can normalize in Premiere Pro with this dialog box.

On the other hand, if Figure 74a was a song (or wedding ceremony) with loud applause at the end, normalizing the entire file wouldn't increase the volume in the lower regions, which might be the bride or groom softly stating their vows. In these instances, normalize in Audition to target specific portions of your audio clip.

To increase low-volume regions in Audition, do the following:

1. In the Display area, click and drag in the waveform to select the quiet regions.
2. Choose Effects > Amplitude > Normalize (process).
3. If the default parameters shown in **Figure 74c** suit your needs (usually, they will), click OK to apply the effect.

Note that the selected region in the audio file in Figure 74c has already been normalized, and if you compare the volume to Figure 74a, you'll see that it has been substantially increased by the normalization effect.

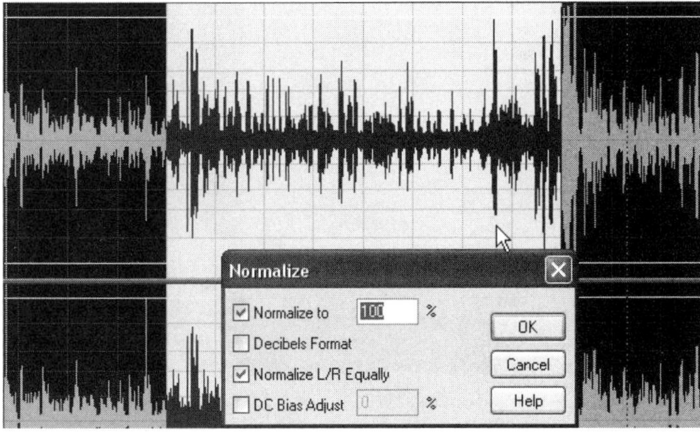

Figure 74c Audition's Normalize dialog box. Note that the audio has already been normalized using the selected region, with substantially increased volume compared to Figure 74a.

Need to Normalize Multiple Files?

If you have multiple files to normalize, load them into Audition, select the files in the Files panel, right-click, and choose Edit Group Waveform Normalize from the pop-up menu that appears. Audition will analyze the files and normalize their respective volumes.

Working Through a Long Audio File?

When working through a long audio file (say 2 minutes or more), you might find it helpful to use markers to break the file into regions and then edit them individually. To set a marker, move the current-time indicator to the target location, right-click, and choose Add to Marker List. You can divide the regions by duration, or use natural breaks like songs or scenes.

#75 Reducing Noise in Audition

Noise Reduction removes consistent noises from audio files like the hum of an air conditioner, or similar noise produced by using sub-par microphones. It does not work on irregular noises like applause, horns honking, or people laughing.

Applying the filter is a three-step process. As you might expect, Audition can't tell a "good" noise from a "bad" noise on its own, so first you have to tell the program what the unwanted noise is and isolate it. To do so, select a region in the waveform that contains just the noise to remove. This creates what Audition calls the Noise Reduction Profile. Then, you preview and adjust the controls to fine-tune the application of the filter. Finally, you apply the filter. Here are the details.

1. Click and drag your pointer to select a region that contains only the background noise (Figure 75a). Generally, you can find areas in the beginning or end of the clip, or during pauses, that have a thick line around the middle of the waveform, but no spikes.

2. After selecting the region, click Play in the Transport panel to make sure that the region contains only noise.

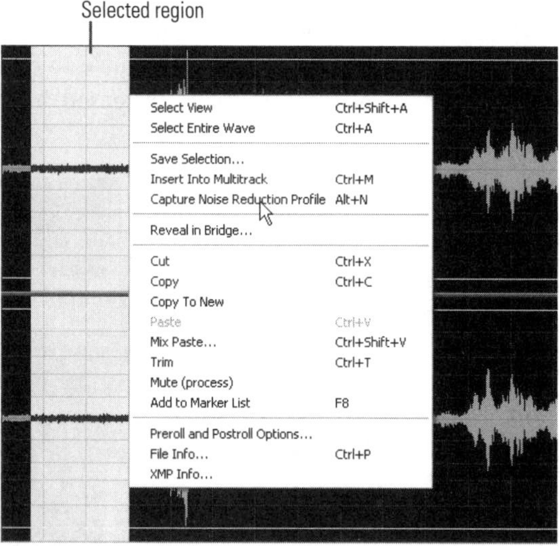

Figure 75a Click and drag to select a region that contains only the noise you're attempting to eliminate.

Got Headphones?

Noise Reduction can be a very subtle effect, especially when you're hunting for audio distortion. While you can edit audio using computer speakers for some operations, noise reduction definitely calls for your best set of headphones.

Noise Reduction? Noise Gate?

Noise reduction removes the noise identified in the Noise Reduction Profile from the entire audio file. In contrast, a noise gate filter simply mutes regions in the file that don't meet a specified threshold and doesn't touch the other regions. Audio corrected with a noise gate filter often sounds artificial, because the filter removes ambient noise the listener hears in other regions of the audio file.

3. Right-click and choose Capture Noise Reduction Profile from the pop-up menu that appears.

4. Choose Effects > Restoration > Noise Reduction (process) to open the Noise Reduction dialog box (**Figure 75b**).

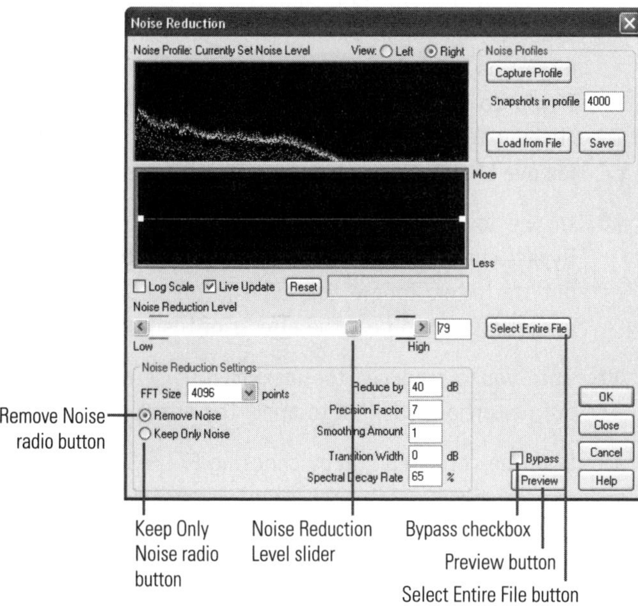

Figure 75b Here are your configuration options for the Noise Reduction effect.

5. Click the Select Entire File button to apply the effect to the entire file. Otherwise, Audition will apply the file only to the selected region.

6. In the lower-left corner of the dialog box, click the Keep Only Noise radio button.

7. In the bottom-right corner of the dialog box, click the Preview button.

8. As the audio plays, drag the Noise Reduction Level slider to the right until you start to hear some of the audio you're attempting to clarify in the filtered file. For example, if the

continued on next page

The Right Profile

If you shoot at the same location on multiple occasions (like a wedding venue or concert hall), odds are you'll encounter the same humming air conditioning system or other intrusive noises—at the same level—each time. To reduce your time spent tweaking and applying Audition's Noise Reduction effect in the future, save your Noise Reduction profile for future use. To save the profile, locate the Noise Profiles box in the upper-right corner of the Noise Reduction dialog (Figure 75b), click the Capture Profile button, and then click Save.

file is from an interview, you would start to hear talking. This indicates that you're filtering too much and removing elements of the audio that you want to keep, so move the slider back to the left until you hear only the noise you're attempting to remove.

9. In the lower-left corner of the dialog box, click the Remove Noise radio button. You should hear only the audio you're attempting to preserve. If you still hear noise in the audio, and no distortion, try dragging the Noise Reduction Level slider to the right. Drag it until you start to hear some distortion, and then stop until the distortion disappears. If you do not click the Remove Noise radio button before clicking OK to apply the effect (Step 11), Audition will remove the "good" audio and leave the noise intact.

10. In the lower-right corner of the dialog box, select the Bypass checkbox and click Preview to play the audio without the filter. Toggle this on and off both to check for distortion and to hear the effects of the filtering.

11. Once you're produced the maximum noise reduction without distortion, click OK to apply the effect.

12. Save the corrected clip by choosing File > Save.

#76 Removing Irregular Pops and Clicks in Audition

The Repair Transient filter removes pops and clicks—i.e., noises that are transient, rather than persistent, like those we addressed with the Noise Reduction effect (#75)—from a range of sources. Typical transient noises may arise from clicking a camera setting during shooting or accidentally kicking the tripod (in which case a pop or click in the audio may be the least of your troubles). Unlike some programs that completely mute the audio track for the selected period, Audition retains more of the background audio, which sounds much better. Here's how to apply the filter:

1. In the Zoom panel, click the Zoom In Horizontally icon (**Figure 76a**) to zoom in until the transient noise is clearly viewable in the waveform.

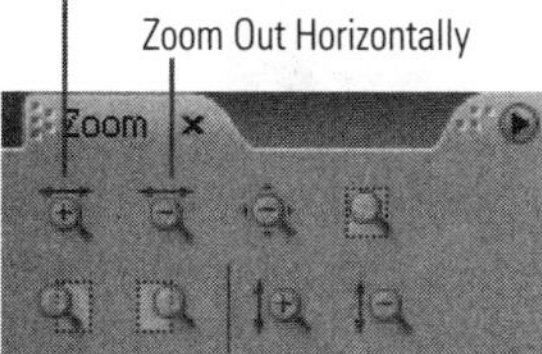

Figure 76a Use these tools in the Zoom panel to isolate the transient noise.

2. Click and drag your pointer to select only the transient noise (**Figure 76b**). After selecting the region, click Play in the Transport panel to make sure that the region contains only that noise.

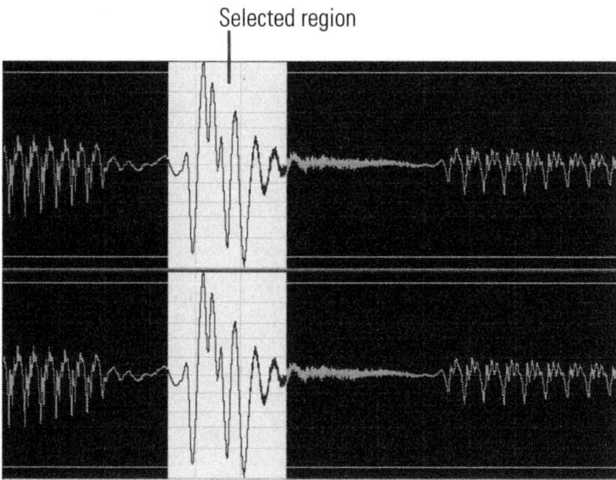

Figure 76b Click and drag to select the transient noise in the waveform.

continued on next page

Playing Favorites

Remove Transient is one of four effects that Adobe has placed in the Favorites menu by default because it's one of Audition's most frequently used features. If you find yourself using other Audition effects often enough that you'd rather not have to sort through Audition's extensive effects lists each time to find them, you can add them to the Favorites panel. Choose Favorites > Edit Favorites, and click the New button. Then select them from the lengthy Audition Effects drop-down menu, type a name under Properties, and click Save.

3. Choose Favorites > Repair Transient. There are no configurable controls, so the dialog box shown in **Figure 76c** will appear briefly, then close.

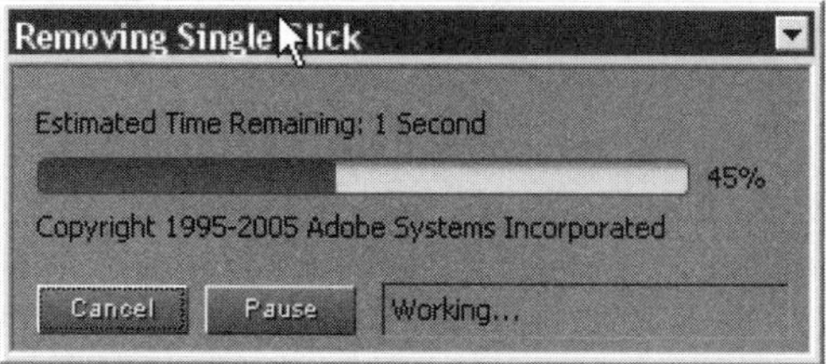

Figure 76c Here's the screen you should see flash before your eyes while Audition is removing the transient noise.

You should see a significant change in the waveform, as shown in **Figure 76d.**

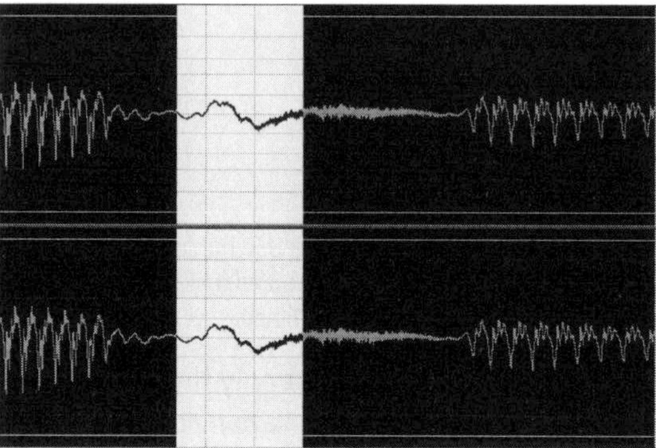

Figure 76d Here's the newly repaired waveform.

#77 Creating Narrations in Audition

Creating narrations has two basic steps: using Windows controls to select your input source and control volume, and then using Audition to capture the audio. I'll assume your microphone is already installed; unfortunately, because of the almost infinite variety of microphones, sound systems, and connections, it's impossible to provide detail on getting this connected.

1. Start by identifying your input source. In Windows XP, click Start > All Programs > Accessories > Entertainment > Volume Control to open the Master Volume Control.
2. Choose Options > Properties to open the Properties dialog box.
3. From the Mixer device drop-down menu, choose your audio input (**Figure 77a**). If there is no Mixer device menu, click the Recording radio button.

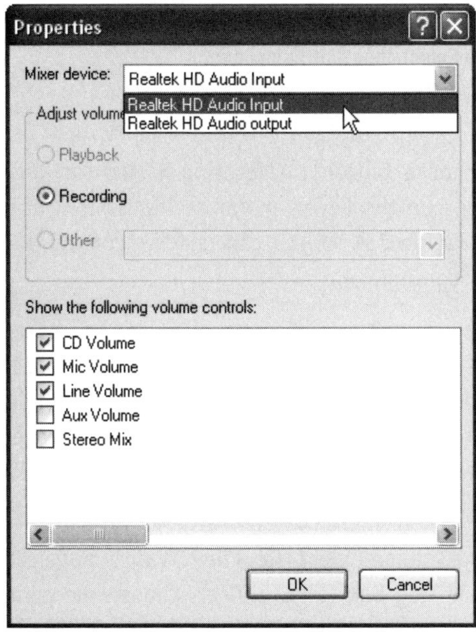

Figure 77a Select your input source from the Mixer device drop-down menu.

4. Be sure the Mic Volume checkbox is selected; you can also select any of the other checkboxes.

continued on next page

If You're Not Hearing Audio

As mentioned above, there are simply too many audio input configurations to provide you with any meaningful help in setting up or connecting your recording hardware. However, if you're having a problem, the first place to look is the Audio Hardware Setup dialog box accessed by choosing Edit > Audio Hardware Setup.

Audio-File Recording Strategy

Audition will record into the same audio file until you close it. You can record over any portion of the file by moving the current-time indicator to the target spot and clicking Record. That said, it's best simply to record your second take at the end of the audio file, and then replace the first take during editing.

It's Better to Be Too Low than Too High

If your audio volume is too low, you can use the Normalize tool to boost volume without introducing distortion. On the other hand, if it's too loud, the file is probably already distorted, which is impossible to fix. For this reason, it's better for your volume to be too low than too high.

5. Click OK to close the dialog box. Windows opens the Recording Control dialog box.
6. In the Recording Control dialog box, select the Select checkbox below the Mic Volume control (**Figure 77b**). Leave the dialog box open; you'll use it to control incoming audio volume when testing your recording.

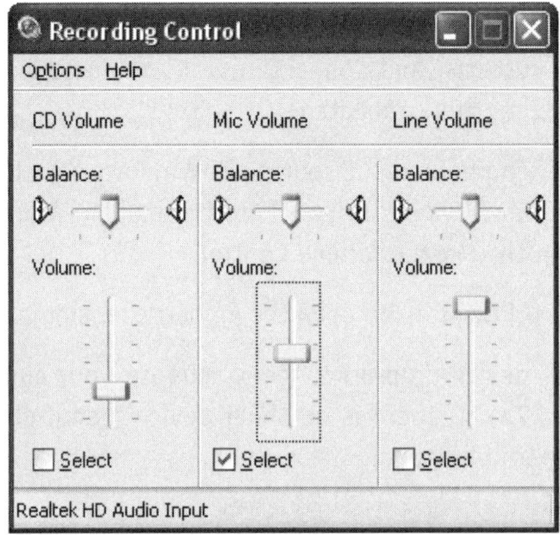

Figure 77b Select the Select checkbox below the Mic Volume control.

7. In Audition, choose Options > Metering > Monitor Record Level. This turns on the Levels meter at the bottom of the interface (see Figure 73) so you can check incoming audio levels before recording.
8. Speak into the microphone in a normal voice. The peak in the Levels meter should reach between –12 and –9 db, but should not reach 0 db, which is too loud and will produce clipping (and turn the box to the right of each Levels meter red). Use the Recording Control dialog box (see Figure 77b) to adjust volume levels.
9. After setting the volume, select File > New. Audition opens the New Waveform dialog box (**Figure 77c**). Choose the parameters that match your project, which typically will be those shown in Figure 77c unless you recorded DV audio at 32kHz.

Note

- *If you have an audio file open in Audition before narrating, Audition will record into that file using the file's audio parameters.*

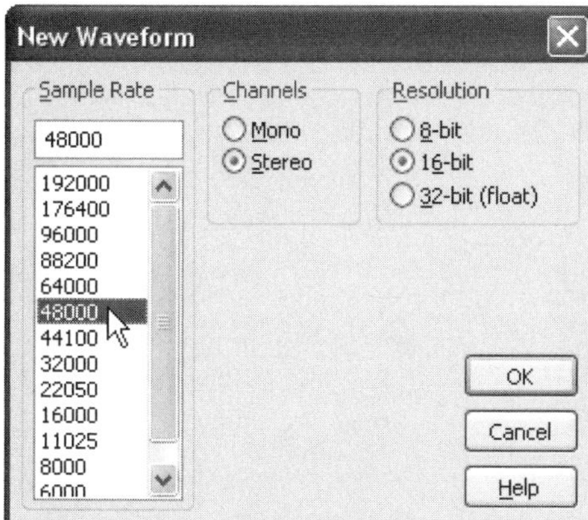

Figure 77c Choose the audio parameters for your soon-to-be-recorded audio file here.

10. Click OK to return to Edit View.

11. Click the Record button in the Transport controls (the red circle), and Audition will start recording.

12. Click the Stop button in the Transport panel (the black square) to stop recording.

13. Analyze the captured waveform (**Figure 77d**), and listen to your file with headphones. The peaks should come close to but not reach 0 dB. Regions that contain no speech should have as flat a line as possible, since fuzziness around the midline represents noise. Though you may be able to remove this with the Noise Reduction filter (#75), it's better if you can find the source of the problem and eliminate it before recording.

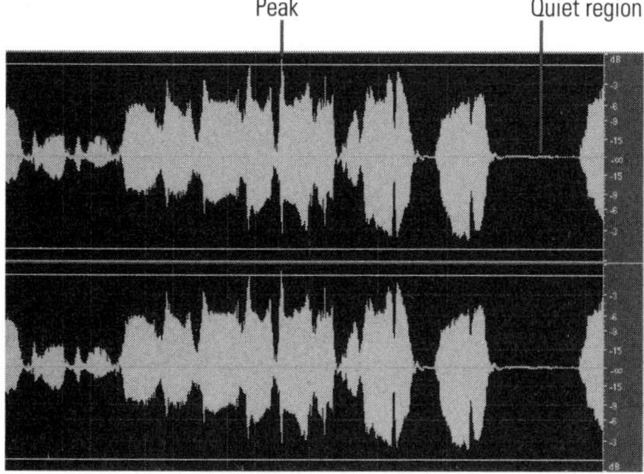

Figure 77d A reasonably healthy waveform. The highs come close to 0 dB, while the quiet regions show only a touch of noise.

CHAPTER TEN

Sharing, Rendering, and Encoding Your Projects

As much as we love editing our projects, there comes a time when we must share them with others, and this and the next two chapters detail how. Sometimes it's helpful to unveil your project before it's completely finished. You may want to solicit feedback from your client or other stakeholders. This chapter starts by describing how to use Premiere Pro's Clip Notes to do just that.

The balance of this chapter discusses how to render your projects into digital video files, first in Premiere Pro, and lastly from After Effects. Whether you're rendering a section of your project or the entire thing, this is the output step that moves your project from editing to delivery. Along the way, you'll learn how to use Adobe's encoding tool, the Adobe Media Encoder, and how to produce Flash Video files from both Premiere Pro and After Effects.

Chapter 11 details how to produce DVDs from within Adobe Premiere Pro, a feature Adobe greatly expanded in the latest version of Production Studio, while Chapter 12 describes the finer points of Adobe Encore.

#78 Sharing and Reviewing with Adobe Clip Notes

Premiere Pro's Clip Notes enables producers to send video files to reviewers in a PDF structure that lets them play the video and add comments at any location. Once returned, these comments appear as markers at that location on the production timeline, where they can easily be viewed in context by the producer.

Using Clip Notes involves three steps. First, you create the PDF file and transmit it to the reviewer. Then, the reviewer enters his or her feedback and returns a file with comments and timecode location. Finally, you import the package and review the feedback in Premiere Pro.

When creating the video file, you can choose either to embed it in the PDF file, or create a separate file you can make available on the Web for streaming. This task describes the first alternative.

1. To create the Clip Notes PDF File, choose Sequence > Export for Clip Notes. Premiere Pro will open the Export for Clip Notes dialog box shown in **Figure 78a**.

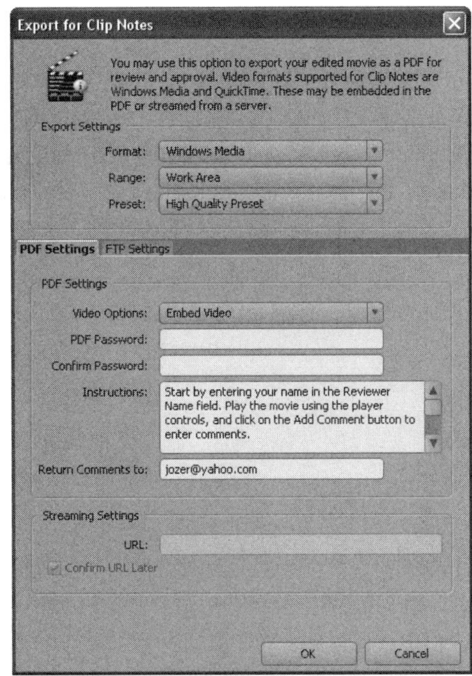

Figure 78a Choose your Clip Notes export options in this dialog box.

Required Acrobat Version

Clip Notes work in any version of Acrobat, from Acrobat Professional to the free Acrobat Reader. Clip Notes are relatively new, however, so consider advising your reviewer to download the most recent updates to his or her Acrobat program.

QuickTime vs. Windows Media

If your reviewer is running Windows, consider using QuickTime, which has superior playback controls, including the ability for the reviewer to move through the video file frame by frame. That said, Windows Media is certainly an acceptable alternative. On the Mac, however, many users have experienced problems playing the latest version of Windows Media, making QuickTime a safer choice for reviewers running the Mac OS.

- Format—Choose either Windows Media (a good choice when your reviewer is running Windows) or QuickTime (good when your reviewer is running either Windows or the Mac OS).
- Range—Choose either Work Area or Entire Sequence, depending upon what you want the reviewer to see. In general, given how large compressed video can be, choose the smallest possible segment.
- Preset—Choose High Quality Preset (720x480 resolution, 30fps, 1650Kbps), Medium Quality Preset (360x240, 30fps, 850Kbps), or Low Quality Preset (360x240, 30fps, 300Kbps).

Note

If you choose to Embed the video into the PDF file and plan to email the file to the reviewer, choose a preset that produces a file within the file size limits imposed by your email provider (typically no higher than 10MB). Our 13-second test file, at the High Quality setting, yielded a 3.8MB file when rendered. If streaming the video, you have more latitude, especially when your reviewer connects via broadband.

- Video Options—Choose Embed Video or Stream Video. If you choose the latter, enter a URL in the Streaming Settings area, and Premiere Pro will automatically link the video to the PDF file from that URL. Also consider clicking the FTP Settings Tab (which is not discussed here) to have Premiere Pro automatically upload the file to your FTP site.
- PDF Password—If desired, enter a password, which Acrobat will require to open the PDF file.
- Instructions—If desired, modify the text in the Instructions box.

Note

The text in the Instructions box pops up when the reviewer opens the PDF File. The default text Adobe provides includes useful information for first-time users, so you should consider using the default text with minimal modification the first few times you send Clip Notes to a new reviewer.

continued on next page

Smaller Is Better

Clip Notes-related video files can quickly become large and unwieldy. For example, the 13-second video sent for approval in the example was about 4MB at the High Quality preset. When possible, consider sending multiple smaller files that contain discrete scenes rather than the entire production.

XFDF Files Are Compact

While the original PDF file can be quite large, the XFDF files are text only. Though getting the original PDF and video files to the reviewer might be a logistical pain, unless the reviewer is Tolstoy or Stephen King, the returned XFDF file should be very compact.

Consider Optical Media

For reviewing an entire production, consider sending your Clip Notes via optical media like CD or DVD. Choose the Embed Video option (Figure 78a), and burn the PDF file created by Premiere Pro to CD or DVD using any recording program. Send it to the reviewer, who can enter comments and store the XFDF file on his or her hard drive for returning to the producer.

- Return Comments to—If desired, type an email address in the Return Comments to text box. If you enter an address, Acrobat will automatically create an email message to that email address, and attach the comments file, when the reviewer exports his or her comments.
- Click OK, and Premiere Pro will open a new dialog box, where you can choose a name and storage location for the PDF file. Click Save in that dialog box, and Premiere Pro will start producing the video and PDF files.

Note

Depending upon the duration of the file and the speed of your computer, producing the PDF and video file can be very time-consuming, since Premiere Pro has to compress the file into the selected streaming format. When finished, transmit the PDF file to the reviewer via email or other medium.

2. To review the video and make Clip Note comments, double-click the saved PDF file to open it in Acrobat (**Figure 78b**). Once in Acrobat, do the following:

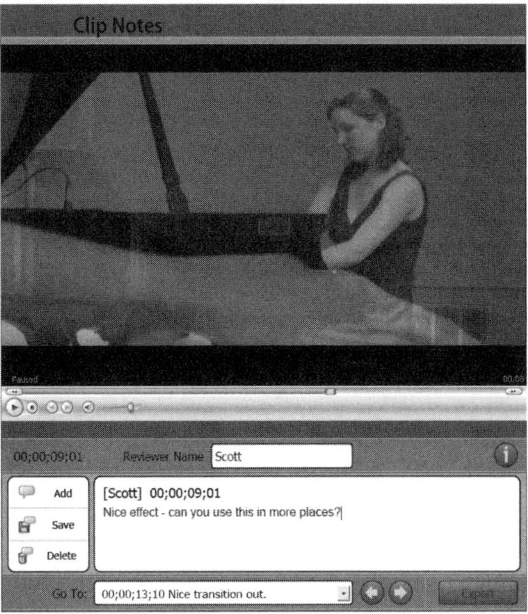

Figure 78b Reviewers enter their comments in any Acrobat version, including the freely downloadable Reader.

- Enter your name or initials in the Reviewer Name box.

- Use the player controls to play the file. To add a comment, start typing in the text box area (you don't need to click the Add button to add a comment; just start typing).
- When your notes are complete, click Export in the bottom-right corner of the dialog box. Acrobat will open the Export Form Data As dialog box, where you can name and store the file in XFDF format. Click Save to store the file and transmit it back to the video producer via email or other medium.

3. To import the Clip Notes comments into Premiere Pro, choose Sequence > Import Clip Notes Comments. Premiere Pro will open the Import Clip Notes Comments dialog box that enables you to navigate to and select the XFDF file created by your reviewer. After selecting the file, click Open to import it into Premiere Pro.
   - Reviewer comments appear as markers above the Premiere Pro timeline. To open a marker and review the comment, double-click the marker. After reviewing, you can leave the marker in place or delete it by clicking Delete.

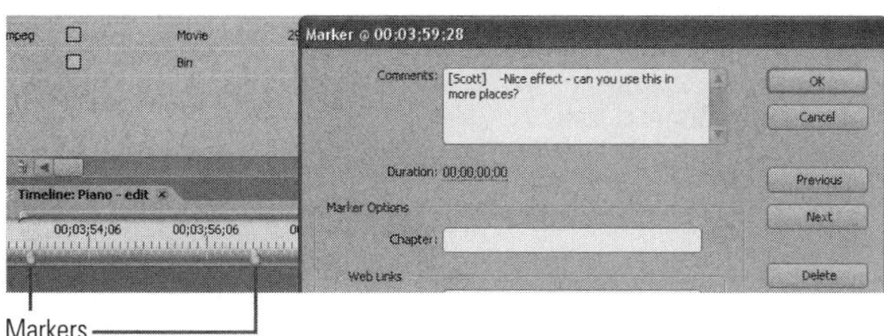

Figure 78c Reviewer comments appear as markers, which you double-click to open.

   - Click Next or Previous to jump to another marker. Click OK to close the dialog box.

#79 Exporting Frames from Premiere Pro

Why BMP?

GIF is a compressed format better created in an image editing application that provides preview and discrete customization controls. Targa is a great name for a Porsche, but has fallen into disuse for most digital image–related applications. I personally have had problems importing TIF files created by Premiere Pro into image editing and other applications, which is why BMP is usually the best option.

DV and HDV Frame Sizes

When exporting DV frames, export in 720x480 resolution at the appropriate aspect ratio—4:3 for regular footage, and 16:9 for widescreen (which should be the defaults for DV projects using the respective aspect ratios). For HDV, export at either 1920x1080 or 1280x720 resolution. Your choice of resolution will depend on which version of HDV, (1080i or 720p) your camcorder uses. Using a Square Pixel Aspect Ratio produces better results than the default, which outputs a 1440x1080 frame from 1920x1080 video using the HD Anamorphic 1080 (1.333) Pixel Aspect Ratio.

Video frames are useful for creating DVD menus and/or disc labels, or even titles for your video. Here's how to export a frame in Premiere Pro.

1. Use player controls to navigate to the target frame, which should appear in the Program Monitor.
2. Choose File > Export > Frame. Premiere Pro will open the Export Frame dialog box.
3. Click the Settings button. Premiere Pro will open the Export Frame Settings dialog box open to the General tab (**Figure 79a**).

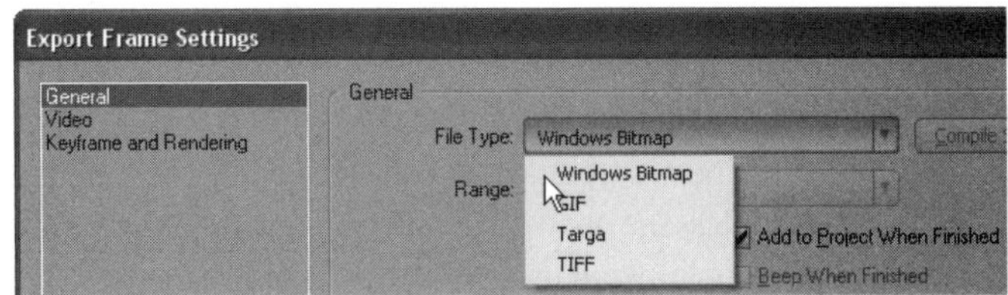

Figure 79a The General tab, where you choose file type and whether to add the frame to the project.

4. In the General tab:
   - Choose the desired File Type in the File Type drop-down menu.
   - If desired, select the Add to Project When Finished checkbox to add the frame to the Project panel after exporting. Unless you plan to use the image in your video project, these frames can quickly clog your Project panel, so deselecting this option may be a better choice.
   - On the left side of the dialog box, click Video to open that tab.
5. In the Video tab (**Figure 79b**), do the following:

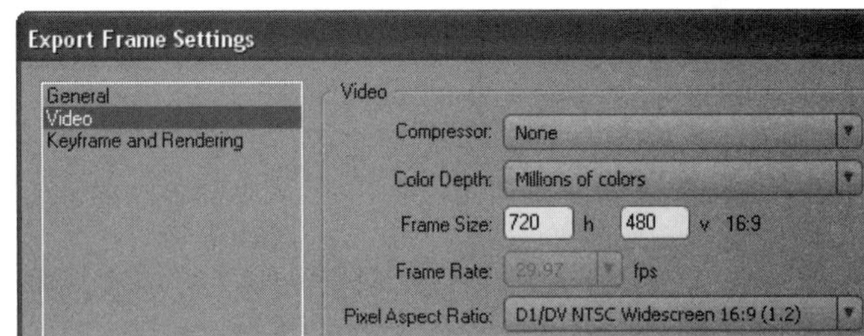

Figure 79b The Video tab, where you choose setting options from the Compressor, Color Depth, Frame Size, and Pixel Aspect Ratio drop-down menus.

- Choose None for Compressor (your only option).
- Choose the desired Color Depth drop-down menu options (which vary with the format chosen in the General tab). Unless you have a compelling reason to the contrary, Millions of colors is typically a good choice and may be your only option.
- Choose the desired Frame Size and Pixel Aspect Ratio drop-down menu options.

Note

It's generally simplest to choose the default settings for Frame Size and Pixel Aspect Ratio (which matches the project settings), and then, if necessary, edit the file to the ultimate target frame size in Photoshop. In other words, if you want a 320x240 image, export a 720x480 frame from Premiere Pro, and adjust it to the target resolution in Photoshop.

- On the left side of the dialog box, click Keyframe and Rendering to open that tab (**Figure 79c**).

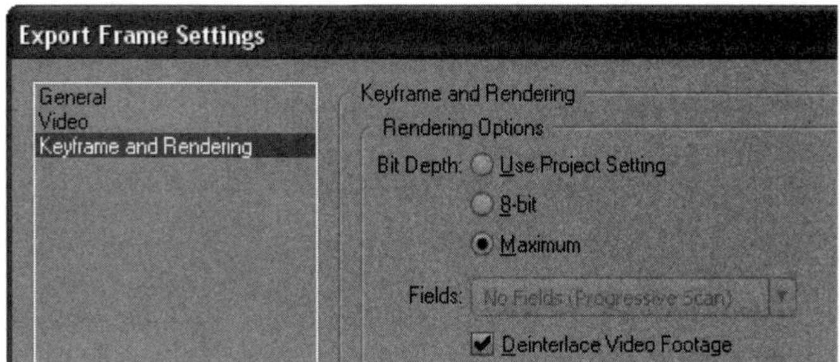

Figure 79c The Keyframe and Rendering tab, where you choose Bit Depth and whether or not to deinterlace.

6. In the Keyframe and Rendering tab:
   - Click the Maximum radio button for Bit Depth.
   - If desired, select the Deinterlace Video Footage checkbox and Premiere Pro will deinterlace the frame during rendering.
7. In the Export Frame Settings dialog box, click OK (not shown) to return to the Export Frame dialog box, where you can name and choose a storage location for your file. Click Save when finished, and Premiere Pro will render and store the frame.

Deinterlace in Premiere Pro or Photoshop?

Premiere Pro appears to use the same deinterlacing filter as Photoshop, producing identical results in several tests. If you're not satisfied with the still-image quality produced by Premiere Pro, deselect the Deinterlace Video Footage checkbox (Figure 79c) and deinterlace in Photoshop (Filter > Video > De-Interlace), but don't expect vastly different results.

#80 Exporting Audio from Premiere Pro

For Multi-Scene Projects with Different Audio Sources

Consider exporting the entire audio file and importing it into Audition where you can view the composite waveform. This will highlight which scenes have lower or higher volume than the others, and you can fix the problem in Premiere Pro or Audition (#74).

Exporting audio is useful for creating audio menus for DVDs or CD-Audio discs, or for editing your audio in an editor other than Adobe Audition (which you can always access via right-click commands). You can export either a work area or an entire sequence, so if you're exporting just a work area, create that first (#14).

Here's how to export audio from Premiere Pro.

1. Choose File > Export > Audio. Premiere Pro will open the Export Audio dialog box.

2. Click Settings. Premiere Pro will open the Export Audio Settings dialog box open to the General tab (**Figure 80a**).

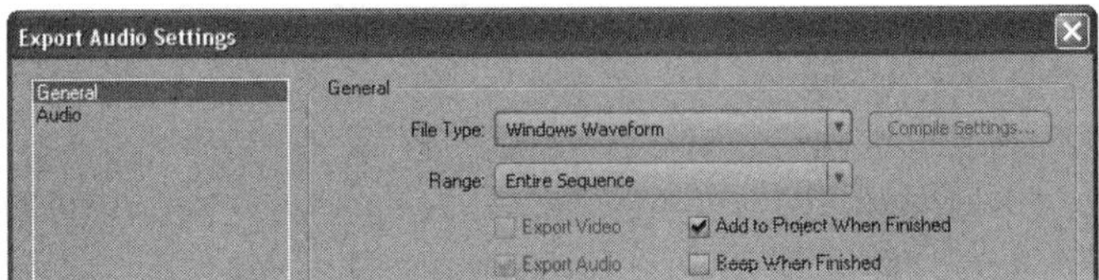

Figure 80a The General tab, where you choose File Type, Range, and other options.

3. In the General tab, do the following:

   - Choose the desired file type in the File Type drop-down menu.
   - If desired, select the Add to Project When Finished checkbox to add the audio file to the Project panel after exporting.
   - If desired, select the Beep When Finished checkbox, and Premiere Pro will beep after completing the export.
   - On the left side of the dialog box, click Audio to open the Audio tab.

4. In the Audio tab (**Figure 80b**), do the following:

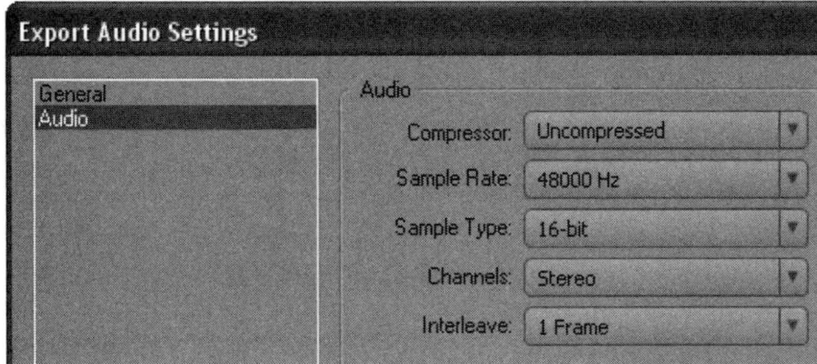

Figure 80b The Audio tab, where you choose Compressor and other options.

- Choose the desired settings for Compressor, Sample Rate, Sample Type, Channels, and Interleave.

Note

It's generally simplest to choose the default settings for all Export Audio Settings parameters and edit to your final target in Audition or other audio editor.

5. In the Export Audio Settings dialog box, click OK (not shown) to return to the Export Audio dialog box where you can name and choose a storage location for your file. Click Save when finished, and Premiere Pro will render and store the audio file.

#81 Working with the Adobe Media Encoder

If Export is Grayed Out ...

...click the Timeline to select it. If you're working in the Effect Controls panel or Source Monitor, for example, Premiere Pro will deactivate Export.

The Adobe Media Encoder is a flexible tool that can export your video project to a range of formats, including MPEG-1, MPEG-2, Macromedia Flash Video (FLV), QuickTime, RealMedia, and Windows Media. Though each format has its own peculiarities, the basic workflow is the same for all of them, which is what is covered here. You can export either a work area or an entire sequence, so if you're exporting just a work area, create that first (#14).

1. Choose File > Export > Adobe Media Encoder. The Adobe Media Encoder dialog box will appear.
2. In the Export Settings area located in the upper-right corner of the dialog box, choose the desired format (**Figure 81a**).

   Note

   Once you choose a format, Premiere Pro customizes the tabs on the bottom half of the Export Settings dialog box to match the available options. This technique reviews the options for the MPEG-2 DVD Format.

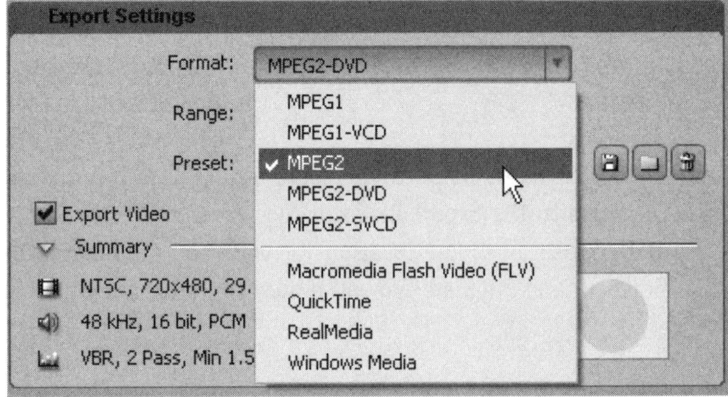

Figure 81a Choose your options from the Format, Range, then the Preset drop-down menus.

3. In the Export Settings dialog box, choose the target range (select either Entire Sequence or Work Area from the Range drop-down menu).
4. In the Export Settings area, choose the target preset from the Preset drop-down menu. If you have previously created any custom presets, they will appear at the top of the Preset list.

Note

If you're an inexperienced user, you should stick with the presets, lest you change a parameter that renders the file unusable. If you're experienced, continue with Steps 5–9. Note that once you change any parameter, Premiere Pro will force you to save the encoding parameters into a new custom preset.

5. Click the Filters tab to open the Noise Reduction option (not shown). Avoid applying this filter unless your video is extremely noisy.
6. Click the Video tab to open the Video settings (**Figure 81b**).

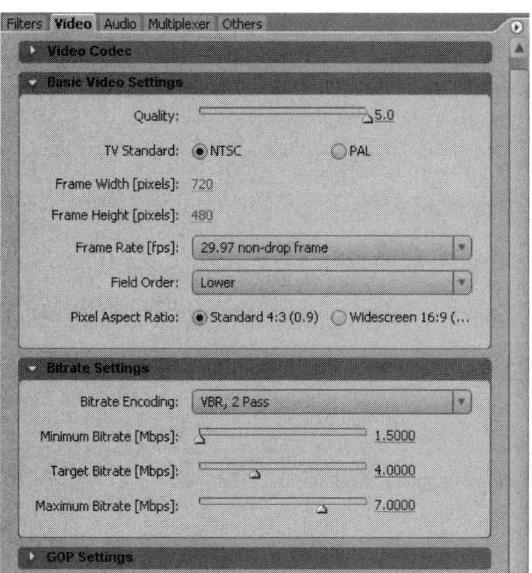

Figure 81b The Video Tab contains multiple parameters, some of which you can adjust, and others that you should leave at the default settings.

- Review the Basic Video Settings to ensure that they are correct.

continued on next page

Outputting MPEG-2 Files—When and Where

When rendering video in Premiere Pro for Encore, you have two choices: outputting a DV-AVI file or outputting an MPEG-2 file. If you're working in DV and have made minimal edits, output in DV-AVI format and import that into Encore. If you've introduced significant or pervasive edits like color correction or brightness adjustments, or you're working with HDV video, consider outputting from Premiere Pro in MPEG-2 format (with PCM audio). Here's why.

In the first example, minimal edits, Premiere Pro will simply output the original DV-AVI files, making only required changes, so you're not adding a generation of processing. In the second example, with pervasive edits, if you output DV-AVI, Premiere Pro will have to apply the effects, then re-encode back into DV-AVI format. If you then encode that file into MPEG-2, you've added a compression generation. Ditto when producing SD DVDs from HDV video, since Premiere Pro will convert that to DV-AVI. If you encode directly to MPEG-2 in both cases, you avoid that generation.

Will the difference be noticeable? Perhaps not, but the best practice is to introduce as few encoding generations as possible into the process.

Creating Custom Presets

If you change any parameters in the selected preset, Premiere Pro will prompt you to save all selected parameters as a custom preset with a unique name. Consider naming these for the project (e.g., Taylor wedding) or by the parameters (e.g., 7.5Mbps VBR with PCM audio).

When Producing Multiple-Format Files

Premiere Pro does a good job producing single-format files in the supported formats. However, if you need to produce multiple-format files (e.g., QuickTime, RealMedia, or Windows Media) to make your streaming video accessible to a wider audience, consider a batch-capable tool like Sorenson Squeeze or Autodesk Cleaner XL that can accept one input file and produce multiple output formats. Also consider these tools in a streaming production environment, where you're creating multiple-bitrate files.

Note

Premiere Pro's streaming presets can be very conservative. For example RealMedia resolution maxes out at 320x240 resolution, even when data rates exceed 1Mbps. To produce higher-resolution streaming videos, change the Frame Width and Frame Height parameters here. Don't change MPEG resolutions (especially DVD), however, since you might produce a file that won't import into Encore.

- Review the Bitrate Settings. It's relatively safe to customize many of these parameters, for example, changing constant bitrate encoding (CBR) to variable bitrate encoding (VBR), which will authorize Adobe Media Encoder to conserve bits on more easily compressed (e.g., low-motion) segments of your video and apply more bits to more dynamic sections while achieving the same average bitrate overall. When producing MPEG2 files for DVD, however, your Target Bitrate shouldn't exceed 7Mbps, and your Maximum Bitrate shouldn't exceed 7.5Mbps, or the encoded file might contain data spikes that will interrupt playback on some DVD players.
- Unless you're an experienced compressionist, don't change the GOP settings for any compression formats.

7. Click the Audio tab to review the Audio settings (**Figure 81c**).

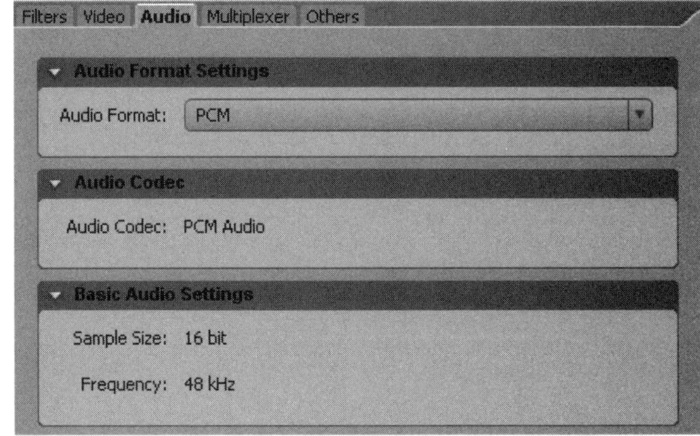

Figure 81c Stick with PCM when producing MPEG-2 files for Encore, and compress your audio when producing the DVD in Encore.

- Review the Audio Settings. When producing MPEG-2 files for DVD, choose PCM in the Audio Format drop-down menu (as shown) and then encode to Dolby Digital Format in Encore.
- When producing streaming formats, adjust both Audio Codec and Bitrate here. Note that whatever Bitrate you select for your audio, Adobe Media Encoder will add to the overall bitrate of your audio/video file; so 256Kbps video with 96Kbps audio, for example, will yield a 352Kbps streaming file.

8. Click the Multiplexer tab to review the Multiplexer settings.
   - When producing MPEG-2 files for DVD, accept the defaults.
   - When producing QuickTime files, this tab changes to Alternates, which contains several QuickTime specific parameters. When producing Windows Media and RealMedia files, this tab changes to Audiences, with settings that vary by compression technology. When producing files in these formats with the Adobe Media Encoder, click all tabs to make sure you've addressed all relevant parameters.
9. Click the Others tab to enter FTP settings that will automatically upload the file after Premiere Pro finishes encoding.
10. When you're finished customizing your encoding parameters, click OK in the bottom-right corner of the Export Settings dialog. Premiere Pro will open the Save File dialog box where you can name the encoded file and choose a storage folder.
11. Click Save, and Premiere Pro will start producing the file.

#82 Producing Flash Output

For Better Flash Video Quality

Premiere Pro uses one-pass, constant bitrate (CBR) encoding for Flash video, which works well for low-motion (talking-head) videos at higher data rates. If your projects involve high-motion video or low bitrates, or you're not satisfied with the quality produced by Premiere Pro, consider a third-party encoder like On2's Flix Pro or Sorenson Squeeze. These tools utilize 2-pass, variable bitrate techniques that produce better quality than the single-pass, CBR output produced by Premiere Pro.

Flash video is a popular streaming format for Internet and intranet use. The Adobe Media Encoder can produce Flash video in the FLV format, but not the SWF format, which contains the metadata required to make a Flash video executable online.

If you've used the Flash 8 Video Encoder, the process will look very familiar, since Premiere Pro uses many of the same controls. Even if you're a total newbie, however, you'll find the controls very simple. Assuming you've got your project completed and ready to render, here are the steps.

1. Choose File > Export > Adobe Media Encoder.
2. In the Export Settings area located in the upper-right corner of the dialog box, click the Format drop-down menu and choose Macromedia Flash Video (FLV).
3. In the Export Settings area, click the Range drop-down menu and choose the target Range (either Entire Sequence or Work Area).
4. In the Export Settings area, click the Preset drop-down menu and choose the target Preset (**Figure 82a**).

Note

The FLV7 presets use the older Sorenson Spark Codec, which produces far less quality than the On2 VP6 codec used in the FLV8 presets. Only choose FLV7 if required for backward compatibility with older players or computers.

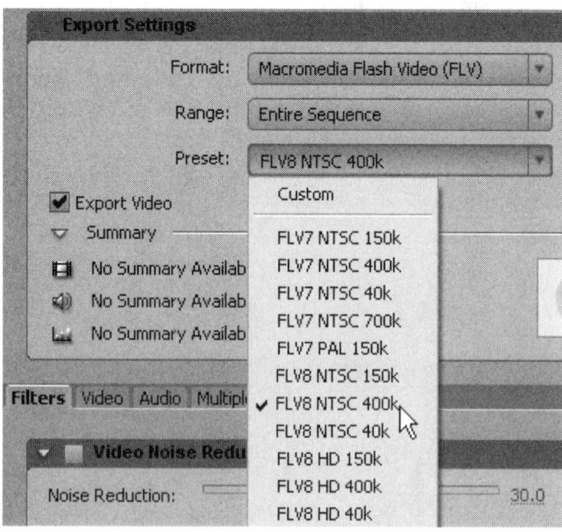

Figure 82a FLV encoding presets separated by codec, video standard, and data rate.

5. Click the Video tab to open the Video settings.

6. In the Video tab, click the Options button to open the Flash Video Encoding Settings dialog box.

7. In the Flash Video Encoding Settings dialog box, click the Show Advanced Settings button. This reveals all encoding options and changes to the Hide Advanced Settings button (**Figure 82b**).

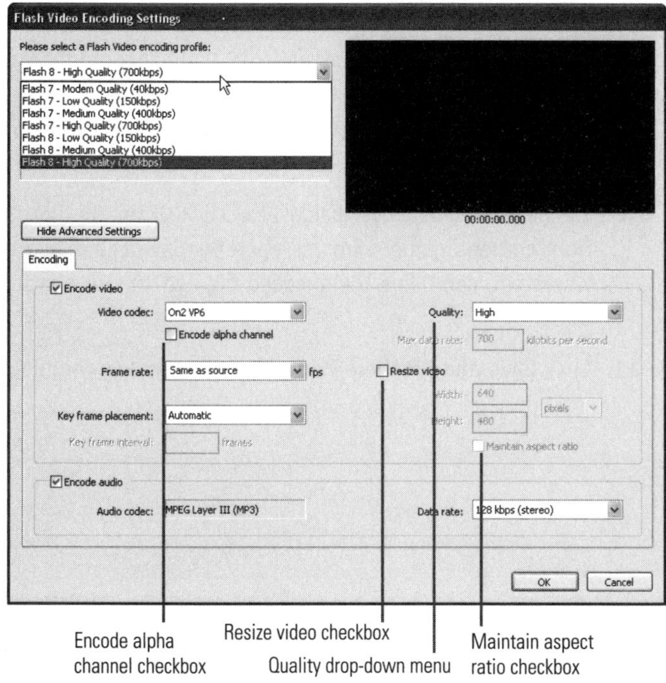

Figure 82b The Flash Video Encoding Settings dialog box is identical to the Adobe Flash 8 Video Encoder.

8. In the upper-left corner of the Flash Video Encoding Settings dialog box, choose a profile. If you customize any parameters, Premiere Pro will change the preset to Custom. Most

continued on next page

More on Producing an Alpha Channel for Flash Video

Step 8 on this page includes only the final step of producing an alpha channel with Flash video; here's the overview. First, shoot your video against a green or blue screen; then use Premiere Pro's Chroma Key filter (#48) to key out the background. Then encode as described above, making sure to select the Encode alpha channel checkbox (Figure 82b).

parameters work as you would expect, so they are not detailed here. Controls worth noting include the following:

- To create Flash video with an alpha channel, select the Encode alpha channel checkbox (this option will be grayed out if you select the Sorenson Spark Video codec).
- To input a custom Max data rate, select Custom in the Quality drop-down menu.
- Select the Resize video checkbox to insert custom Width and Height parameters. Then select the Maintain aspect ratio checkbox to avoid distorting your video.

9. When you're finished customizing your encoding parameters, click OK in the bottom-right corner of the Flash Video Encoding Settings dialog box to return to the Export Settings dialog box.
10. In the Export Settings dialog box, click OK in the bottom-right corner. Premiere Pro will open the Save File dialog box where you can name the encoded file and choose a storage folder.
11. Click Save and Premiere Pro will start encoding the file.

#83 Deinterlacing Video for Progressive Output

Most video acquisition formats like DV and the 1080i HDV codec used by the Sony and Canon HDV cameras are interlaced formats that contain two fields for every frame, usually shot 1/60th of a second apart (1/50th for PAL). In contrast, most streaming formats are frame-based. To produce frame-based video from interlaced sources involves combining the two fields into a single frame, which can produce the artifacts shown at the top of **Figure 83a**.

Figure 83a The top frame sample is not deinterlaced; the bottom sample is.

To avoid artifacting and produce video more like the bottom of Figure 83a, you have to tell Premiere Pro to deinterlace the video. Here's how you do it:

1. Right-click the video source on the timeline, and choose Field Options from the pop-up menu. Premiere Pro will open the Field Options dialog box.
2. Select the Always Deinterlace radio button (**Figure 83b**).

continued on next page

Deinterlacing Large Projects

If your project has multiple video files, or multiple sections of the same video file, you have to deinterlace each instance on the timeline. If your project includes hundreds of files on the timeline, it may be faster to output the entire project into one file in DV-AVI format, then deinterlace that file before outputting into your final format.

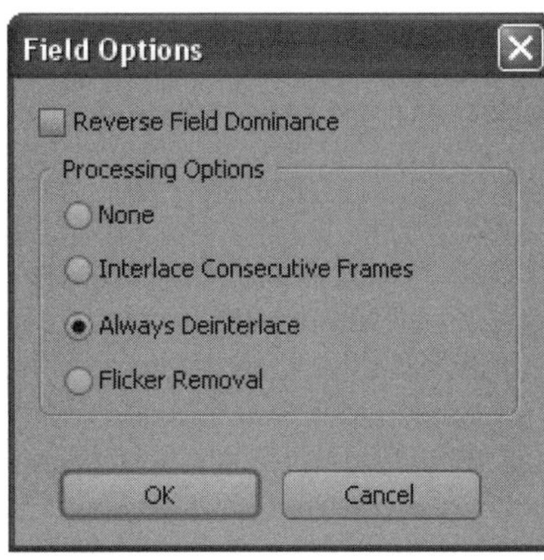

Figure 83b Choose Always Deinterlace to deinterlace all frames in a clip bound for progressive streaming formats.

3. Click OK to close the dialog box and render your video.

Note

*Selecting the Deinterlace checkbox in the Output tab of the Export Settings dialog box (**Figure 83c**) doesn't deinterlace the footage; you must deinterlace it on the timeline. The Export Settings preview screen does provide an accurate preview, however, so if your video isn't deinterlaced there (as shown in Figure 83c), the final file won't be deinterlaced either.*

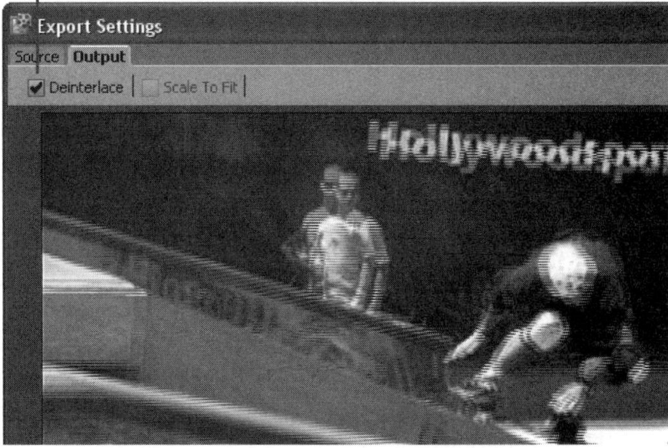

Figure 83c As you can see, selecting the Deinterlace checkbox doesn't resolve the problem, as the deinterlacing artifacts are still evident.

#84 Rendering in After Effects

Assuming that you're using After Effects for simple, discrete tasks, like those described in Chapters 4 and 6, rendering from After Effects is relatively simple, with many encoding chores handled by the Adobe Media Encoder, detailed in #81. This technique details the high-level workflow for rendering in After Effects, assuming that you've got your composition loaded and ready for output.

1. Choose Composition > Add to Render Queue. After Effects adds the composition to and will open the Render Queue (**Figure 84a**).

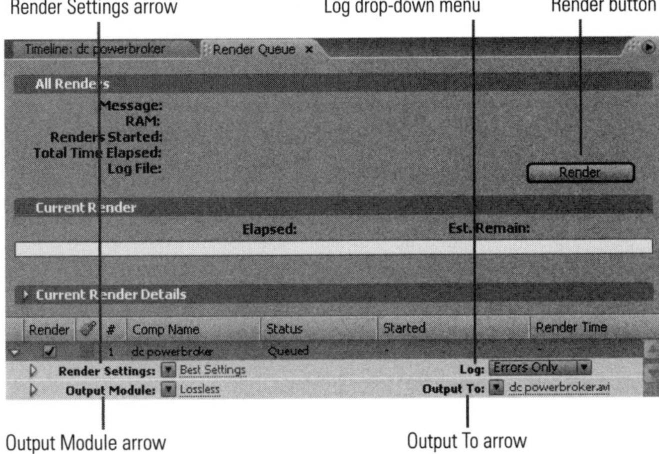

Figure 84a After Effects' Render Queue.

> ***Note***
> *For most simple projects, you can accept the default settings for both Render Settings and Log.*

2. Click the downward-pointing arrow next to Lossless in the Output Module. After Effects will open the Output Module Settings dialog box (**Figure 84b**).

continued on next page

Batch Encoding

The Render Queue supports batch encoding. Simply queue multiple compositions as described above, and click the Render button to start encoding.

Producing Flash Files in After Effects

After Effects doesn't use the Render Queue to produce FLV Flash videos. Instead, with the composition selected, choose File > Export > Flash Video (FLV), and After Effects will open the Flash Video Encoding Settings dialog box shown in Figure 82b. You can also produce SWF files by clicking File > Export > Macromedia Flash (SWF), with simple dialog boxes for setting relevant encoding parameters.

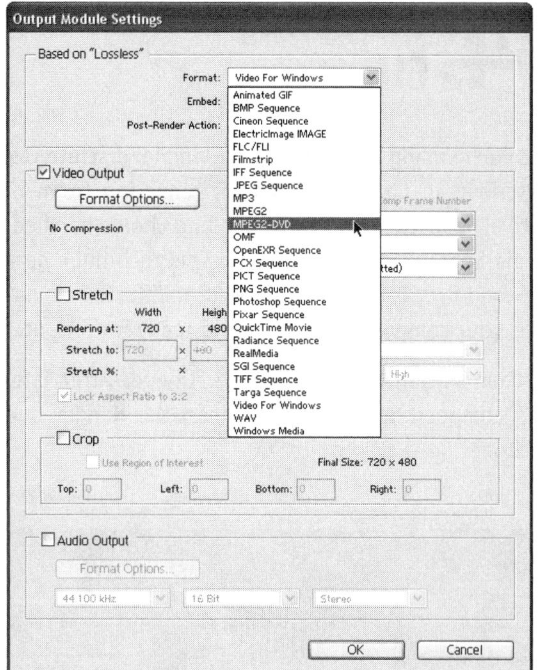

Figure 84b Choose your target format first, then click the Format Options button. Note the currently blank Audio Output checkbox. If you don't select this checkbox, you'll produce a silent movie.

3. Click the Format drop-down menu and choose the target format.
4. Click the Format Options button.
    - If you select RealMedia, MPEG2, MPEG2-DVD, or Windows Media, After Effects will open the Adobe Media Encoder window (Figures 81a, 81b, and 81c). Choose the target parameters as detailed in #81, Steps 4–9.
    - For other formats, After Effects will open format-specific dialog boxes that are beyond the scope of this book.
5. Click OK to close the dialog box and return to the Output Module Settings dialog box.
6. In the Output Module Settings dialog box, select the Audio Output checkbox to encode audio with the video, and adjust audio settings as desired.
7. Click the Format Options button and choose your output options and compression parameters. Click OK to close the dialog box.

8. In the Output Module Settings dialog box, click OK to close the dialog box and return to the Render Queue.
9. In the Render Queue, click the name in the Output To control to open the Output Movie To dialog box where you can name your file and designate a storage location. Click Save to close that dialog box.
10. Click the Render button to start rendering.

#85 Creating Custom Output Presets in After Effects

When rendering multiple files to common encoding parameters in After Effects, you'll save oodles of time and irritation by creating custom output presets. The process is very simple once you've specified your output parameters as described in #84. After selecting all of your encoding parameters, and before clicking the Render Button, do the following:

1. In the Render Queue, click the downward-pointing arrow next to Output Module to open the Output Module drop-down menu and choose Make Template (**Figure 85a**). After Effects will open the Output Module Templates dialog box.

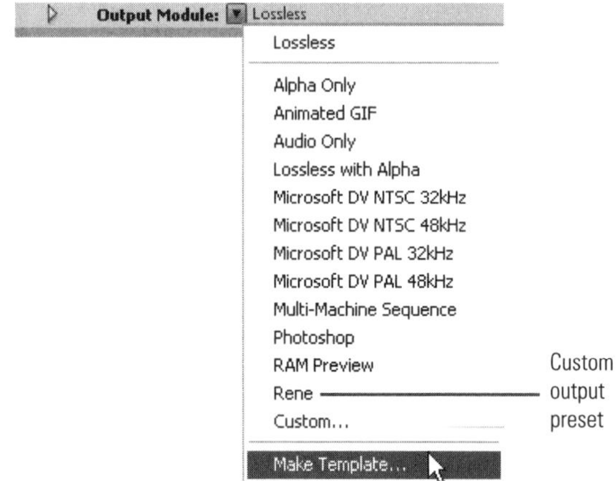

Figure 85a Click Make Template to create a new Template. Note the Rene preset, a previously created custom preset.

2. In the Settings Name text box, enter a name for the setting (**Figure 85b**).

   Note

   If you have not already set your encoding parameters before starting this process, click Edit, which will open the Output Module Settings dialog box shown in Figure 84b. Choose your settings as described in #84, click OK to close the dialog box, and move to the next step.

3. Click OK to save the setting. Thereafter, you can select the preset by choosing it in the Output Module drop-down menu (like the Rene preset shown in Figure 85a).

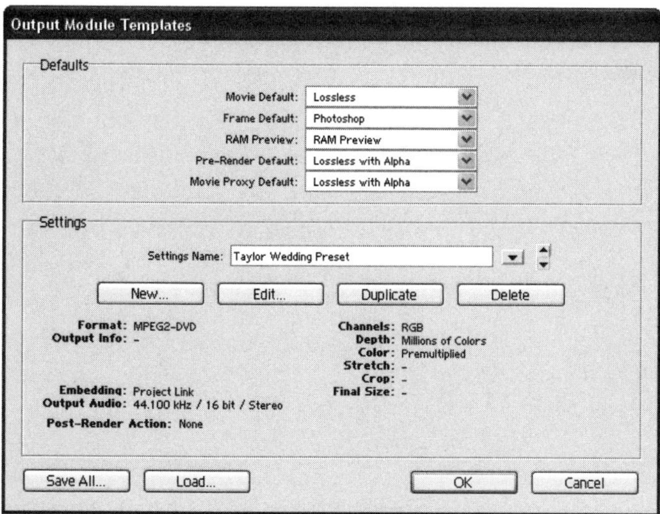

Figure 85b Name your preset in the Settings Name text box.

CHAPTER ELEVEN

DVD Production in Premiere Pro

One feature that distinguishes Premiere Pro from other editors is the ability to produce DVDs from the timeline, reducing the authoring time for a review copy of your video to zero. In Premiere Pro 2.0, Adobe expanded this capability to include basic menu creation and editing, allowing producers to burn simple DVDs without using Encore DVD, which is another timesaver.

This chapter starts by describing Premiere Pro's DVD authoring capabilities and its limitations, so you'll know when to author in Premiere Pro and when to use Encore. Then the chapter describes how to access and use Premiere Pro's DVD authoring capabilities.

Even when producing DVDs in Encore DVD, you should insert your DVD chapter markers in Premiere Pro, since titles or audio waveforms that you can't easily see in Encore DVD guide your efforts. The final technique discussed in this chapter details how.

#86 Using Premiere Pro vs. Encore DVD

Supported DVD Formats

Premiere Pro supports only single-layer DVD-Recordable disks in the DVD+R, DVD+RW, DVD-R, and DVD-RW formats. If you have a dual layer–capable drive, Premiere Pro can create a single-layer disc with any of these media. Premiere Pro cannot author or burn HD DVD or Blu-ray discs.

Adobe Encore DVD is an exceptionally feature-rich DVD authoring program that provides virtually unlimited artistic and navigational flexibility. You also get a fast and easy to use slide show creation tool, and playlists, which allow you to further customize the viewer experience. You can also burn your DVD on single or dual-layer media.

Premiere Pro's internal DVD authoring capabilities are similar to those of its consumer sibling, Premiere Elements. You can customize menus with images or video backgrounds, and add audio. However, if the selected template has three buttons per menu, you're limited to three buttons on that menu, which can frustrate your customization efforts.

From a navigational perspective, Premiere Pro's authoring capabilities support sequential Scenes Menus from the Main Menu, with no menu branching. While you can link scenes directly to the Main Menu, again you're limited to the number of buttons supported on that menu. If you're trying to consolidate six scenes onto a single Main Menu, for example, you won't be able to do it.

All that said, for many simple projects with limited customization, especially for consumer audiences, Premiere Pro's authoring features will do just fine and save you a rendering and authoring step. For more fully featured productions, you'll want to use Encore DVD, which is covered in Chapter 12.

#87 Producing a Menu-less DVD in Premiere Pro

Oftentimes during production you need a quick-and-dirty DVD to send to a client or to view on your own DVD/TV combination to verify color correction or other adjustments. Here's how to quickly produce a menu-less DVD in Premiere Pro:

1. Click the target sequence on the Timeline.
2. Insert a blank DVD disc into the target drive.
3. Choose File > Export > Export to DVD. Premiere Pro will open the Burn DVD dialog box (**Figure 87**).

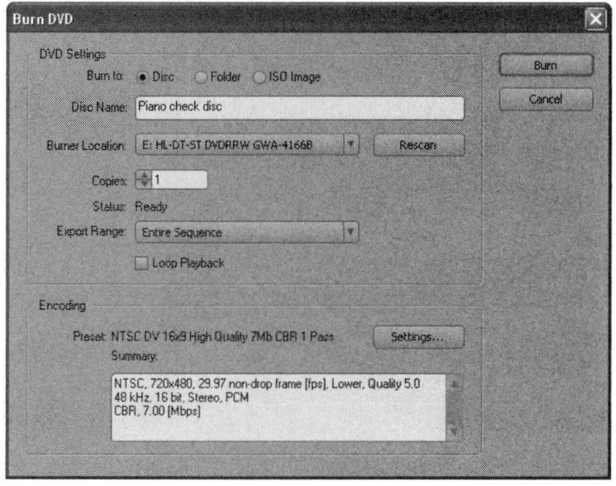

Figure 87 Here's where you select your DVD burning options.

4. In the DVD Settings area, choose your Burn to: options by clicking the radio button for target output device and format.
   - Choose Disc to burn a DVD.
   - Choose Folder to encode and save all files in the specified folder where you can preview them with a software DVD Player on your computer.
   - Choose ISO Image to create and save an ISO image that you can use to burn additional DVDs with most disc-burning programs.

continued on next page

Auto-Play

The disc Premiere Pro creates with this process is an "auto-play" disc that will start playing as soon as placed in a DVD drive. No menu will appear.

Hard Drive Space Requirements

To produce any DVD with Premiere Pro (or Encore DVD for that matter), you'll need sufficient hard drive space to store all compressed files and menus before they are written to disc. In Premiere Pro, this means 4.7GB, and in Encore DVD, which can produce dual-layer discs, this means up to 8.5GB of free space if you plan to use the full capacity of your target disc.

5. If desired, enter a name in the Disc Name text box.

6. If your computer has multiple DVD recorders, click the Burner Location drop-down menu to select the target.

Note

Premiere Pro scans the default DVD recorder before opening the Burn DVD dialog box, and will display the message "Media not present" in the Status box if a suitable blank DVD disc is not in the target drive. If you add media after opening the dialog box, or change drives in Step 6, click the Rescan button to have Premiere Pro rescan the drive for suitable media.

7. If desired, enter the number of desired copies in the Copies field.

8. In the Export Range dialog box, choose to produce either the Entire Sequence or the Work Area Bar.

9. Select the Loop Playback checkbox to have the video loop after finishing. Otherwise, the DVD will simply stop after the video finishes playing.

10. Click the Settings button to change the encoding settings. This opens the Adobe Media Encoder discussed in #81.

11. Click the Burn button to start the encoding and burning process.

#88 Creating Scene Markers in Premiere Pro

You have two options for creating scene markers in Premiere Pro: You can insert them automatically or manually. To insert them automatically, choose Marker > Auto-Generate DVD Markers, and adjust the simple controls as desired. Here's how to insert them manually.

1. In the timeline, drag the current-time indicator to the target location for the marker.
2. Right-click the current-time indicator, and from the pop-up menu that appears, choose Set DVD Marker and the chapter marker type—either Scene, Main Menu, or Stop (**Figure 88a**).

Figure 88a These are your choices for manually creating scene markers.

- Scene marker—Creates a marker that appears in the scene submenus automatically created by Premiere Pro.
- Main Menu marker—Creates a text-only marker that appears in the Main Menu. Note, however, that each template can contain only a specific number of menu items and that if you exceed this number, Premiere Pro will create additional Main Menus.
- Stop marker—Creates a marker that returns the viewer to the menu once reached on the timeline. Stop markers are useful when you want to break video playback into discrete scenes, rather than having the viewer play through to completion irrespective of entry point.

Once you select any of these markers, Premiere Pro will insert a small DVD icon in the Time ruler above the timeline. Scene markers are distinguished by a small blue arrow

continued on next page

Scene Markers and Chapter Markers

Note that scene markers inserted to create DVDs in Premiere Pro won't show up in video exported for use in Adobe Encore DVD. To create chapter markers for Encore DVD in Premiere Pro, see #91.

Note the Previous and Next Buttons in the DVD Marker Dialog Box

These are the fastest and easiest ways to move from chapter point to chapter point.

Adjusting Scene Markers

Scene markers attach to timecode, not a specific video scene. For this reason, if you add markers and then make an edit that changes a video's location on the timeline, you'll have to adjust the location of the scene marker. It's easy enough; just click and drag the marker to the desired location.

Short Button Names Are Better

Though the Name text field in the DVD Marker dialog box is very large (Figure 88b), menu real estate is always limited, so try to restrict the button names to two or three short words at most. You can edit them later, but to get it right the first time, keep them short.

below the icon, Main Menu markers by a green arrow, and Stop markers by a red arrow.

3. To edit the marker, double-click it in the Time ruler. Premiere Pro will open the DVD Marker dialog box (**Figure 88b**).

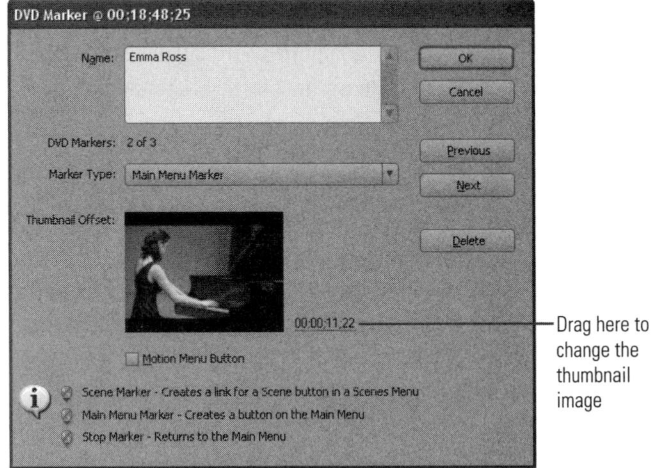

Figure 88b The DVD Marker dialog box. Note that you can easily change the frame displayed in the Scenes Menu by dragging the timescale to the right of the Thumbnail Offset.

4. Enter a name for the marker in the Name text box. With Scene and Main Menu markers, this text becomes the button name in the menu.

5. If desired, change the marker type in the Marker Type drop-down menu.

6. If desired, drag the timecode to the right of the Thumbnail Offset window to display another frame in the Scenes Menu. This is especially helpful when a scene is fading in from black, since the first frame of the scene is black. Note that this doesn't change the location of the marker, just the frame displayed in the Scenes Menu.

7. If desired, select the Motion Menu Button checkbox below the Thumbnail Offset window. Rather than presenting a single thumbnail image in the menu button, Premiere Pro will play the first 30 seconds of the video from that file in the menu button.

8. Click OK to close the dialog box.

#89 Choosing DVD Templates in Premiere Pro

All Premiere Pro templates include a "Main Menu" and a "Scenes Menu," and Premiere Pro will create as many menus as necessary for the Main Menu and scene markers you've created. It will also create all necessary links between menus and content. All you have to do is choose a template! Here's how:

1. Choose Window > DVD Layout. Premiere Pro will open the DVD Layout dialog box.

   Note

   If you've not previously added a DVD menu to this project, the dialog box will contain the message "Auto-play DVD with no Menus." If you have previously selected a template, Premiere Pro will display that template.

2. In the DVD Layout dialog box, click the Change Template button. Premiere Pro will open the DVD Templates dialog box (**Figure 89a**).

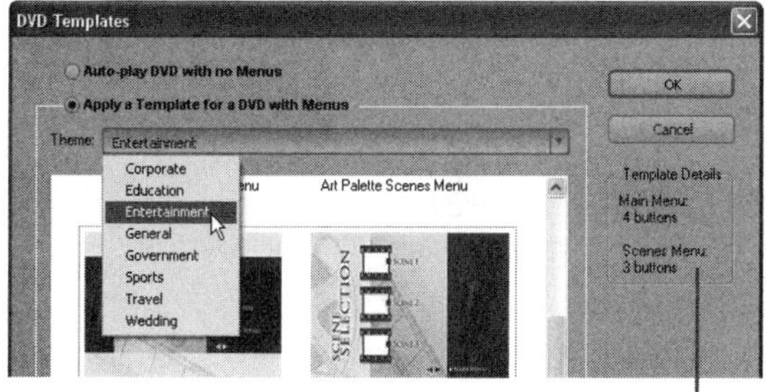

Figure 89a The DVD Templates dialog box, with templates stored in convenient categories.

3. Click the Apply a Template for a DVD with menus radio button.

4. Click the Theme drop-down menu to view and select from the available themes.

   Note

   Note the Template Details box on the right of the DVD Templates dialog box in Figure 89a, which details the number of buttons in the Main Menu and Scenes Menu. Most Main Menus contain four buttons, while Scenes Menus contain between three and six buttons.

continued on next page

When Four Equals Two

All Main Menu templates have four buttons. However, two of these are dedicated to Play Movie and Scene Selection buttons, which you can't change. For this reason, the number of Main Menu markers you can insert in a single Main Menu is two, after which Premiere Pro will create an additional Main Menu to contain any additional Main Menu buttons.

And the Winner Is...

If you're looking to cram as many thumbnail buttons as possible in a single menu, check out the Winter Main Menu in the Travel Theme option, which contains six thumbnails.

5. Click your template of choice.

6. Click OK to close the DVD Templates dialog box and return to the DVD Layout dialog box. Premiere Pro will display the initial Main Menu, with all submenus displayed in the DVD Menus window (**Figure 89b**).

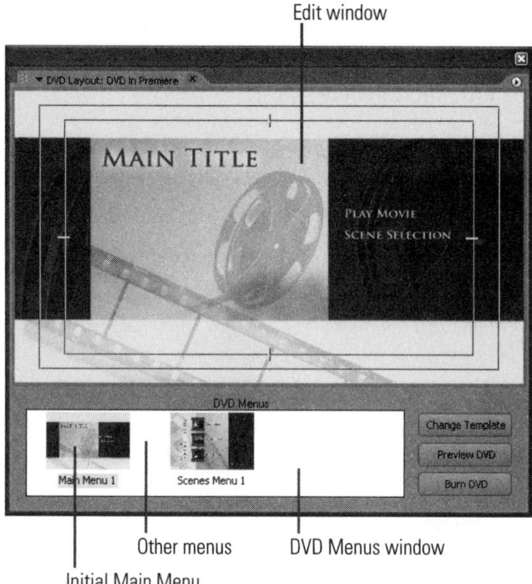

Figure 89b The newly selected template. Premiere Pro initially displays the initial Main Menu in the Edit window, and you can edit other menus by clicking them in the DVD Menus window.

#90 Customizing DVD Menus in Premiere Pro

Premiere Pro offers several DVD menu configuration options. Here's how to access them. Start in the DVD Layout dialog box (choose Window > DVD Layout) with the menu you're editing in the Edit window (Figure 89b).

1. To move any menu item, click and drag the bounding box to the new location.
2. To resize any menu item, click and drag any selection point of the bounding box to the new size.
3. To change any menu-related text, double-click the text box.
   - If the text is part of the template, Premiere Pro will open the Change Text dialog box (**Figure 90a**). Modify the text in the Change Text field and click OK to close the dialog box.
   - If the text is from a marker, Premiere Pro will open the DVD Marker dialog box (Figure 88b). Modify the text in the Name field and click OK to close the dialog box.

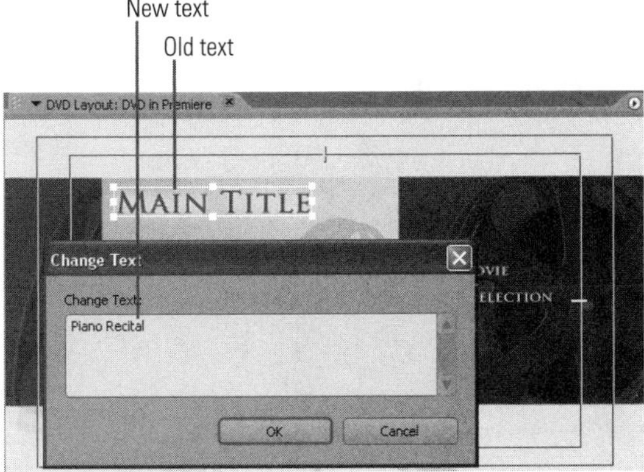

Figure 90a Use the Change Text dialog box to modify template-related text.

4. To change the text font or related characteristics, click the text in the DVD Layout dialog box, then click the Effect Controls tab to open that panel (**Figure 90b**).

   Note

   Note the handy Apply to all Text Items button, which can save lots of time when making universal changes.

continued on next page

Who Wins the Audio Battle?

If the file you've selected for the video background contains audio, and you insert a separate audio file as background for the menu, Premiere Pro will play the audio file exclusively.

Drag and Drop Works Okay Too

If the media you're using for the menu background is already in the Project panel, you can simply drag it into either the selected menu in the DVD Layout dialog, or the video, audio or still image thumbnail in the Effect Controls panel. Premiere Pro will then insert it into the menu.

Create Motion Backgrounds in After Effects

After Effects has a superb library of motion backgrounds that work well as menu backgrounds. See #63 for details.

Figure 90b Change fonts and font-related characteristics in the Effect Controls tab.

5. To change the menu background and audio, click the background (making sure no text or buttons are selected), and then click the Effect Controls tab to open that panel (**Figure 90c**). Here you can add any image or audio track you like to customize your menu.

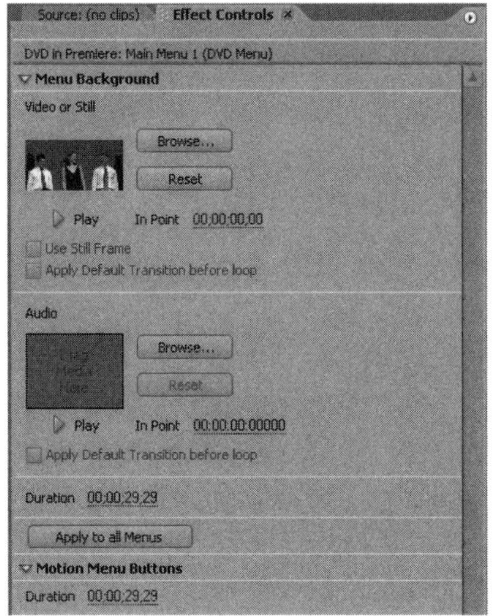

Figure 90c Change the menu background and audio in the Effect Controls tab.

Note

Though controls for the Main Menu and Scenes Menu vary slightly, it's relatively straightforward to choose a still image, video, or audio background. The most significant limiting factor is that all motion menus loop after 30 seconds, which can look and sound very repetitive (I'd say like a broken record, but my copy editor would comment about my age).

#91 Creating Chapter Markers for Encore DVD in Premiere Pro

Even if you author in Encore DVD, you should still insert your chapter points in Premiere Pro, where you have a full timeline and waveforms to guide you. Once you import the rendered file into Encore DVD, the inserted chapter markers will automatically appear on the Timeline, exactly as if you created them in Encore DVD. Here's how to create chapter markers for Encore DVD in Premiere Pro.

1. In the timeline, drag the current-time indicator to the target location.

2. Right-click the current-time indicator, and from the pop-up menu that appears, choose Set Sequence Marker > Unnumbered (**Figure 91a**). Premiere Pro will insert the marker in the Time ruler.

Figure 91a Here's the first step for creating a chapter marker in Premiere Pro that Encore DVD will recognize.

3. Double-click the marker in the Time ruler. Premiere Pro will open the Marker dialog box (**Figure 91b**).

continued on next page

Be Precise

Type the chapter names entered in step 4 *exactly* as you'd like to see them appear in your Encore menu. When you link your chapter markers to buttons in Encore DVD, Encore DVD will use this text for the button name, so you if you enter it properly here, you won't have to mess with it again.

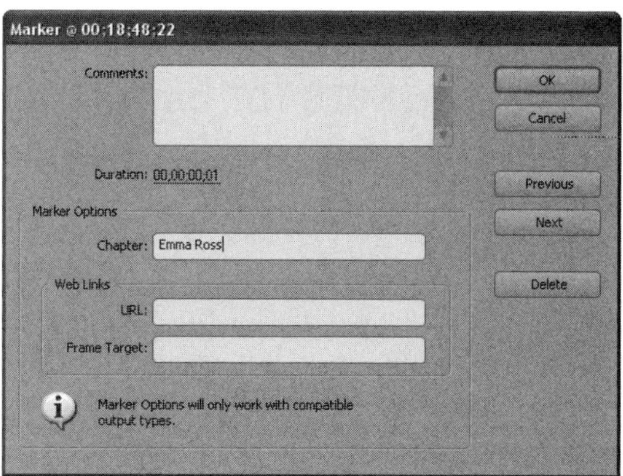

Figure 91b The text you enter in the Chapter field will appear as the chapter name in Encore DVD.

4. Enter the chapter name in the Chapter field. Click OK to close the dialog box.

CHAPTER TWELVE

Producing DVDs in Encore DVD

In many ways, the upgrade from Production Studio 1.5 to 2.0 benefited Encore DVD the most. Not only did Adobe improve the interface, they also enhanced and increased the number of templates, added a slide show feature, and boosted its playlist functionality. Encore's DVD's authoring capabilities extend well beyond Premiere Pro's, allowing you to add customized navigation, a more professional and attractive look, and greater control over your audience's viewing experience to the DVDs you create.

This chapter starts with an introduction to Encore DVD, and then details how to create and enhance menus in Photoshop and After Effects. Next, you'll learn how to control end-user navigation through your DVD, and how to create and use playlists. After reviewing how to manually arrange button routing, the chapter concludes with a checklist for previewing your DVD.

#92 Getting Started with Encore DVD

Import Video Files as Timelines

If you've exported one long video file from Premiere Pro to use as your primary content in Encore DVD, import it as a Timeline (File > Import As > Timeline). Encore DVD will create a timeline from the content (saving you a step) and use the file name as the name of the timeline (saving you another step). If you have multiple video files you intend to combine on a single timeline, import them as assets (File > Import As > Assets), create the timeline (right-click in the Project panel and choose New > Timeline), and drag them to that timeline.

Let's do a quick flyover of the Encore DVD interface and workflow to make sure we're on the same page regarding panel names and general procedures (**Figure 92a**).

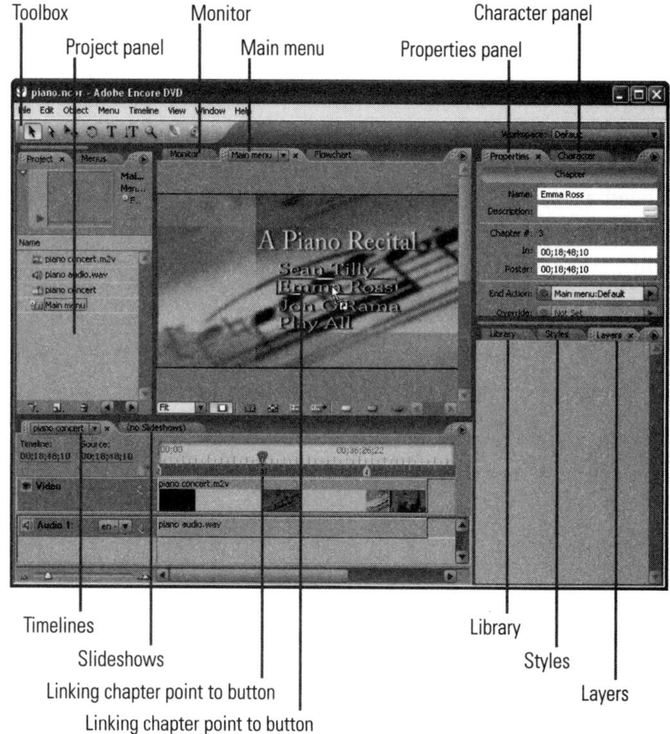

Figure 92a Adobe Encore DVD in all its glory.

1. Import your content into Encore DVD by choosing File > Import As and the target content type. Navigate to and select your content and click Open.
2. Create your menus and buttons. Options here include:
    - Import PSD menus created in Photoshop.
    - Choose a template from the Library and modify it for your use.
    - Import a still image as a menu background and add text (from the Toolbox) or buttons (from the Library).

- Customize text properties in the Character panel.
- Customize navigational properties (like End Action) in the Properties panel.

3. Add chapter points to your content. Options here include:
   - Add chapter points in Premiere Pro (#91).
   - To add chapter points in Encore DVD, click Monitor or double-click the Timeline asset in the Project panel to preview video on the timeline. Drag the current-time indicator to the target location, right-click it, and choose Add Chapter Point.
   - If desired, customize the chapter point name and navigational properties in the Properties panel.
4. Link buttons to content. Options here include:
   - Click and drag the chapter point to the button in the menu (Figure 92a).
   - Drag the pick whip from the button Properties panel to the target chapter point (**Figure 92b**).
   - Click the arrow to the right of the button link in the Properties panel, then choose the target link via menu selections.

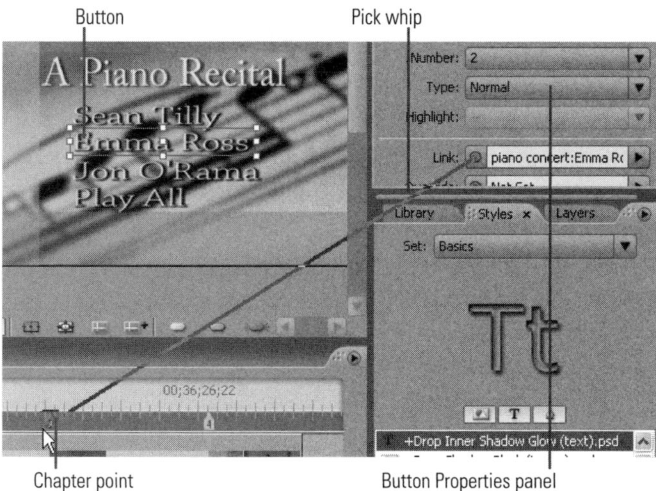

Figure 92b The pick whip is a simple, visual way to link buttons and content.

continued on next page

Link Chapter Points to Multiple Menus with Chapter Indexes

If your DVD design involves multiple chapter points accessible via sequential chapter menus, you can automate the design and linking process by using Chapter Indexes. See page 140 of the Encore DVD manual for details.

5. Choose File > Preview to preview the DVD. See #100 for more details.

6. Choose File > Check Project to open the Check Project dialog box (**Figure 92c**). Click Start to have Encore DVD check all selected project characteristics.

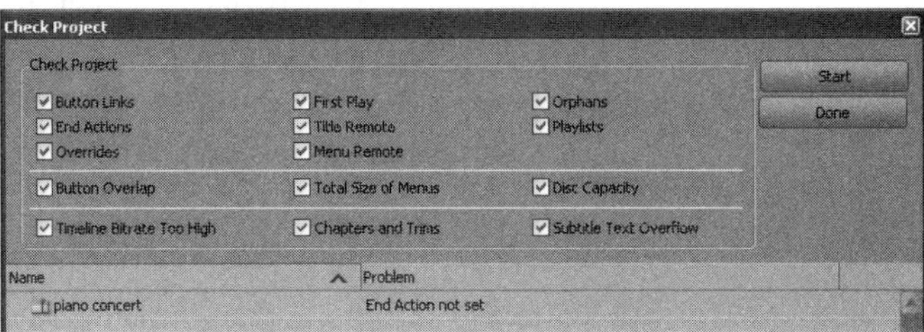

Figure 92c Encore DVD's ability to detect a range of potential errors is one of its strongest features.

7. After resolving all issues identified in the Check Project dialog box, choose File > Build DVD and the desired option (DVD Disc, DVD Folder, DVD Image, or DVD Master). Encore DVD opens the Build DVD dialog box.

8. Select your project options and click Build to build the project (**Figure 92d**).

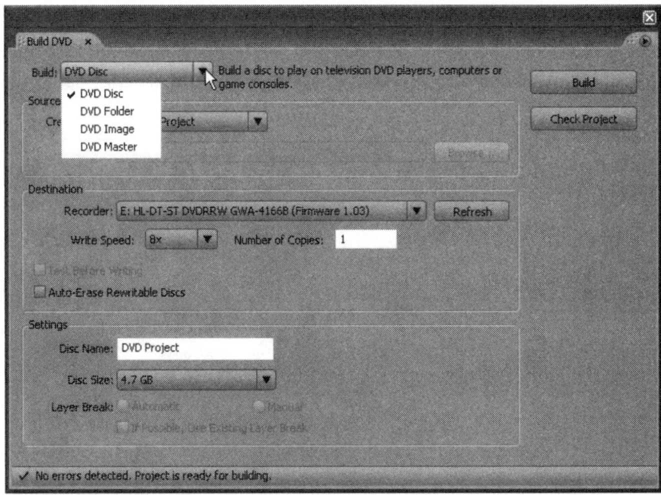

Figure 92d Select all recording options here, then click Build to start the process.

#93 Creating Text Buttons in Encore DVD

For many projects, a simple menu composed of a video frame grab for background and text buttons will suffice. Here's how to create the text buttons.

1. Click the Text tool in the Toolbox (**Figure 93a**).

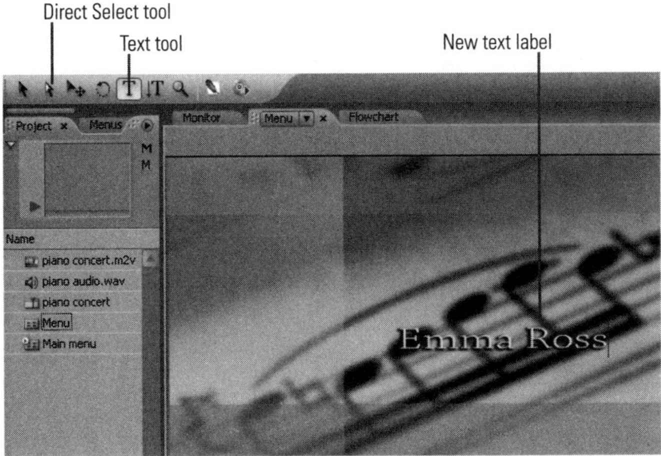

Figure 93a Click the Text tool and start typing to add text to a menu.

2. Click the Menu at the target location and enter the desired text.
3. To customize the text, click the Character tab in the Properties panel and drag over the text with your cursor (Encore DVD will display a yellow highlight box over the text). You can modify target font, font size, color, and other characteristics as desired (**Figure 93b**).

continued on next page

Encore DVD Retains Previous Text Characteristics

Once you get the desired "look" for your text buttons, type all of your buttons at once. Encore DVD will keep the same text characteristics until you change them, ensuring a consistent appearance.

Watch Your Button Order

DVD navigation works most smoothly when your buttons are sequentially numbered (See #100). To accomplish this, insert all text labels first, position them as desired, and then convert them to buttons in the order in which you'd like the viewer to browse.

Try Encore DVD's Libraries

Encore DVD has an extensive library of buttons in the Library panel (Figure 92a). Rather than starting from scratch with the Text tool, you can experiment with this content by dragging a button into the menu and modifying that button.

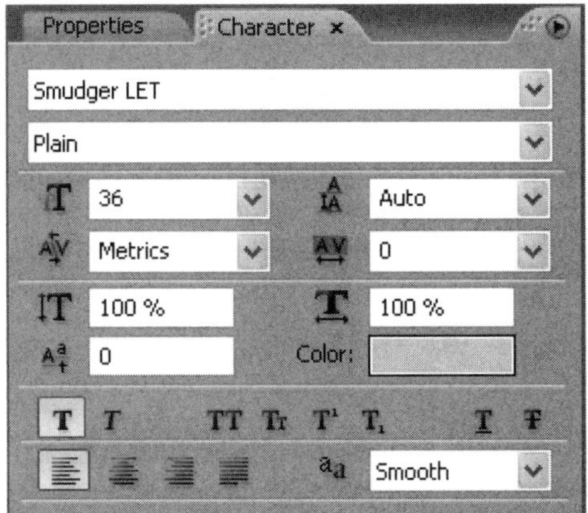

Figure 93b Modify font and other characteristics in the Character tab of the Properties panel.

4. Click the Direct Select tool in the Toolbox (Figure 93a).
5. Click the new text label. Encore DVD will place a bounding box around the text.
6. Choose Object > Convert to Button. Encore DVD will convert the text to a Normal button that you can link to either another menu or other content.

#94 Editing Text Buttons in Photoshop

When you create text buttons, Encore DVD automatically assigns a color set that controls button appearance when selected and activated. Sometimes, you'll want to augment these colors with highlights of your own, especially when producing DVDs for older or visually impaired viewers. To accomplish this, you'll need to edit in Photoshop. Here's how.

1. In Encore DVD, right-click the menu and choose Edit Menu in Photoshop from the pop-up menu that appears. Photoshop will run and load the menu file.

   Note

   Photoshop may display messages about updating text layers for vector output (click Update) and also warn you that pixel aspect ratio correction is enabled (click OK).

2. In the Photoshop Layers panel, click to select the text button layer set, and if necessary, twirl the triangle to the left of the layer set to open the set and reveal the text label.

3. Click the Create a new layer button at the bottom of the Layers panel (**Figure 94a**).

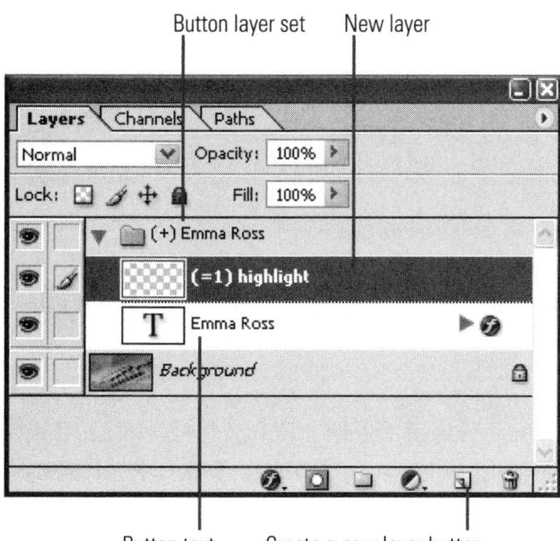

Figure 94a Adding a highlight layer above the text.

continued on next page

Undo Edit in Photoshop

If you don't like the new menu after Encore DVD inserts it, you can always undo the changes in Photoshop by choosing Edit > Undo Edit.

Choose Highlight Colors Carefully

Adobe doesn't define how Encore DVD chooses the automatic color set applied to custom highlights, so you can't control the colors; however, the selection process does take into account (but isn't controlled by) the colors you select in Photoshop. Be sure that you preview the buttons in both the highlighted and selected states before finalizing your settings to ensure that the assigned colors are acceptable. See page 162 of the Encore DVD manual for details.

Avoid Very Thin Lines

Avoid very thin lines (like underlining text) for your highlights, since these tend to flicker on some television sets. Try to use shapes that are at least 3 pixels wide.

Encore DVD Doesn't Use the Original Photoshop File

Encore DVD creates a new PSD file for all menu edits and does not change the original file imported into Encore DVD. If you make several layers of round-trip adjustments via this process, your original menu file will be totally different from the final menu. If you're using it as a template, or plan to create a motion menu with the menu, use Photoshop's File > Save As command to save over your original file or to a new file in a known location.

4. Rename the new layer (=1) highlight. This tells Encore DVD that this is the first highlight layer (you can have up to three).

5. Create the desired overlay or image (**Figure 94b**). Your options here are very broad, subject to the rules discussed in the following notes. The example uses the Custom Shape tool to draw an arrow in front of the button text. This arrow will appear when the button is selected and/or activated.

   Notes

   The overlay or image can contain only one solid color (no gradients) with no feathering or anti-aliasing.

   You can create up to three layers, each with an individual color. All three layers will appear when the button is selected and/or activated, and Encore DVD will automatically assign a color set for all three states. See page 154 of the Encore DVD manual for details.

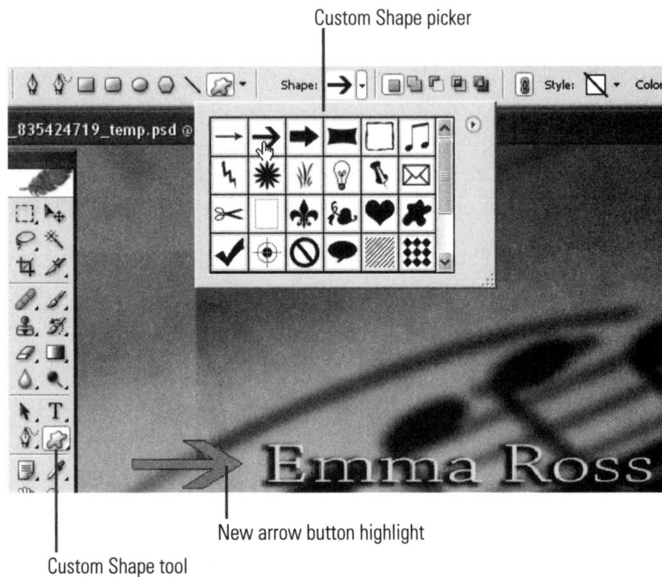

Figure 94b Creating an arrow that will appear when the button is selected and/or activated.

6. To change the color of the highlight, double-click the color chip in the highlight layer (**Figure 94c**). Photoshop will open the Color Picker dialog, which features an eyedropper tool that you can use to choose a color from the menu or from the Swatches panel. Click OK in the Color Picker dialog box to set the color.

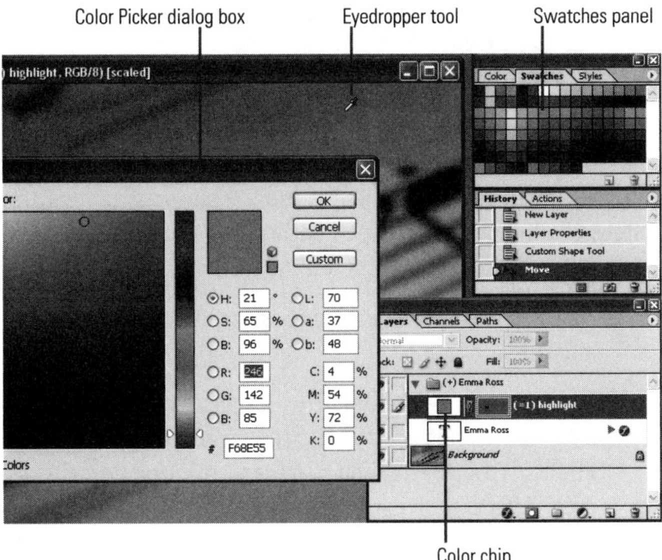

Figure 94c Changing the color of the highlight layer.

7. In the Photoshop menu, choose File > Save to save the file. Encore DVD will automatically update the menu once the file is saved.

For a Complete List of Photoshop Menu Syntax...

If you'd like to develop your menus and menu templates from scratch in Photoshop, you'll need a complete list of menu-related syntax. See pages 145–146 of the Encore DVD manual for details.

#95 Producing Motion Menus in After Effects

Set the Loop Point

Though your viewers may not be able to see your buttons or their final placement (depending upon the type of animation you produced), the clickable subpictures will remain active unless you deactivate them, which means viewers can click the buttons even if they can't see them. To deactivate your buttons while the animation is playing, check out #96.

The coolest motion menus are those that seamlessly animate into the actual menu that viewers use to view your content. Fortunately, the integration between Encore DVD and After Effects make these very simple to create. Here's the workflow.

1. In Encore DVD's Project panel, select the menu you want to animate.
2. Choose Menu > Create After Effects Composition. Encore DVD will prompt you to save the menu before opening After Effects. Type the desired name and location and click Save. After Effects will run and load the menu as a composition with nested compositions for each button (**Figure 95a**).

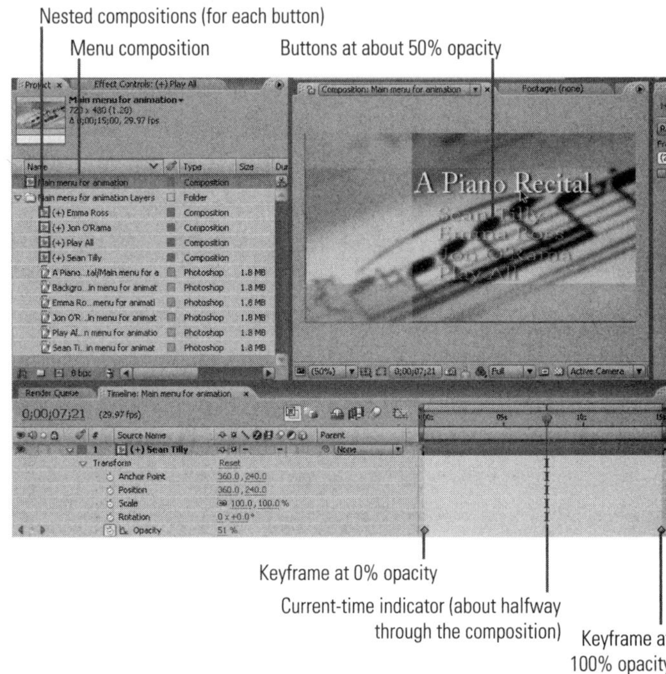

Figure 95a Here's the menu composition in After Effects. With the current-time indicator about halfway through the composition, the buttons are at about 50% opacity, on their trip from 0% to 100% opacity.

3. In the After Effects Project panel, double-click the menu composition to open it on the timeline.

4. Set an ending keyframe (see #43) for each menu parameter that you plan to animate, which will ensure that the final frame of the animation matches perfectly with the original menu. For example, this 15-second menu will fade the buttons in from 0% to 100% opacity. Accordingly, the first step is to set the opacity value for all buttons at 100% on the final frame of the composition.
5. Create the target animation. In the example, this means inserting a keyframe for each button at the start of the composition and adjusting the opacity to 0%.
6. Save the composition in After Effects.
7. In Encore DVD, click File > Adobe Dynamic Link > Import After Effects Composition. Encore DVD will open the Import Composition dialog. Navigate to and insert the main composition into Encore DVD (see #20).
8. Click the original Menu to make it active; then open the Properties panel (Figure 92a) and click the Motion tab.
9. In the Motion tab, drag the pick whip from the left of the Video settings to the imported After Effects composition. Release the pick whip once Encore DVD highlights the target composition (**Figure 95b**).

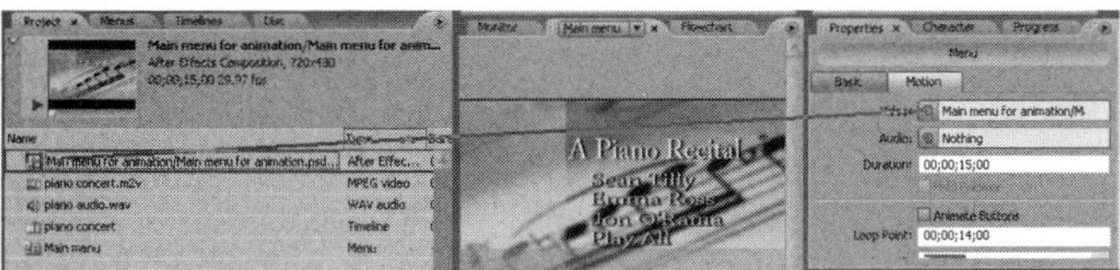

Figure 95b Use the pick whip to select the After Effects composition as the video background for the menu.

10. Click the Layers tab for the menu, and deselect the Eye icons next to all visible layers in the menu to make them transparent (**Figure 95c**).

continued on next page

Edit the Menu in After Effects

To make further changes in the After Effects composition, select it the Project panel and choose Edit > Edit Original. Note that if you change the original menu file upon which you based the composition in Encore DVD or Photoshop, After Effects won't automatically update the project, which may result in the last frame of your After Effects composition not matching the menu. You may have to start over in After Effects to ensure that the transition between the final frame of the animation and actual menu is seamless.

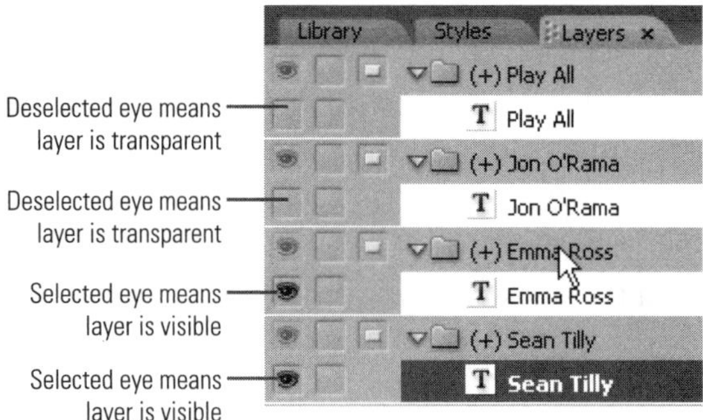

Figure 95c Click the eye icons next to all visible layers in the Encore DVD menu to make them transparent (since they'll show through in the After Effects animation).

Note

This will hide the buttons that will show through from the After Effects composition, but retain the subpictures, so viewers can still click to activate the button.

#96 Controlling Button Behavior in Motion Menus

With some motion menus, especially those with animated buttons, you may wish to deactivate the buttons until the animation finishes playing. To accomplish this, set a Loop Point for the video at the time the buttons should become active. The first time the viewer plays the menu, Encore DVD will deactivate the buttons until the Loop Point. During subsequent replays of the video, Encore will play the video after the Loop Point and keep the buttons active.

Here's where and how to set the Loop Point.

1. In the Project panel, click the Menu to make it active.
2. In the Menu Properties panel, set the Loop Point at the point you want the buttons to become active (**Figure 96**).

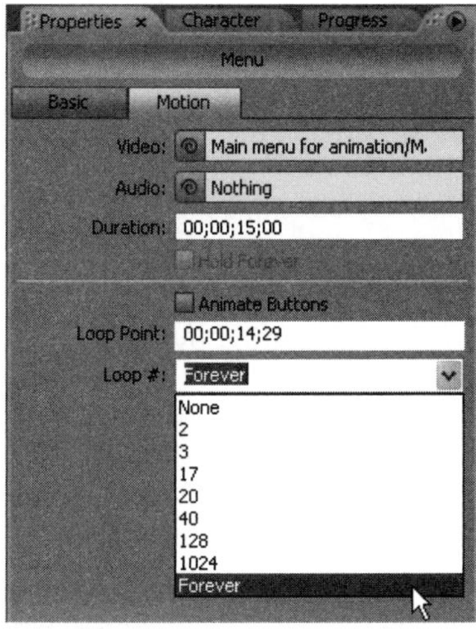

Figure 96 Setting the Loop Point and number of loops.

3. From the Loop # drop-down menu, set the desired number of times for the menu to loop.

Loop Point Recurrence

Each time the viewer plays the DVD, the cycle starts again, and the viewer must wait for the Loop Point before clicking any buttons. While this is probably acceptable for entertainment DVDs (if the cycle duration is short enough), waiting for the Loop Point may be irritating for some business or educational customers. For these customers, remember that just because you can loop your animation doesn't mean you should.

#97 Controlling the DVD Viewing Experience

Keep Your First Play Short

Your first play should be about 15 seconds or less. Not only will your viewers have to wait until it finishes playing each time they insert the disc—you will, too, each time you test or preview the disc.

What About "Overrides?"

Most Encore DVD End Actions have an "Override" option, which you can see in Figure 97. This was designed to provide an alternative End Action depending upon the button used to access the content. To be honest, I never really understood how it worked, and thankfully Adobe let me off the hook when they introduced playlists, covered in #98, in Encore version 1.5.

Whether your DVD is entertainment-oriented or educational, you'll optimize its impact if you control the viewing experience. Here are the questions you should ask yourself when producing the DVD, and the steps necessary to produce the desired results.

1. What happens when the viewer inserts the DVD?

   This is the "First Play" item, which can either be a menu or a video (like the FBI anti-piracy warnings on Hollywood DVDs, or a quick teaser or intro video). Designate the First Play by selecting the target content in the Project panel, right-clicking it, and choosing Set as First Play.

2. What happens after the First Play item concludes?

   This is the "End Action" for each piece of content or menu, i.e., where the DVD goes next—whether content, chapter, menu, or submenu. If you choose a menu for the First Play, you can set a duration for the menu by selecting it, clicking the Motion tab of the Menu Properties panel, and choosing a duration. Then choose an End Action in the Basic tab of the Menu Properties panel, say launching into the first movie on the menu. For example, you can display the menu for 30 seconds (the default), then launch the first video, which can be particularly useful when creating DVDs for kiosks or trade show use.

   If you choose a video for First Play, you must select an End Action to take place when the video finishes playing. In addition, you must choose an End Action for each timeline, playlist, slide show, and chapter point, or Encore will note the lack of an End Action during the preburn error check.

   You choose the End Action for all content in the respective Properties panel for that content. You can choose a button within a menu as an End Action (**Figure 97**), or a chapter point within a timeline, slideshow, or playlist. You select an End Action directly in the Properties panel using the End Action drop-down menu, or, when possible, by clicking and dragging the relevant pick whip.

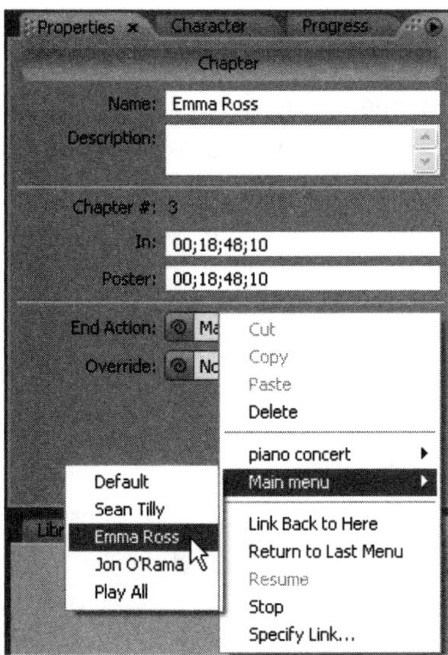

Figure 97 Choosing an End Action for the Emma Ross Chapter Point. You can use the menu as shown, or the pick whip.

3. Where does the viewer go when she clicks the Title button on her DVD remote?

   The default here is to proceed to the main menu with the default button selected, which is acceptable for most projects. You can change this disc default in the Disc Properties panel. (The Disc Properties panel appears automatically in the Properties panel when no menus, timelines, or assets are selected in the Project panel.)

4. Where does the viewer go when she clicks the Menu button on her DVD remote?

   The default here is to return to the originating menu (called the Last Menu in Encore DVD-speak), which, again, is acceptable for most projects. This is a timeline-specific default that you can change in the timeline Properties panel.

Think Through Your End Actions

End Actions exercise significant control over your viewer's experience. For example, when producing a wedding DVD, you probably have multiple chapter points that allow the viewer to directly access certain scenes, like the ceremony. But what happens when they reach the end of that scene? You can let the viewer continue to the next scene, or return to the originating menu, preferably with the button he or she just selected. It all depends upon how you think the viewer would want to enjoy the experience, and how you want the viewer to move through the content.

My practice varies by project. For example, for concerts, weddings, and training DVDs, where viewers may want to enjoy a specific scene, I tend to send the viewer back to the originating menu at the end of each scene (so the End Action is Return to Last Menu). For concerts and weddings, I also include a "Play All" button that allows the viewer to see the entire project. For ballets and similar performances, I let the viewers play through each scene, forcing them to use the Menu or Title button to return to the menu.

#98 Creating and Using Playlists

Create a Play All Button

Here's a common usage scenario for playlists. You've produced a wedding DVD with separate scenes accessible via chapter points with End Actions that return the viewer to the originating menu after playing each scene. But you also want one button that lets the viewer "Play All." The easiest way to accomplish this is with a playlist that links all chapters together.

Playlists link or group elements of disc content that do not appear sequentially in a DVD's navigational structure (e.g., Chapters 1, 2, 3, or scenes and their assigned End Actions) so that they play sequentially. Once created, a playlist looks like any other piece of content; you play it by linking it to a button, and assign it an End Action so Encore DVD knows what to do when it's finished playing.

Here's how to create such a Chapter Playlist.

1. In the Project panel, right-click and choose New > Chapter Playlist from the pop-up menu that appears. Encore DVD will open all timelines in a Select Timeline dialog (**Figure 98a**).

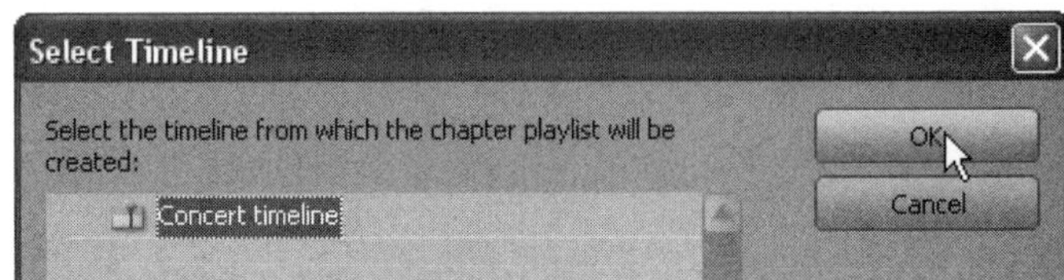

Figure 98a Choose which timeline to use as the basis for the Chapter Playlist.

2. Select the timeline and click OK. Encore creates a new Chapter Playlist and opens a dialog box displaying all chapter points from the Master Timeline (**Figure 98b**).

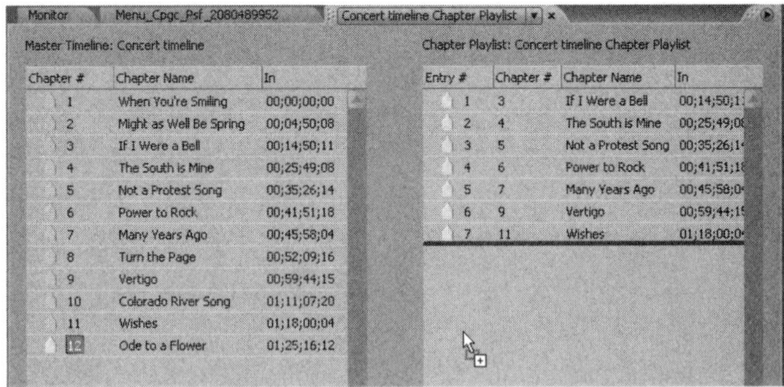

Figure 98b Click and drag the desired chapters from the Master Timeline to the Chapter Playlist in any order.

3. Drag the desired chapter points from the Master Timeline to the Chapter Playlist. You can insert the chapter points in any order, and reorder them in the Chapter Playlist column via drag and drop.
4. As with all DVD content, specify an End Action in the Chapter Playlist Properties panel, and link the Playlist to a button on a menu (or make it the First Play) so viewers can play it.
5. Close the Chapter Playlist dialog box to save your new playlist.

Customize a Concert Experience

Another playlist scenario would be a concert DVD in which the band played original music in songs 1, 3, 5, 7, and 9, and covers of songs written by other artists for the rest. If you want to let the viewer click one button and play only the original material, you would create a playlist that links these songs together.

#99 Manually Arranging Button Routing

Button routing controls where viewers go when using the arrow controls on their remote control. Normally, Encore DVD manages button routing automatically, but if you've added or arranged buttons manually, routings may need a bit of tweaking. Here's how.

1. In the Menu Properties panel, deselect the Automatically Route Buttons checkbox. This allows you to manually route the buttons.
2. Below the Menu window, click the Show Button Routing icon (**Figure 99**). Encore DVD will reveal the button routing in the Menu window.

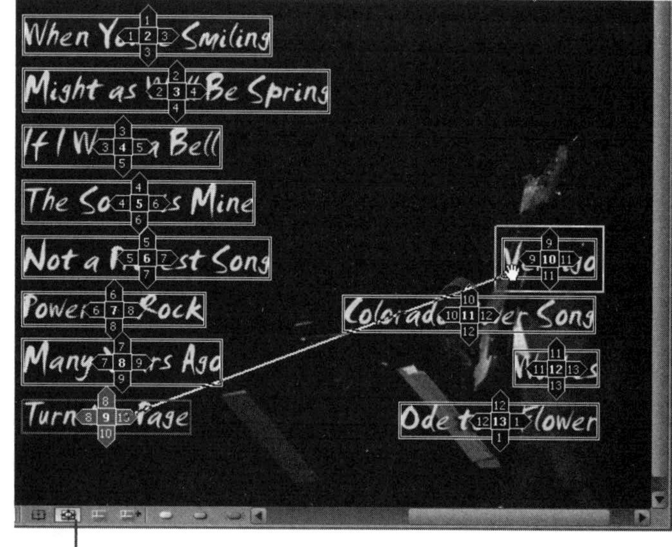

Figure 99 Click and drag the link to the target button.

Note

In the cross over each button, the center number is the number of that button, while the other numbers are the buttons currently assigned to that arrow key. For example, for button 13 in the lower-right corner of Figure 99, clicking the up arrow key would move the viewer to button 12, the right and left arrow keys to button 9, and the down arrow key to button 1 (not shown).

Consistency? Ease of Access?

With menus like the one shown in Figure 99, I typically choose consistency over ease of access, and cycle the viewer through all buttons in numerical order rather than by position. This means that the down and right arrow keys always send the viewer to the same button, as do the up and left arrow keys. I'm not advocating this approach as much as encouraging you to choose a navigational paradigm and stick to it.

3. To change the target for any button, click the arrow key and drag it to your button of choice. For example, in Figure 99, the right arrow key for button 9 is being reassigned from button 13 to button 10.
4. When finished, click the Show Button Routing icon to return to normal viewing mode.

#100 Previewing Your DVD

Here's a checklist of tests I perform before burning a DVD. Click File > Preview and join in (**Figure 100**).

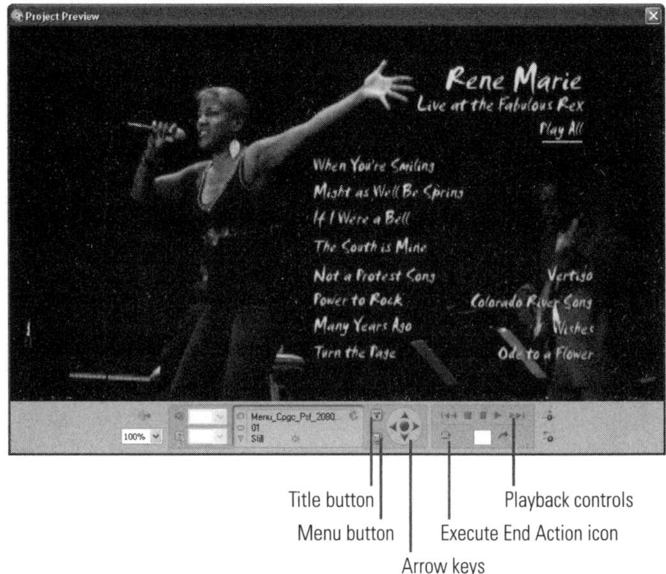

Figure 100 Encore DVD's very capable Project Preview panel.

1. Check First Play by addressing the following:
   - Does the correct video or menu appear (with the desired audio or video background).
   - If a menu, does it time out or loop as desired (if appropriate).
   - If a video, is the End Action correct? Click the Execute End Action icon to test it.
2. For each menu, check the following:
   - When you arrive at the menu, is the proper button highlighted? You control this for each menu in that menu's Properties panel with the Default Button setting.

- Check button routing using all four arrow keys through all buttons in the menu. Is operation consistent and logical? Do all arrow keys access all buttons?
- If a menu, does it time out properly and execute the appropriate End Action?

3. Click all navigational menus to navigate to and from all menus.
4. For all content buttons, check the following:
    - Does it play the target content?
    - Does the content have the correct End Action?
    - Does the DVD go to the correct menu when interrupted with title or remote menu buttons?

APPENDIX

Adobe Production Studio Integration Options

Adobe Production Studio's interapplication integration streamlines and shortens your production cycle while preserving video quality by reducing the number of rendering cycles. I discuss many of these integration features throughout the book, but I wanted to lay them out in one place for the three primary video production applications: After Effects, Premiere Pro, and Encore DVD.

Adobe After Effects

Photoshop

- Create new Adobe Photoshop File automatically creates a file with the proper resolution and aspect ratio and opens the file within Photoshop for editing (File > New > Adobe Photoshop File).
- Import existing Adobe Photoshop file either as Footage, which merges the layers or imports a single layer, or as Composition, which preserves layers for editing (File > Import).
- Edit Original allows you to edit a PSD file in Photoshop, with all edits to *existing layers* (but not new layers) automatically updating within After Effects (Select a PSD file in After Effects, and choose Edit > Edit Original).

Illustrator

- Import existing Adobe Illustrator file, either as Footage, which merges the layers or imports a single layer, or as Composition, which preserves layers for editing (File > Import).

- Edit Original allows you to edit an AI file in Illustrator, with all edits to *existing layers* (but not new layers) automatically updating within After Effects (Select an AI file in After Effects, and choose Edit > Edit Original).

Premiere Pro

- Copy and paste content from Premiere Pro's timeline to an After Effects composition (#18).
- Import a Premiere Pro project into After Effects for further editing (#19).
- Capture within After Effects using Premiere Pro's Capture function (File > Import > Capture in Adobe Premiere Pro).

Audition

- Edit in Adobe Audition allows you to edit an audio file imported into After Effects in Audition, with all edits automatically flowing through to After Effects (Select an audio file in After Effects, and choose Edit > Edit in Adobe Audition).

Adobe Premiere Pro

Photoshop

- Create new Adobe Photoshop file automatically creates a file with the proper resolution and aspect ratio and opens the file within Photoshop for editing (#61).
- Import existing Adobe Photoshop file either as Footage, which merges the layers or imports a single layer, or as Sequence, which preserves layers for editing (#61).
- Edit in Adobe Photoshop allows you to edit a PSD file in Photoshop, with all edits automatically flowing through to Premiere Pro.

Illustrator

- Import existing Adobe Illustrator file as a single layer (#62).
- Edit Original allows you to edit an AI file in Illustrator, with all edits to *existing layers* (but not new layers) automatically flowing through to Premiere Pro (Select an AI file in Premiere Pro, and choose Edit > Edit Original).

After Effects

- Import existing After Effects composition via Dynamic Link allows all subsequent edits in After Effects to automatically flow through to Premiere Pro (#20).
- Create new After Effects composition from within Premiere Pro—The composition uses the appropriate preset and automatically appears in the Premiere Pro Project panel (#20).

Audition

- Edit in Adobe Audition allows you to edit an audio file imported into Premiere Pro in Audition, with all edits automatically flowing through to Premiere Pro (#73).

Adobe Encore DVD

Photoshop

- Import existing Photoshop file as a menu—Layers remain intact, and defined syntax for highlights and other menu elements allow complete menu creation within Photoshop (#92).
- Edit existing menu in Photoshop allows you to edit a menu in Photoshop, with all edits automatically flowing through to Encore DVD (#94).

Premiere Pro

- Insert markers into the Premiere Pro timeline to serve as chapter points in an Encore DVD timeline (#91).

Encore DVD–After Effects

- Import existing After Effects composition via Dynamic Link allows you to import a composition, with all edits in After Effects automatically flowing through to Encore DVD (#95).
- Create new After Effects composition from within Adobe Encore DVD—Choose File > Adobe Dynamic Link > New After Effects Composition. The composition uses the appropriate preset and automatically appears in the Adobe Encore DVD Project panel.

Index

A

Acrobat, 178, 180
Action Safe zone, 99
Adobe Bridge, 14, 140, 141
Adobe Gamma, 47
Adobe Media Encoder, 186–189
After Effects. *See also* compositions
  copying/pasting from Premiere Pro, 41–42
  creating compositions in Premiere Pro, 39, 45–46
  creating title backgrounds in, 140–142
  custom output presets, 198–199
  described, 37
  editing menus in, 223
  effects in, 42
  exporting projects into Premiere Pro, 45–46
  getting started with, 38–40
  image stabilization, 64–66
  importing projects from Premiere Pro, 38, 43–44
  integration with Audition, 236
  integration with Encore DVD, 237
  integration with Illustrator, 235
  integration with Photoshop, 235
  integration with Premiere Pro, 37–46, 236–237
  interface, 38–40
  Keylight Effect, 107–108
  motion backgrounds, 210
  motion tracking in, 117–119
  presets, 40, 198–199
  producing Flash files in, 196
  producing motion menus in, 222–224
  re-editing compositions in, 46
  rendering in, 195–197
  sepia effect, 101
  text animation, 143–145
  timeline, 43
  working in, 38
.ai files, 139
alpha channels, 191, 192
anchor point, 121–122
animation
  deactivating buttons during, 222
  looping, 225
  presets, 144
  text, 143–145
  video clips in Premiere Pro, 114–116
Apply to All Text Items button, 209
arrow keys, 230–233
artifacts, 193, 194
Aspect HD tool, 8
aspect ratio
  correcting, 150, 151–152
  pixel aspect ratio (PAR), 8, 182, 183
  resizing and, 148
  types of, 2, 182
assets, 14, 214
audio, 161–175. *See also* Audition
  clip gain, 162
  distortion, 169–170, 174
  exporting from Premiere Pro, 184–185
  headphones, 168
  importing, 23–24, 164
  microphones, 173–175
  mixing, 163
  narrations, 173–175
  noise, 166, 168–170
  normalizing, 166–167
  playing, 165
  quality of, 2, 161
  removing pops/clicks in, 171–172
  selecting in Source Monitor, 23–24
  streaming, 165
  synchronizing with video, 72–75
  troubleshooting, 173
  volume, 162, 163, 166–167, 174
  working with, 26, 162–163
audio files
  importing, 164
  loading into Audition, 161
  markers in, 167
  as menu background, 209, 210, 214
  naming, 185
  recording, 173–175
  storing, 185
Audio Mixer, 9, 163
audio point, 72
Audio tab, 184–185, 188–189
audio tracks, 6, 78
audio transitions, 163
audio waveforms, 23–24, 72, 83
Audition. *See also* audio
  basics of, 161, 164–165
  creating narrations in, 173–175
  getting started in, 164–165
  importing files, 164
  integration with After Effects, 236
  integration with Premiere Pro, 237
  loading audio files into, 161
  normalizing audio in, 166–167
  playing files in, 165
  reducing noise in, 168–170
  removing pops/clicks in, 171–172
Auto Color effect, 55–56
Auto Levels effect, 51
auto-play DVDs, 203, 207
Autodesk Cleaner XL tool, 188
Automate to Sequence feature, 21, 22, 124

B

B-roll footage, 31–35
background music, 162–163
backgrounds
  aligning with objects, 114–116
  blurring, 103
  compositions as, 223
  menus, 209, 210
  motion, 141–142, 210
  presets, 141, 142
  titles, 131–132, 140–142
backlight issues, 53–54
BackTraxx music library, 163
Balance Angle tool, 57, 62
Balance Gain adjustment, 57, 58
Balance Magnitude tool, 57
Band Wipe transition, 126
"banding," 53
batch encoding, 195
batch processing images, 148–149
behaviors, button, 225
beveled edges, 99
bins, 20
bit depth, 183
Bitrate settings, 188
black-and-white video, 102
black pixels, 101
Blu-ray format, 202
blue frames, 99
blurring, 103, 112, 113
BMP format, 182
bracketing, 51
Bridge, 14, 140, 141
brightness, 48–52, 93, 101
broadcast-legal limits, 49
Browse command, 14
Build process, 216
burning DVDs, 203–204
buttons
  behaviors, 225
  color, 219
  content, 233
  creating in Encore DVD, 214–215
  deactivating, 222, 225

default, 227, 232
hiding, 224
library of, 217
links to, 211, 215
naming, 206
navigation, 230
opacity, 222–223
order, 217, 230
playing animation and, 222
routing, 230–231, 233
states, 219–221
targets, 230, 231
text, 217–221
thumbnail, 207

C

camcorder, 16–18, 71–89
camera angles, 78–83
Camera View effect, 115
"Capture Device Offline" message, 17–18
Capture panel, 16–17
capturing video. *See* video capture
chapter indexes, 215
chapter playlist, 228–229
chapter points, 205, 211–215, 228–229
chapters, 205, 211–212, 228–229
chroma, 48, 49
chroma key effects, 103–107, 191
Cinescore library, 163
Clip Gain, 162, 166–167
Clip Notes, 178–181
Clip Overlap option, 22
clips
adding to sequences, 22
captured, 16
deleting from timeline, 83
layering, 84–85
moving, 84
naming, 16, 19
opacity, 92–93
rearranging in Premiere Pro, 21–22
source, 31–33, 76–77
subclips, 19–20
synchronizing, 72–75
untitled, 16
Closed Bezier, 111–112, 113
Collapse/Expand Track control, 162
color
buttons, 219
converting black-and-white to, 102
highlight, 219–221
intensity, 48, 57
saturation, 57, 102
sepia effect, 100–101
text, 144
titles, 131
Color Balance (HLS) effect, 102
color casts, 57, 60, 76
color correction
with Fast Color Corrector, 57–59
Multi-Camera projects, 62, 76–77
reference monitors, 50, 76
resetting to defaults, 61
setting up for, 50
with Three-Way Color Corrector, 60–61
with YC Waveform scope, 48–49
Color Correction widget, 58, 62
Color Correction workspaces, 50
color depth, 183
Color Finesse feature, 55
Color Picker, 131, 220
color signal, 48
color wheel, 58
comments, 178–181
Composition panel, 39
compositions, 39–42. *See also* After Effects
as backgrounds, 223
copying/pasting content, 41–42
creating, 41, 45–46, 222
duration of, 140, 145
importing into Encore DVD, 223
nested, 222
opening in Premiere Pro, 42, 45
opening on timeline, 222
opening Premiere Pro sequences as, 43–44
settings, 39, 40
computer monitor, 47, 49
constant bit rate (CBR), 188, 190
Constant Gain, 163
Constrain Proportions checkbox, 148
content. *See also* media
adding chapter points to, 215
adding from Source Monitor, 25–26
adding to existing footage, 27–28
copying/pasting to After Effects, 41–42
importing into Encore DVD, 214
linking buttons to, 215
organizing, 20
content buttons, 233
contrast, 49, 51, 52
corrective effects, 68–69
crawls, title, 133–135
Creative Suite Production Studio. *See* Production Studio
credit rolls, 19, 133–135
Crossfade transition, 163
Ctrl key, 28
current-time indicator, 94, 95
Custom Shape tool, 220

D

date/time features, 16
Default Sequence window, 6
deinterlacing, 158, 183, 193–194
design primitives, 111–112, 131–132
Desktop editing mode, 8
Direct Select tool, 217, 218
Disc Properties panel, 227
dissolves, 95, 98
distortion, 150, 169–170, 174
Dolby Digital format, 189
Draft Quality option, 50
drop shadows, 99, 112
drop zones, 11
DV-AVI format, 187, 193
DV format, 193
DV frames, 182–183
DV/HDV camcorders, 17
DV video
resolution, 182
upconverting to HDV, 87
DVD markers, 205–206, 209
DVD menus, 209–210. *See also* menus
checking for errors, 232–233
consistency *vs.* ease of use, 230
creating in Encore DVD, 214–215
customizing with Photoshop, 209–210
duration of, 226
editing, 223
linking chapter points to, 215
looping, 225
main, 227
motion, 222–225
navigation, 233
synchronizing with titles, 127–128
templates for, 207–208
DVD recorders, 204
DVDs
auto-play, 203, 207
building, 216
burning, 203–204
checking for errors, 216, 232–233
concert, 229
controlling viewing experience, 226–227
end action, 226–227, 229, 232, 233
first play, 226, 232
formats, 202
hard disk space requirements, 203
Loop Point, 225
"menu-less," 203–204
menus. *See* DVD menus

DVDs *(continued)*
- naming, 204
- navigation, 217
- playlists, 228–229
- previewing, 232–233
- producing in Encore DVD, 213–233
- remote control, 230–231
- scenes menus, 202, 206, 207
- templates, 207–208

DVI adapter, 12
Dynamic Link, 43–46, 140, 143, 223

E

Ease-In/Ease-Out options, 134
edges, 99, 112
edit point, 125
edit sequence, 71
editing
- essential techniques, 15–35
- four-point, 34–35
- HDV, 86–89
- images, 148
- insert edits, 27–28, 33
- markers, 206
- menus in After Effects, 223
- menus in Premiere Pro, 208
- Multi-Camera projects. *See* multi-camera editing
- overlay edits, 27–28
- overwrite edits, 27
- PSD files, 136
- rolling edits, 82–83
- text buttons, 219–221
- three-point, 31–33
- undoing edits in Photoshop, 219

Effect Controls panel, 9, 39
effect parameters, 142
effects, 91–122. *See also* mattes
- applying to layers, 43
- Auto Color, 55–56
- black-and-white to full-color, 102
- Camera View, 115
- chroma key, 103–107
- copying, 153
- customizing with keyframes, 94–95
- fades, 95
- Fast Color Corrector, 57–59
- importing and, 43
- Keylight Effect, 107–108
- layered, 84–85
- overlay, 84–85, 92–93
- pan, 155–156, 160
- pasting, 67, 153
- picture-in-picture, 98–99
- presets, 68–69
- sepia, 100–101, 109–110
- Three-Way Color Corrector, 60–61
- Track Motion, 117–119
- tracking, 117–119
- zoom, 155–156, 160

Effects and Presets panel, 39
Effects panel, 9, 10–11
ellipses, creating, 111–112
email, 180
Embed Video option, 179, 180
encoding, batch, 195
Encore DVD, 213–233
- chapter markers, 211–212
- creating buttons in, 214–218
- getting started with, 214–216
- importing After Effects compositions into, 223
- importing content into, 214
- integration with After Effects, 237
- integration with Photoshop, 237
- integration with Premiere Pro, 237
- interface, 214
- libraries, 217
- menus in. *See* DVD menus
- playlists, 228–229
- *vs.* Premiere Pro, 202

End Action item, 226–227, 229, 232, 233
end points, 75
Enter key, 30
exporting
- audio from Premiere Pro, 184–185
- for Clip Notes, 178–181
- DV frames, 182–183
- Flash video, 190–192
- frames from Premiere Pro, 182–183
- HDV frames, 182–183
- presets for, 186–187
- streaming audio, 165
- video with Adobe Media Encoder, 186–189

"Extend my Windows desktop" option, 12
eyedropper, 58

F

fade effects, 94, 95, 98, 100
Fast Blur filter, 103
Fast Color Corrector effect, 57–59
favorites, 171, 172
file formats, 4, 8, 18, 150, 202. *See also specific formats*
files. *See also* project files
- .ai, 139
- audio. *See* audio files
- finding, 14
- Flash, 196
- importing as assets, 214
- multiple-format, 188
- naming, 16
- organizing with Bridge, 14
- PDF, 178–181
- project, 3, 16
- PSD, 136–137, 220
- QuickTime, 189
- selecting, 14
- video. *See* video files
- XFDF, 179, 180

filters, 41, 42, 158. *See also specific filters*
finding items, 11, 14
First Play item, 226, 232
Flash 8 Video Encoder, 190
flash cameras, 72
Flash files, 196
Flash video, 7, 190–192
flicker, 56, 160, 220
Flix Pro encoder, 190
FLV format, 186, 190
fonts, 127, 144, 209, 210, 217, 218
footage
- adding content to, 27
- B-roll, 31–33
- deinterlacing, 183, 194
- HDV, 86, 87–88
- importing Photoshop files as, 149
- limiting during rendering, 30
- overlay, 93
- widescreen, 182

Footage option, 149
four-point editing, 34–35
Fractal Type effect, 142
frame-based video, 193
Frame Hold control, 157–158
frame rates, 2
frames
- blue, 99
- deinterlacing, 193–194
- DV, 182–183
- exporting from Premiere Pro, 182–183
- freeze, 157–158
- HDV, 182–183
- size, 183
- splitting, 157–158
- still, 157–158
- video, 182–183

FTP settings, 179, 189

G

gamma values, 51, 56
garbage mattes, 96–97, 105
General settings, 5–6
GIF format, 182
graphics cards, 13

H

handles, 29, 97
HD DVD format, 202
HDV cameras, 4
HDV devices, 4
HDV/DV camcorders, 17
HDV DVDs, 2–4
HDV editing, 86–89
HDV frames, 182–183
HDV video
  interlacing, 193
  mixing with DV video, 87
  panning/zooming, 86, 87–88
  presets, 3
  resolution, 4, 86, 182
  using with SD video, 4, 87, 89
headphones, 168
heads, 124, 125
Highest Quality Output option, 50
highlights, 53–54, 60, 219–221
histograms, 51
History panel, 10
Hold Filters option, 158
Hold On option, 158
Horizontal Type tool, 143
Hue Angle tool, 57

I

Icon view, 21, 22
Illustrator, 139, 235, 236
images
  batch processing, 148–149
  distortion, 150
  duration, 154
  editing, 148
  ISO, 203
  managing in Premiere Pro, 153–154
  moving in 3D space, 115
  panning/zooming, 148, 155–156, 160
  preprocessing in Photoshop, 148–149, 159
  resizing, 148
  rotating, 114
  royalty-free, 14
  scaling, 153–154
  stabilizing, 63–66
importing
  After Effects compositions into Encore DVD, 223
  After Effects projects into Premiere Pro, 45–46
  assets as timelines, 214
  audio, 23, 164
  Clip Notes comments, 181
  content into Encore DVD, 214
  files as assets, 214
  Illustrator files, 139
  image size and, 148
  logos into Titler, 132
  Photoshop files, 136–137
  Photoshop layers, 136, 138
  Premiere Pro projects into After Effects, 38, 43–44
  projects into other projects, 5–6
  as sequences, 136–137
  single-layer Photoshop files, 149
  titles with Dynamic Link, 140, 143
  video assets, 214
  video files as timelines, 214
In/Out points, 24, 31–35
indexes, chapter, 215
Info panel, 10, 39
insert edits, 27–28, 33
"Insufficient media" message, 125
interpolation, 87–88, 116
IRE (International Radio Engineers), 48
ISO images, 203

K

key frame values, 88
keyframes
  adding, 88, 89, 94–95, 163
  adjusting volume, 162
  customizing effects with, 94–95
  interpolation, 87–88
  removing, 163
  setting to "Hold," 87, 88
  smoothing motion, 116
Keylight Effect, 107–108

L

layered effects, 84–85
layering clips, 84–85
layers
  applying effects to, 43
  creating, 85
  multiple, 43
  Photoshop, 136
  transparent, 223–224
level adjustments, 51–52
lighting, 76
linear interpolation, 88
List view, 21
locking tracks, 27
loop point, 222, 225
looping playback, 204, 225
luma, 48
luminance signal, 48, 49

M

Magic Bullet plug-in, 101
main menu, 205–207, 227
markers
  in audio files, 167
  chapter, 205, 211–212
  DVD, 205–206, 209
  editing, 206
  Main Menu, 205, 206
  scene, 205, 207
  snapping, 74
  Stop, 205–206
  synching clips with, 72–73
  text, 209
mattes. *See also* effects
  creating for titles, 146
  creating in Photoshop, 112
  creating in Premiere Pro, 111–112
  creating with design primitives, 111–112
  garbage, 96–97, 105
  Track Matte Key, 113
  working with in Premiere Pro, 109–110
media, 125, 204. *See also* content
Menu button, 227
menus. *See also* DVD menus
  audio in, 209
  backgrounds, 209, 210
  editing, 208, 209
  motion, 210, 222–225
  scenes, 202, 206, 207
  templates, 127–128
microphones, 173–175
midtones, 56, 60
mixed target feature, 26
Mixer device, 173
mixing audio, 163
monitors, 12–13, 50, 76. *See also* television
Mosaic filter, 113
motion
  adding to text, 135
  in background, 141–142, 210
  in menus, 210, 222–225
  smoothing, 116
  stabilizing, 63–66
Motion Controls, 135
motion tracking, 117–122
MP3 format, 165
MPEG-1 format, 186
MPEG-2 format, 186–189
Multi-Cam events, 71
multi-camera editing
  adding transitions, 82
  camera angles, 78–83
  editing sequences on timeline, 82–83
  HDV editing, 86–89
  overlay effects, 84–85
  perfecting source clips, 76–77
  playing audio tracks, 78
  synching clips on timeline, 74–75

multi-camera editing *(continued)*
synching clips with markers, 72–73
tips for, 81
Multi-Camera Monitor
color correction with, 77
fixing mistakes in, 81
illustrated, 79
opening, 79
overlay effects, 84–85
playing audio tracks in, 78
tips for using, 81
multi-camera production, 71–89
Multi-Camera projects
color correction, 62, 76–77
editing. *See* multi-camera editing
mixing HDV/DV in, 87
synchronization, 79
Multi-Camera workflows, 79
multi-scene projects, 184
multi-track mixing, 163
multiple-format files, 188
Multiplexer settings, 189
music, 162–163

N

narrations, 173–175
navigation, 217, 230, 233
nested compositions, 222
nested sequences, 78, 137–138
Next button, 205
noise, 166, 168–172, 175, 187
normalization, 166–167, 174
NTSC DVDs, 2–3
NTSC monitor, 47, 106

O

On2 VP6 codec, 190
opacity, 92–93, 95, 222–223
optical media, 180
overexposure, 53
overlay edits, 27–28, 33
overlay effects, 84–85, 92–93, 98–99
Overlay icon, 27
Override option, 226
overwrite edits, 27

P

pan-and-zoom effect, 155–156, 160
panels, working with, 9–11
panning, 86, 87–88
PCM format, 188, 189
PDF files, 178–181
Pen tool, 112
photos, stock, 14
Photoshop
aspect ratio and, 148
creating mattes in, 112
customizing menus with, 209–210
editing text buttons in, 219–221
integration with After Effects, 235
integration with Encore DVD, 237
integration with Premiere Pro, 236
layers, 136
preprocessing images in, 148–149, 159
resizing in, 148
title creation, 136–138
transparency, 136
"piano-edit," 71
pick whip, 215, 223
picture-in-picture effect, 98–99
pixel aspect ratio (PAR), 8, 182, 183
pixelation, 86
pixels
"banding," 53
black, 101
brightness, 48, 49, 51
contrast, 49, 51, 52
"crushed," 51
overexposed, 58
rectangular, 150
square, 8, 150–152, 182
white, 58, 62, 101
Play All button, 227
Play Movie button, 207
playback, looping, 204, 225
Playback Settings control, 13
playing audio, 165
playlists, 228–229
Position property, 87–89
Postroll option, 134
Premiere Elements, 18, 202
Premiere Pro
animating clips in, 114–116
Clip Notes, 178–181
converting clips to sepia, 100–101
copying/pasting from After Effects to, 41–42
creating After Effects compositions in, 45–46
creating After Effects projects from, 39
creating chapter markers for Encore DVD, 211–212
creating mattes in, 111–112
creating scene markers in, 205–206
creating slide shows in, 159–160
customizing DVD menus in, 209–210
deinterlacing in, 183
DVD production, 201–212
DVD templates, 207–208
exporting audio from, 184–185
exporting frames from, 182–183
image stabilization, 63
importing projects from After Effects, 45–46
importing projects into After Effects, 38, 43–44
integration with After Effects, 37–46, 236–237
integration with Audition, 237
integration with Encore DVD, 237
integration with Illustrator, 236
integration with Photoshop, 236
interface, 9–11
managing images in, 153–154
"menu-less" DVDs, 203–204
multi-camera production in, 71–89
normalizing audio in, 166–167
opening After Effects compositions in, 45
organizing content, 20
pan effects, 155–156, 160
preprocessing images in Photoshop, 148–149, 159
project presets, 2–4
stabilizing images in, 63
storyboarding in, 21–22
supported formats, 150
title templates, 129–130
using tracking data in, 120–122
using with After Effects, 37–46
vs. Encore DVD, 202
working with dual monitors, 12–13
working with mattes in, 109–110
zoom effects, 155–156, 160
Premiere Pro projects. *See* projects
Preroll option, 134
presets
After Effects, 40, 198–199
animation, 144
applying, 68, 69
backgrounds, 141, 142
capture, 8
Clip Notes, 179
corrective effects, 68–69
custom, 7–8, 188, 198–199
effects, 68–69
export, 186–187
FLV7, 190
naming, 68, 188, 199
output, 198–199
picture-in-picture effect, 98
projects, 2–4, 7–8
storing, 68–69
streaming video, 188
Presets folder, 68–69
previews
DVD, 232–233

NTSC monitor, 106
resolution, 50
on television, 47, 106
with work area bar, 29–30
Previous button, 205
primitives, 111–112, 131–132
Production Studio
described, 1
integration options, 37–46, 235–237
program incompatibilities, 43
programs included in, 1
updates to, 2
Program Monitor, 9, 48
progressive output, 193–194
project files, 3, 16. *See also* files; projects
Project panel, 9, 10–11, 22, 39
projects
importing from Premiere Pro to After Effects, 43–44
importing into other projects, 5–6
multi-scene, 184
nonstandard, 7
organizing, 20
presets, 2–4, 7–8
saving compositions as, 42
PSD files, 136–137, 220

Q

quality
audio, 2, 161
video, 47–69
QuickTime files, 189
QuickTime format, 178, 179, 186

R

Razor tool, 157–158
RealAudio format, 164, 165
RealMedia format, 186, 188, 189
recording audio, 173–175
rectangular pixels, 150
reference monitors, 50, 76
remote control, 230–231
remote menu buttons, 230–231, 233
rendering, 30, 195–197
Repair Transient filter, 171–172
Reset button, 61
resolution
4:3, 13
16:9, 3
DV, 182
HDV, 4, 86, 182
multiple output resolutions, 7
nonstandard, 7
previews, 50
video, 2, 7
reviewer comments, 178–181
RGB Parade scope, 62
RGB values, 101
rolling credits, 133–135, 157
rolling edits, 82–83
rotation, 114
rubber band controls, 95

S

Safe Margins, 99
saturation, 57, 102
Scale property, 87–89
scaling images, 153–154
scene changes, 59
scene detection, 16
scene markers, 205–207
Scene Selection button, 207
scenes menus, 202, 206, 207
scrolling credits, 157
SD DVDs, 2–4
SD video, 3–5, 87, 89
search function, 11, 14
sepia effect, 100–101, 109–110
sequences
adding clips to, 22
adding source clip sections to, 31–33
importing Photoshop files as, 136–137
jumping between, 87
nested, 78, 137–138
opening as compositions, 43–44
Shadow/Highlight filter, 53–54, 101
shadows, 53–54, 60, 99, 112
Show/Hide Effects button, 93, 98, 114, 155
slide shows, 147–158
SmartSound, 163
Snap Neutral Midtones option, 56
snapping markers, 74
Sorenson Spark Codec, 190
Sorenson Squeeze tool, 188, 190
source clips, 31–33, 76–77
Source Monitor
adding content from, 25–26
audio selection in, 23–24
choosing scopes in, 48
illustrated, 9
video selection in, 23–24
sourcing overlay footage, 93
special effects. *See* effects
split screens, 96–97
Split View options, 57–59
square pixels, 8, 150–152, 182
Stabilize Motion tool, 64–66
steadycam, 63, 66
still frames, 157–158
stock photos, 14
Stop markers, 205–206
storyboarding, 21–22, 154
streaming video, 8, 128, 179, 188, 193
subclips, 19–20. *See also* clips
SWF format, 190, 196
synch points, 72
synch sequence, 71
synchronization
audio/video, 72–75
clip deletion and, 83
clips to target tracks, 74
clips with markers, 72–73
moving clips and, 84
Multi-Camera projects, 79
titles with DVD menus, 127–128

T

tails, 124, 125
Targa format, 182
target tracks, 74
targeting tracks, 25–26
targets, button, 230, 231
television. *See also* monitors
broadcast, 49
flicker on, 220
previewing on, 47, 106
remote control, 230–231
text size, 127
templates
DVD menus, 127–128
DVDs, 207–208
output module, 198–199
title, 129–130
temporal interpolation, 87–88
Temporal Smoothing parameter, 53, 56
text
adding motion to, 135
animating, 143–145
color, 144, 217
credits/crawls, 19, 133–135
customizing, 217
diagonal, 131
fonts, 127, 144, 209, 217, 218
highlights, 219–221
marker, 209
size, 144, 217
vertical, 131
text buttons, 217–221
three-point editing, 31–33
Three-Way Color Corrector, 60–61
thumbnails, 22, 207
TIF format, 182
time codes, 16
Time Controls panel, 39
time/date setting, 16
Timecode Display, 155
timeline
adding content to existing footage, 27–28

timeline *(continued)*
adding source clip sections to sequences, 31–33
After Effects, 43
deleting clips from, 83
editing multi-camera sequence on, 82–83
importing assets as, 214
importing video files as, 214
moving to points on, 155
synching clips on, 74–75
Timeline panel, 9, 39
Timeline Timecode Display, 155
timeline tracks, 77
Tint Effect, 100–101
Title button, 227, 233
Title Safe zone, 99
title templates, 129–130
Title tool, 99
Titler
creating mattes in, 111–112
design primitives, 131–132
importing logos into, 132
interface, 132
rolling credits, 133–135
titles
backgrounds, 131–132, 140–142
color, 131
creating in Illustrator, 139
creating in Photoshop, 136–138
credits/crawls, 133–135
fonts, 127
full-screen, 129
importing with Dynamic Link, 140, 143
inserting into video, 25–26
lower-third, 129
matte effects, 146
rolling text, 133–135
saving, 130
storage of, 129
streaming video, 128
synchronizing with DVD menus, 127–128
templates for, 129–130
text size, 127
tonal ranges, 60–61
Track Matte Key, 113
Track Motion effect, 117–119
Tracker controls, 64–65
tracking data
After Effects, 117–119
Premiere Pro, 120–122
tracking motion, 117–122
tracks
audio, 6, 78
default number of, 6
locked/unlocked, 27, 28
naming/renaming, 77
order, 77
shifting of, 27
targeting, 25–26
video, 6, 25–26
transitions
adding to edit point, 125
audio, 163
in beginning/end of credits, 133
default, 124, 126
dissolves, 95
duration, 124, 126, 159
inserting, 82
keyboard shortcuts, 82
pan-and-zoom effects and, 156, 160
slide shows, 159
tips for, 124–126
transparency
clips, 94–95
Illustrator and, 139
layers, 223–224
Photoshop, 136
Trim tool, 85
tripods, 63, 71
troubleshooting
audio, 173
black lines on bottom of screen, 63–66, 86
"Capture Device Offline" message, 17–18
Type tool, 133

U

Undo Edit command, 219
unlocked tracks, 27, 28
updates, downloading, 2

V

variable bitrate encoding (VBR), 188
VGA-to-DVI adapter, 12
video
black-and-white to full-color, 102
blurring portion of, 113
capturing. *See* video capture
converting to sepia, 100–101
deinterlacing, 193–194
DV, 87, 182
exporting. *See* exporting
Flash, 7, 186–189
flicker, 56
frame-based, 193
frame rate, 2
HDV. *See* HDV video
importing, 214
picture-in-picture effect, 98–99
quality of, 47–69
resolution, 2, 7
SD, 3–5, 87, 89
selecting in Source Monitor, 23–24
sepia, 100–101
shaky, 63
split screens, 96–97
streaming, 8, 128, 179, 188, 193
synchronizing with audio, 72–75
video assets, 214
video capture
capture device offline, 17–18
formats for, 4, 17, 18
naming files and, 16
presets, 8
scene detection, 16
video clips
animating in Premiere Pro, 114–116
converting to sepia, 100–101
importing audio from, 23–24
Video Effects folder, 51
video files, 178–181, 214
video frames, 182–183. *See also* frames
video loop, 204
video stabilization, 63–66
Video tab, 187–188
video tracks, 6, 25–26
volume, 162, 163, 166–167, 174

W

WAV format, 165
waveforms
audio, 23–24, 72, 83, 175
video, 48–49
white, "pure," 58
white balance, 57–59, 60
white pixels, 58, 62, 101
widescreen footage, 182
Windows Media format, 178, 179, 186, 189
Wipe border, 126
WMA format, 165
work area, 29
work area bar, 29–30
workflows, 71, 72, 76, 79, 184, 220
workspaces, 9–11, 50

X

XFDF files, 179, 180

Y

YC Waveform Scope, 48–49

Z

zebra pattern, 126
zoom effects, 86–88, 155–156, 160
Zoom tool, 157